365

★ LIFE DEVOTIONS ★

for TEEN

Girls

B&H
PUBLISHING GROUP
Nashville, Tennessee

1

God Speaks To You

So, when Gentiles, who do not have the law, instinctively do what the law demands, they are a law to themselves even though they do not have the law. They show that the work of the law is written on their hearts Their consciences confirm this. Their competing thoughts will either accuse or excuse them. (Romans 2:14–15)

You've seen those movies or shows where a person has a small devilish figure on one shoulder and a small angelic figure on the other, both trying to persuade the person to make one decision or another. Discounting the impish figures on the shoulders, is that scene true-to-life? How would you define *conscience*? What do you think is the purpose of your conscience? God gave you a conscience to help you know right from wrong. However, because your conscience can be flawed or weak, there must be a higher standard to which it answers.

What's the danger of depending just on your conscience to determine what is right and wrong? Your conscience instinctively questions whether something is right or wrong, but what ultimately answers the question? Or rather Who answers the question? Who sets the standard? God does. You may face difficult situations and issues today in which you struggle to know right from wrong. How will you determine what's right?

Thank God for giving you a conscience to help you determine right from wrong. Express to God your desire for Him to guide your conscience to follow His ultimate and absolute standard.

2

God Sets The Rules

*Then God spoke all these words: I am the LORD
your God, who brought you out of the land of Egypt,
out of the place of slavery. (Exodus 20:1–2)*

What rules do you have at your house? Why do those rules have
meaning? Look over Exodus 20. What is this chapter about? Why do
these commandments have meaning?

The commandments are powerful because of the Authority behind
them. Moses didn't call a meeting of all the people and say, "So . . . what
do you guys think should be the rules?" Chaos would have followed a
rule-making meeting. Instead, the perfect, almighty God gave absolute
rules for living. They are backed by Him, by His character and authority.
That being the case, they are worth following.

What changes will you make to live by God's standards? How will your
living by God's standard be a witness to your friends and family? Submit
to God today and commit to living by His standards.

3

God Stays the Same

A voice was saying, "Cry out!" Another said, "What should I cry out?" "All humanity is grass, and all its goodness is like the flower of the field. The grass withers, the flowers fade when the breath of the Lᴏʀᴅ blows on them; indeed, the people are grass. The grass withers, the flowers fade, but the word of our God remains forever." (Isaiah 40:6–8)

The comic strip *Calvin and Hobbes* features a game called "Calvinball" —a game where they made up the rules as they went along. The rules would be changed mainly by Calvin—always in his favor, of course. Would you like to play "Calvinball"? Would you enjoy a game where the rules change on the whimsy of the person in charge? Why would that be frustrating?

What if God decided to rewrite the Scriptures and change the rules? Would that be frustrating? Why? How can we know God's rules won't change? What comes to mind when you hear the word *forever*?

Isaiah wrote that God's Word will remain forever—this is not just a length of time. The word *forever* speaks to the quality and integrity of God's Word. It will always last, and it will never change. How can you know God's Word won't change? Read Hebrews 13:8, 1 Samuel 15:29, and James 1:17. What is the message of these verses? God's Word won't change because God does not change. His Word is backed up by His character. A relationship with God isn't like playing "Calvinball"— you have His word on it.

4

He Is God—You Are Not

Our God is in heaven and does
whatever He pleases. (Psalm 115:3)

Reflect on that verse for a moment. The message is simple and straight to the point. He is God, and you are not. How does that truth hit you? Does that statement seem a little arrogant? Why or why not? How does Psalm 33:6–11 support the truth that God has the right to set the rules?

When was the last time you spoke anything into existence? Do your plans always work out? Why? When God speaks, things are created. When God plans, it comes to pass. NO ONE compares to Him. He's the King. The Creator. The Master. The Almighty. Always has been. Always will be.

Now you have a choice. If you want to be in charge and set your own rules, He'll let you. But heed the warning; the results probably won't be pretty. Usually when you put yourself in charge, the best thing you make is a mess. When you set the agenda, the plans fall apart.

What is your best and most appropriate response to such a great and awesome God—worship, trust, love, submission, adoration, praise, or even bowing in reverence? Pick one. Better yet, pick them all. What is a specific way you will live out your response this week?

5

The Faithful One

Happy is the nation whose God is Yahweh—the people
He has chosen to be His own possession! (Psalm 33:12)

God's greatness, power, and sovereignty are emphasized in Psalm 115:3. It is His right as God to make the rules. But if you stop there, you might start thinking that God's just a strong dictator with His thumb pressed down on the little people. However, that is not the case.

What emotion is mentioned in today's verse? Why would a nation be happy when God is in charge? To find out, read verses 13–22. What are the reasons a nation—and you—can be happy when God's in charge?

God is not a distant dictator who hands down edicts and stays uninvolved. He is a concerned, attentive, and loving Father who watches over you. What should be your response to this kind of God? Pay close attention to verses 20–22. When you respond with waiting, trusting, and hoping, you find help, joy, and peace.

Rewrite Psalm 33:20–22 as your prayer response to God. The Father, not the dictator, waits for you.

6

Give Praise To The Lord

*I exalt You, my God the King, and praise Your name
forever and ever. I will praise You every day; I will
honor Your name forever and ever. (Psalm 145:1–2)*

You have a relationship with a God who is sovereign, loving, powerful, and attentive to you personally. What are some other words of praise you would use to describe God? When you truly realize the character of God and understand the depth of His love for you, what should be your response?

Check out Psalm 145:1–7. The psalmist was so overwhelmed with God, he couldn't hold it in. Look at the different ways the writer desired to express His feelings about God. The psalmist was excited and joyful about his relationship with God. Are you that excited and joyful? Can you hardly keep the joy inside? Why or why not?

Why is it important that you declare, praise, sing, and express the greatness of God?

When you express praise about God, good things happen. God is honored, believers are encouraged, unbelievers are enlightened, and you worship. In what ways will you proclaim Him this week? Our God is a great God and worthy to be praised. Don't hold it in!

7

A Perfect Book

All Scripture is God-breathed and is useful for teaching, rebuking, correcting and training in righteousness. (2 Timothy 3:16 NIV)

"I pledge allegiance to the Bible, God's holy Word. I will make it a lamp unto my feet, a light unto my path, and will hide its words in my heart that I may not sin against God."

Those words have been said by millions of children (maybe even you) during Vacation Bible School. Let's look closely at the pledge to see if it's just a cute saying or if it is still a valid commitment you need to make.

What does it mean to pledge allegiance to something? Why should you make a commitment to the Bible? Why not make a commitment to the latest Harry Potter book or the dictionary? Our commitment is based on the truth that the Bible is God's holy Word. That's what sets it apart—authorship.

How would you define "God-breathed"? It's His Word. There are no contributing authors. Of course humans wrote it down, but they didn't think it up on their own. They weren't robots, but they were being led by God's Spirit. God placed the words He wanted on their hearts, and they performed the physical task of writing them down.

Why did God give you His holy Word? There are lots of answers. However, the ultimate reason is found in 2 Timothy 3:15. The Author gave you His book so you can know Him. It's His story, and when you read it, listen to it, and study it, it leads you to Him.

8

A Book of Wisdom

*Your word is a lamp for my feet and
a light on my path. (Psalm 119:105)*

"I pledge allegiance to the Bible, God's holy Word. I will make it a lamp unto my feet, a light unto my path, and will hide its words in my heart that I may not sin against God."

Ever go camping? What's one essential item for the trip, especially if you need to go to the bathroom in the middle of the night? No, not toilet paper. Well, yes, that's pretty essential too, but not the answer we're looking for. We're talking about a flashlight. You need the flashlight to keep yourself from falling over roots, tent stakes, firewood, bears, and other stuff. The flashlight illuminates your path. It helps you know where and how you should walk.

How is the Bible your spiritual flashlight? Why do you need a spiritual flashlight? The clouds of big decisions, tragedies, pressures at school and home, and relationship troubles can cause your way to seem very dark. You need the light of God's Word to show you the way. There are also lots of things you can spiritually fall over, sins that can trip you up and cause you to stumble. God's Word helps guide you through and around those things.

Is your path dark right now? Are you spiritually stumbling? You don't have to stumble in the dark. Open His Word and let the light shine!

9

A Reliable Book

*I have treasured Your word in my heart so
that I may not sin against You. (Psalm 119:11)*

"I pledge allegiance to the Bible, God's holy Word. I will make it a lamp unto my feet, a light unto my path, and will hide its words in my heart that I may not sin against God."

Quick . . . what is 6 x 7? 7 x 7? 8 x 7? 9 x 7? 10 x 7? You probably could rattle off the correct answers without using your calculator or your fingers and toes. As a child, you learned the multiplication tables by memorizing them. Memorization is also a wonderful tool when it comes to knowing Scripture.

Consider the different versions of Psalm 119:11. Some translations use the words "treasured Your word," while others use "hidden Your word." How do you hide or treasure God's Word in your heart? How does hiding God's Word in your heart keep you from sinning? Memorizing God's Word does not form a temptation force field around you, and it's not an immunization against sin. However when faced with a tempting situation, the Spirit of God can use the Scripture you've tucked away to remind you of what is right and best. What Scripture will you memorize this week? Hide that Scripture in your heart.

10

Questions & Decisions

Now if any of you lacks wisdom, he should ask God,
who gives to all generously and without criticizing,
and it will be given to him. (James 1:5)

Your world is filled with questions and decisions. How do you know what is the right thing to do in every situation? You need wisdom—not worldly wisdom; God's wisdom. If you ask Him for wisdom, God gives it to you. So, when you ask God for wisdom, do you sit around and wait for Him to spring it on you? One day you're ignorant, then *poof!* the next day you're wise. Is that how it works? Not quite. God does give wisdom, but our waiting on His wisdom is active, not passive.

Read Proverbs 2:1–6. What does Solomon say you must do? Notice all the active words in that passage: *store up, listen, direct, call out, lift, seek, search.* God gives you wisdom as you seek Him, as you study His Word, and as you listen for His voice. As you grow closer to God, you become more like Him, wisdom included.

There is no magic formula to gain God's wisdom. It comes to the student who seeks Him.

11

Always Faithful

So whether you eat or drink or whatever you do,
do it all for the glory of God. (1 Corinthians 10:31 NIV)

What does *Semper Fidelis* mean? It is a Latin phrase translated "Always Faithful," and it is the motto of the United States Marine Corps. What is the purpose of a motto? Mottos are more than just concise and clever sayings that look good on a t-shirt. The USMC motto is never far from the heart of a marine. The saying *Semper Fi* is a motivational phrase and a guide. It is a constant reminder of who they are and what they do. It is a statement of character and purpose.

Do you have a personal motto? How about *eis doxan theou*? Any idea what it means? You can find it in today's verse. What phrase do you think it is? The language is Greek, and is translated "to the glory of God." What does it mean? As a follower of Christ, everything you do should be motivated by your desire to bring glory to God. Every action, word, or decision should be filtered through that motto. What would your life look like if *eis doxan theou* was your motto? What needs to change for it to be your motto? Reflect on these words today. Let them drive you and define your purpose.

Eis doxan theou. Live it.

12

The Gray Areas

So then, we must pursue what promotes peace and what builds up one another. (Romans 14:19)

Making decisions in those gray areas can be a real pain. It would have been much easier if God had just given us a rule about everything. Why didn't He? Being a Christian is not about following rules. Everything you do is done in the context of relationships—how you relate to God and how you relate to others. If there was a rule about everything, you would be more concerned with legalism than love, and procedures and protocol would take precedence over people. That describes the Pharisees, and that's not what God intended.

Read Mark 2:1–3:5. How do these stories illustrate that Jesus was more concerned with relationships than rules? While it's true that God has given some very specific truths for you to live by, even those non-negotiables are given to point you to a better relationship with Him and others. Relationships are important.

Your first consideration when facing a gray area should be how your decision affects your relationship with God. If it dishonors Him or is contrary to His Word, you don't do it. Period. How does Romans 14:13–19 speak to the second consideration? You must choose what leads to peace and unity. Even when the decision is contrary to what you want or inconveniences you, you must put other Christians first.

13

Beware of Lions

*But your iniquities have built barriers between you and
your God, and your sins have made Him hide His face
from you so that He does not listen. (Isaiah 59:2)*

Sin. It is a powerful word, but what does it mean? Webster's dictionary defines *sin* as "an offense against God." How would you define *sin*?
What does today's verse say is the result of sin?

As a child, were you ever separated from your parents in a crowded
place? How did it make you feel? Frightened? Alone? Vulnerable? Were
you afraid that someone might harm you? If we are separated from
God, we should feel all of those things. God wants us to stay near to
Him because if we don't, we are making ourselves vulnerable to attacks
from Satan.

Read 1 Peter 5:8. Why are you to be on guard? What does Satan want
to do to you? God wants you to stay close to Him. Sin prevents this from
happening. Just like a parent looking for a lost child, God longs for you.
He wants you to be with Him. He loves you.

Everyone sins (Romans 3:23). It is a cold-hard fact that we all sin, but
there is hope. Jesus is your hope. He is your salvation. Take a moment
and think of all the things in your life right now that are separating you
from God. Pray and ask God to forgive you for your sin.

14

Not Even Holy Rollers

As it is written: There is no one righteous,
not even one. (Romans 3:10)

Virtue. Decency. Uprightness. Honesty. What do all of these words have in common? They are synonyms for the word *righteousness*. When you hear that word, what comes to mind? Do-gooders? Holy Rollers? Preachers? Goody-Goodies? "Holier-than-thou" types?

According to the Bible, who is righteous? So does that change your view? Does it make you think *Oh great, if even they aren't righteous, then there is no hope for me!*? Well, don't think that! There is always hope!

Read Romans 3:22–24. What is the hope? Wow! Now doesn't that make you feel better? Everyone has sinned, but we all have the chance of redemption through Jesus Christ.

Read Romans 1:16–17. What is a great way to describe what it means to be righteous? If you live by faith—faith in Jesus as your Lord and Savior—then you are righteous! Remember, no one is perfect, but your goal in life should be to strive to be like Jesus—who was perfect!

What does it mean to you to live by faith? Reflect on your day and week. Have you been living by faith? Have you been showing others that you are striving to live a righteous life? Why or why not? Take a moment and thank God for His Son and the great sacrifice He made for you.

15

Sin Sick

*If we say, "We have no sin," we are deceiving
ourselves, and the truth is not in us. (1 John 1:8)*

Prisoner. Thief. Liar. Drug pusher. Gang member. Backstabber. Next-door neighbor. Sunday school teacher. Preacher. Christian recording artist. Me. You. What do all these people have in common? Well, if you said "nothing," then you are wrong. These people share one thing . . . sin!

Are you thinking that it is horrible to compare a Sunday school teacher to a drug pusher or a preacher to a gang member? Sorry, but it's the truth. Read Romans 3:23. Who is identified in this verse as a sinner? Notice it says "all". That's me, you, and even sister Sally at the piano.

According to 1 John 1:8, what are you not supposed to do? Sin will always be around while you walk the planet. Granted, you can be forgiven for your sin, but the fact is, sin is everywhere. No matter how hard you try, you will sin.

Read Romans 3:12–18. Have you ever thought about yourself this way? Does it seem harsh? Why? We are all sinners—yep, even you. Plain and simple. Cold-hard fact. It is the reality of being human, but God still loves you. His love is amazing. Ask God to make you aware of all the sin in your life. Praise Him for His willingness to forgive you through His Son, Jesus.

16
We Can't Fix It

He made the One who did not know sin to be sin for us, so that we might become the righteousness of God in Him. (2 Corinthians 5:21)

Have you ever taken a test and received a perfect score? Was it easy for you, or did you study extra hard for it? Can life be like that? Can we live a perfect life? Why or why not? Wouldn't it be easier to live a perfect life if you could make your own rules? What rules would you make?

Read Romans 10:1–5. Why is making up our own rules for perfection not an acceptable way to live? The Israelites didn't understand God's righteousness. They thought that they could gain righteousness by their own methods and works. They didn't understand that no matter how hard they tried, it is impossible to gain righteousness on your own.

What's the only true way to gain God's righteousness and become right with God? God sent His perfect and sinless Son, Jesus, to live on the earth to take your sin, so that you might become the righteousness of God. Aren't you glad you're not the one responsible for earning your righteousness? It's a precious gift from God through His Son, Jesus! Submit your life to God, and thank Him for His perfect Son's sacrifice for you.

17

Impossible Perfection

I thank God through Jesus Christ our Lord! So then,
with my mind I myself am a slave to the law of God,
but with my flesh, to the law of sin. (Romans 7:25)

Have you ever seen a child, after being told something was hot, walk over and touch it? It seems like it's human nature to have to test things out and see if something is really true. Are you ever like that with God? You know something is wrong, but you have to test your limits to see how far He'll let you go—or wonder how far you can actually go before you sin. It's proof that you can't live a perfect life on your own.

What did Paul describe about his life in Romans 7:15–23? Sound familiar? Everyone experiences moments when they do things they know they aren't supposed to be doing—or they don't do things they know they should do. Is "Oh, I just can't help it" an acceptable excuse for bad behavior? Our heart's desire should be to live for God and strive to be more like Jesus in everything we do. Can you do this by yourself? Only by the power of God can you be freed from your bondage to sin, and only through your faith in Jesus can you be completely cleansed.

No one can live a perfect life, yet, with God's help, you can make every effort to live in a way that pleases God. Read Romans 7:24–25. What does it mean to be a slave to God's Word? Surrender your entire life to God today. Be willing to let Him help you strive toward perfection.

18

Model Jesus

You know that He was revealed so that He might take away sins, and there is no sin in Him. (1 John 3:5)

Can you name at least one person that you know who leads a perfect life? It needs to be a person with no flaws, no shady secrets, and absolutely no imperfections. Possibly this person could be a friend at school, someone at church, or maybe even a family member.

It's very unlikely that you were able to think of anyone that is completely perfect because everyone has flaws and imperfections. Everyone has sin.

Who is the only person to ever be without sin? Why is that important? Only Jesus, the Son of God, was able to come to this earth and live a perfect, sinless life. What does that mean to you? Why is His perfection important to us?

We read in 1 John 2:1–2 that Jesus is our Mediator. When we sin, and we all do, He speaks to God in our defense. Only Jesus can help you overcome your sin problem. His perfection gives you eternal hope. Thank God for sending His Son to live the perfect life so that He could be your Mediator and your "defense attorney."

19

Diamonds on The Inside

He did not even spare His own Son but offered Him up for us all; how will He not also with Him grant us everything? (Romans 8:32)

Have you ever wanted something so badly that you were willing to give up your most prized possession for it? Did you go through with it? Imagine diamonds on a table. The jeweler says you can have the entire bag if you hand over your most prized possession. Inside the bag are diamonds of all sizes. Some of them are beautiful and smooth. Others are jagged and sharp. And some are lost in the lining of the bag and may never be found. Would you do it? Why?

God did. Why would God do that? Before you answer, read Romans 3:21–24 and John 3:16. God sent His Son to pay the price for our sin—for your sin. He knew we were unlovable, rebellious, and difficult, but He still gave His most prized possession—His Son, Jesus. Do you think God regrets His decision? Why or why not? Praise God for Jesus and His willingness to pay the price for you to be one of God's precious diamonds.

20

Perfect Sacrifice

God presented Him as a propitiation through faith in His blood, to demonstrate His righteousness, because in His restraint God passed over the sins previously committed. (Romans 3:25)

Would you ever confess to a crime you didn't commit? Would you ever take a punishment for something you didn't do? Why or why not? Have you ever thought about the fact that Jesus was completely innocent but willingly accepted a death sentence? Why do you think He did that for you?

What does the word *propitiation* mean? Jesus bore the sins—past, present, and future—of the entire world. His broken body on the cross was for your sin and mine. Had you ever thought about it that way? We are the ones that helped nail Jesus to the cross. No, we weren't actually there with nails and hammer, but our sin kept Him on the cross.

How would you define sacrifice? How does 1 Peter 2:22–25 describe Jesus as a willing sacrifice? No one forced Jesus to the cross. His love for us—for you—led Him there and held Him there.

Find a quiet place and read chapters 18–20 in the Gospel of John. Read how Jesus took the punishment for your sin. Surrender your mind and heart to God today as you read so that He may fill your spirit with love and a new recognition of the sacrifice He paid for you.

21

Sinner Crossing

*Jesus told him, "I am the way, the truth, and the life.
No one comes to the Father except through Me. (John 14:6)*

Are you afraid of heights? Spiders? Snakes? Darkness? Death? What is your greatest fear? Imagine you are standing on the edge of a huge canyon. Looking down, you see your greatest fear, and it's coming closer to you. On the other side of the canyon is God with His arms reaching for you to come to Him for safety, but the only way to Him is over your fears.

You look and see Jesus by a tiny bridge. It's the only way to get to God. Would you cross it? Why or why not? Suddenly there's a roaring lion behind you. What do you do now? Do you face the lion, run away from the lion, or run to Jesus?

Is Jesus the only way to God, or is there another way? Why? Why is it so hard for many people to think of Jesus as the only way to God? If you cross the bridge, you will never be the same. If you walk over, your life will be forever changed. Are you still willing to go?

The lion stands growling, the fears are even closer, and the only hope for survival is the bridge. What are you waiting for? Pray and praise God for Jesus, because He is the only way to God. Only through Him can we be made clean.

22

Amazing Love

But I received mercy for this reason, so that in me,
the worst of them, Christ Jesus might demonstrate
His extraordinary patience as an example to those who
would believe in Him for eternal life. (1 Timothy 1:16)

How would you define unconditional love? How do you see examples of either conditional or unconditional love in the people and relationships around you? How about in God's relationship with humanity?

Unconditional love is a love without condition. A love that will always be there no matter what you have done or will do. You can't earn it, and you can't lose it.

Do you believe that God has unconditional love for you? Why or why not? Read Romans 5:6–8. When have you ever felt unworthy of such amazing love? You will never be unlovable to God, and there is not anything you can do that would keep God from loving you. Even when we are at our worst, God still loves us!

Read 1 Timothy 1:15–16. It's God's mercy and grace that shows us His unconditional love. Even though we are sinners, Jesus still died for us. Can you accept the fact that God loves you unconditionally? Do you believe it? Remember John 3:16. That is outstanding love. God knew some would never love Him back, but He still was willing to make the sacrifice for those who would. He loves you! Close your eyes. Be still and know that you are forever loved by your heavenly Father.

23

Prove It!

"For God loved the world in this way: He gave His One and Only Son, so that everyone who believes in Him will not perish but have eternal life." (John 3:16)

Is it possible to prove that you love someone? Why or why not? If so, is it always easy to do? What do you believe would be the best and most convincing way to prove your love for someone?

God loves you! God has proved His love for you. His love can be seen by reading Romans 8:31–34, 1 John 4:9–10, and 1 John 4:15–19. What is the recurring theme in these passages?

Think of someone you love. Now magnify the love you have for that person by one million. Multiply that by ten thousand. Do you think that is a lot of love? Even that doesn't come close to the amount of love God has for you. Do you still need proof? Imagine Jesus on the cross. Think of God watching His Son become a willing sacrifice. He did it for you. He did it for everyone. He gave His one and only Son. He loves you!

What is your reaction when you consider the great love that God has for you? Thank God for His unfailing love. Praise Him for the Bible and its reminders that His love is always there.

24

Always and Forever

*Look at how great a love the Father has given us that we should
be called God's children. And we are! The reason the world
does not know us is that it didn't know Him. (1 John 3:1)*

What do you think can separate you from the love of God? Drugs?
Premarital sex? Alcohol? Fear? Doubt? Disbelief? Lies? Anger? Mistakes?
Can you think of anything else? Do you realize that nothing can separate you from the love that God has for you? That's right—nothing.
Zilch. Nada. Even if you choose not to love God, He still loves you. Nobody
can influence God into not loving you; nobody can make God love you
any less.

Read Romans 8:35–39. What things are listed? Why? There is absolutely nothing you can do that will keep God from loving you. His love is
sufficient. His love is abundant.

What things in your life do you fear are keeping God from loving you?
Everyone makes mistakes. We all sin, but we can never fall away from
God's love.

Read Ephesians 2:4–7. What words are used in these verses to
describe God's love for you? Because of God's mercy and grace, we are
able to know that nothing will ever separate us from the outstanding and
powerful love of God. Thank God for being one of His precious children.
You're a child of the King, and nothing you can do will ever change His
love for you!

25

Relationship Rescue

"No one has greater love than this, that someone would lay down his life for his friends." (John 15:13)

A United States Coast Guard rescue team was sent to a ship that had run aground on some dangerous shoals. The people onboard were in great danger of drowning. The Coast Guard rescue leader was quoted as telling a crew member, "You have to go out, but you don't have to come back!" What did he mean?

Read John 15:9–17. According to Jesus, what is the greatest example of love? How did Jesus demonstrate this type of love for you? Take a moment to create two gift lists. In the first column, list the greatest gifts you've ever received. In the second column, list the greatest gifts you've ever given. Which list was longer and easier to create? An easy excuse to claim as a teenager is, "I don't have any money to buy gifts." Is it possible to give without spending money? What kinds of gifts can you give that have nothing to do with money?

If you struggled with the last question, think about the gifts you have received that had nothing to do with money. Some of the best gifts you can give and receive are based on relationships, love, and prayer. The price tag for such gifts is time. What has God given you, and what did it cost? Pray and ask God to show you what He wants you to give.

26

Word Wounds

Above all, maintain an intense love for each other,
since love covers a multitude of sins. (1 Peter 4:8)

"Wow, how could you have failed that test?" Words, especially when spoken, can have an incredible impact on others. Unfortunately, many of us use words as arrows to shoot at others. If your best friend had asked you that question, what would you have thought and felt? What if someone who dislikes you had asked the same question? Would your thoughts and feelings have been different? Why? Why is it so easy to overlook a hurtful comment from a friend? Love makes forgiveness so much easier, and forgiveness makes love so much greater!

Read Luke 7:41–48. According to this passage, whom should you forgive? What would be the response of an enemy if you chose to forgive him or her for hurtful remarks and demonstrated love? There is an expression that states, "Hurting people hurt people." Many times hurtful words come from hurting hearts. We need to listen beyond the words someone may speak and hear the hurt, fear, or insecurity that may be stirring within them. Being insulted, whether intentional or accidental, could be an excellent opportunity God has given you to pray for someone.

27

Love Never Fails

*Keeping our eyes on Jesus, the source and perfecter
of our faith, who for the joy that lay before Him endured
a cross and despised the shame and has sat down
at the right hand of God's throne. (Hebrews 12:2)*

"FREE muscle cramps, blisters, sweating, calluses, bruises, and aching. Call 123-4567." Would you respond if you saw that ad while online? Why? Not many people would intentionally seek to undergo such distress, yet many of us experience such things. We do so as part of a training program to be on a sports team. We are willing to endure some temporary discomfort in order to obtain a greater prize.

Read Hebrews 12:1–2. These verses explain that Jesus endured the cross because of the "joy that lay before Him." What was the "joy" that was before Him? Jesus viewed your salvation with such joy that He was willing to endure death on a cross. His primary focus was not on the physical pain and agony He was facing but on your salvation. Why did Jesus find such joy in providing salvation for mankind? Jesus' love for all of us was His motivation. The love He demonstrated for you can and should motivate you to love others.

Love never quits. What about you? Do you persevere in showing God's love to others, or do you quickly give up at the first sign of discomfort? Are you ever ashamed or embarrassed to share God's love? Pray and thank God that Jesus persevered through the cross. His joy became your salvation.

28

Believable Billboards

*But God proves His own love for us in that while
we were still sinners, Christ died for us! (Romans 5:8)*

When driving along any major highway you can see endless billboards advertising a lot of different things. What makes an advertisement on a billboard believable? One of the main things that make an advertisement believable is personally using that product. What you read in an advertisement or what someone tells you is just information. However, when you experience a product yourself, then you are convinced about whether or not it is true. What would a billboard advertising God's love look like?

Read Romans 5:6–8. God's demonstration of His love was by giving His only Son, Jesus, for our sins. This is only information, though, unless you personally experience His forgiveness and commit your life to an ongoing relationship with Him. If you were given a billboard to advertise your life, what would be included on it? What kinds of pictures or slogans would best advertise your life? Is your commitment to Christ believable, or are you guilty of false advertising? Do you personally experience God's love, or just know a lot of religious information? Pray and ask God to help you move from information to personal experience of His love.

29

Love Warranty

He did not even spare His own Son but
offered Him up for us all. (Romans 8:32)

Have you ever been hurt by someone you loved? Just about anyone who has ever loved has, at some time, been hurt by the person they cared for. After being hurt by someone you loved, what were your first thoughts? People who are hurt in love will often proclaim, "I will never love again." They believe if they don't love then they won't get hurt like this again. What is wrong with this view? Choosing not to love leads to a lonely life. One of the main reasons people vow they will never love again is their fear of being hurt and rejected again. This fear is like a wall that blocks the building of future relationships.

Wouldn't it be great if there were guarantees on love? There is one love that can be perfectly trusted to never hurt, never quit, and never end. Read Romans 8:31–39. God knew that loving us would be risky and hurtful. What did it cost Him? Even though it cost God His own Son, God did not quit loving. Perhaps someone has hurt you in the past. Pray for them right now and ask God to help you show His love to them.

30

Boomerang Love

"Love the Lord your God with all your heart, with all your soul, and with all your mind." (Matthew 22:37)

Take a moment and list the first five things or persons that come to mind that you love. Now look at your list again and think of the reasons you love those things or persons. A sad truth is that many times our love is based on what we have gotten, or will get, in return. If we only love when we get roses, compliments, physical pleasure, or attention, then our focus in on self.

Perhaps you included God in your love list from above. Why do you love God? Is it for what He has, can, or might do for you? What is the right reason to love God? Perhaps that question could be answered with a different question: Why does God love us? God does not love us for what we do but for who we are.

Read Matthew 22:37–40. What are the two great commandments? Why should we love God and others? We should love God for who He is, not for what He can do for us. We should also practice loving others for who they are in God's eyes or who they can become through God's grace, rather than loving just for what they give us in return.

31

Crossing Cliques

But wanting to justify himself, he asked Jesus,
"And who is my neighbor?" (Luke 10:29)

Just like files on a computer, every school has an inner subsystem of cliques. Can you name some of the cliques in your school? Which cliques do you feel you belong in? Which cliques would you never want to be a part of? Which cliques do you wish you could belong to? How do you feel about the individual people in these cliques? In high school most cliques are formed by a stereotype, so acceptance is based on whether or not you fit the stereotype. Why is it difficult to accept someone who is "different"?

Read Luke 10:25–37. What are the different people or cliques that are identified in the story? Read the story again, and choose which character you most easily identify with. Are you one of the robbers who bullies and intimidates others? Are you too good to associate with a victim who may be unpopular because he's poor, dirty, and wounded? Are you the innkeeper who will help if there's something in it for you? If you do not see yourself as the Samaritan in this story, then what needs to change? "Go and do the same."

32

Photo Negatives

Because if anyone is a hearer of the word and not a doer,
he is like a man looking at his own face in a mirror.
For he looks at himself, goes away, and immediately
forgets what kind of man he was. (James 1:23–24)

Have you ever had a picture taken of yourself that you hated? Most everyone has. What specifically made you dislike the picture? Since the picture was an accurate reflection of how you looked at that time, why were you unhappy with it? Many people will throw away or hide pictures of themselves they don't like. We don't want to dwell on what is wrong with our looks or with our lives. Throwing away a bad picture, though, does not change how we look. The same is true of our hearts.

Read James 1:22–25. What is the difference in the focus of verse 24 and verse 25? Much of the character we reflect depends on whether we are focused on self or God's Word. If someone held a camera to your heart, what characteristics would be reflected? Compare your list with the list in Colossians 3:12–14. Are there any characteristics missing in the picture of your heart?

The next time you get dressed, think about your reflection. Do your clothes and heart reflect the character of God? Pray and ask God to show you if something is missing in your spiritual wardrobe, then listen. God wants to talk with you today.

33

Selfish Giving

"They devour widows' houses and say long prayers just for show. These will receive harsher punishment." (Mark 12:40)

School involves so much more than books and classes. Much of what occurs in school involves a broad variety of activities, teams, and organizations. Many scholarship applications take into consideration an individual's social and community contributions, so many students work toward compiling a lengthy list of such activities. What extracurricular activities are you currently involved in or what do you plan to join in the future? Now here's a more difficult question. For each activity or group listed above, why are you involved in it? If nobody would ever know of your involvement in these activities, would you still do them?

Read Mark 12:38–44. What was the main difference in the actions of the scribes and the actions of the widow? The most notable difference is the focus of their actions. The scribes were serving to draw attention to themselves, mainly because that is who they loved the most. The widow was giving out of her love for God.

Now read Matthew 6:19–21. Where is your heart? Are your treasures for self or eternity? Ask God to capture your heart in such a way that you will give out of love for Him, rather than love for self or this world.

34

Contagious Christianity

Therefore, if anyone is in Christ, he is a
new creation; old things have passed away,
and look, new things have come. (2 Corinthians 5:17)

Are you part of the "in" crowd? That's an old term, but actually everyone is "in" something. People can be "in" love, debt, school, trouble, or sports, just to name a few. What does it mean to be "in Christ"? Unlike many earthly situations that are temporary, being in Christ brings changes that are permanent.

Look at the example in John 4:1–42. As you read, imagine yourself being there and watching this story unfold. This woman genuinely became "in Christ." Look again at verse 28. The woman had come for water, but left her water jar behind. Why? She had found something much more important than getting a drink. When the woman left the "old" behind, what was the "new" result? (Look again at vv. 39–42.) It's hard to keep good news a secret. She ran to town to share with everyone that she had met Jesus. Her excitement was so great it made others want to check out Jesus for themselves. What about you? Is your walk with Jesus so exciting that others want to know more? Ask God to fill you with a contagious joy that will draw others to Him.

35

Taking Both Sides

*That is, in Christ, God was reconciling the world
to Himself, not counting their trespasses
against them, and He has committed the message
of reconciliation to us. (2 Corinthians 5:19)*

Have you ever found yourself in a relationship where you ended up stuck between two friends? What were the circumstances and how was the situation eventually resolved? In such situations we often experience a great deal of pressure to take sides with one of the parties involved. Is it possible to remain neutral and be friends with both? How? There are companies today who hire people called reconciliation specialists. It is a big title that basically means they help two differing sides come together. They can be viewed much like a bridge connecting two separated pieces of land.

Read 2 Corinthians 5:18–21. How are we reconciled to God? The greatest reconciliation specialist in the Bible is Jesus. Jesus became the bridge to reconcile us to God. More than being reconciled to God, though, these verses also say that God has given us the ministry of reconciliation. How can God use you in reconciliation? The next time you feel stuck in the middle in a situation, remember God has called you to the ministry of reconciliation. God can use you to bring friends together. More importantly, He wants to use you to bring friends to know Jesus.

36

News Headlines

Therefore, we are ambassadors for Christ, certain that
God is appealing through us. We plead on Christ's behalf,
"Be reconciled to God." (2 Corinthians 5:20)

Are you good at keeping secrets, or are you the kind of person who could one day be a television news anchor? What is there about news that makes it so difficult to keep quiet? When you read news online or watch the news on television, do you hear more negative or positive stories? It seems that most of today's news is focused on negative stories involving pain, destruction, or death. Why do you think there is so much more focus on bad news? Perhaps the news is mostly negative because those with good news don't share it!

Read 2 Corinthians 5:14–21. What are you doing with this news? These verses say that we are compelled by Christ's love to be ambassadors. What does it mean to be compelled by Christ's love? The love of Christ is so great that we have to tell others. It should be something we just can't keep to ourselves. As a believer, you have the information to help people each day who are spiritually in a life-or-death situation. Will you share the good news of salvation? Pray and ask God to give you boldness in sharing how He has changed your life.

37

Your Heart Focus

*I have suffered the loss of all things and consider
them filth, so that I may gain Christ. (Philippians 3:8)*

Martin Luther lived in Germany in the early 1500s. As a monk, Luther became frustrated with the church's ignorance of spiritual truth and their focus on status and wealth. Luther called Christians to realign with the Bible. Because he spoke against church leaders, he was kicked out of the church and lost many of his friends. Still, he clung to his relationship with God as his main focus. Luther declared, "Whatever your heart clings to and confides in, that is really your god." To what does your heart cling these days?

Read Philippians 3:8–9. Why is what Christ offers you superior to any other use of your time? What you value determines how you spend your time—hobbies, interests, and aspirations. None of those things is bad in and of itself. Problems arise when those things become more important than your personal relationship with God. If Christ is your Savior and Lord, you should consider Him so valuable that everything else looks like garbage in comparison.

What things in your life have you put before God? What steps do you need to take to realign your life to make God your heart focus? Ask God to give you a desire for Him that surpasses your love for anything else in your life.

38

Time Well Spent

I want their hearts to be encouraged and joined together in love,
so that they may have all the riches of assured understanding
and have the knowledge of God's mystery—Christ. (Colossians 2:2)

When you are trying to get to know someone, where do you start? Check out his or her profile? Invite him or her to hang out? Ask other people about him or her? Strike up a conversation and ask lots of questions? Watch to see what he or she does or says? There are lots of ways to get to know someone. The more time you invest in discovering what someone is like, the more you find out and the more accurate your impression will be of that person.

How would you rate your understanding of who God is? Read Colossians 1:25–27. What is the mystery that is revealed to us through God's Word? Skip down to Colossians 2:2. What type of understanding does Scripture promise? A relationship with God is just like any other relationship. The more time you invest in digging into His Word—the Bible—the more you discover about who He is. Each thing you learn helps you piece together His nature, heart, and desires. Every bit of knowledge you gain about God helps you develop an intimate relationship with Him. So what are you waiting for? Dig in! It is time well spent.

39

Look Alikes

"I am the vine; you are the branches. The one who remains in Me and I in him produces much fruit, because you can do nothing without Me." (John 15:5)

You've seen it a hundred times. A friend starts hanging out with someone new, and the more time they spend together, the more similar they become. Their language, mannerisms, and clothing begin to be very similar—they even say the same thing at the same time, and they may not even realize they are doing it. Who do you act like?

For a plant to bear fruit, there must be a consistent flow of nutrients. It doesn't happen overnight, and many things can stunt its growth. How is this similar to what happens in your walk with Christ? The more consistent time you spend with God, the more He's going to rub off on you. You'll find yourself thinking, acting, and talking more like Him because you've grown to know Him and understand more about how He would respond. Pray that God will help you abide in Him—and that you will become more like Him.

40

Safe on Your Knees

*He leads the humble in what is right and
teaches them His way. (Psalm 25:9)*

In *Indiana Jones and the Last Crusade*, adventurer Indiana Jones must make it safely through a series of deadly traps in order to complete his quest. Following a cipher, he safely navigates each hazard. When his clue reads, "The penitent man shall pass," Indy drops to the ground, narrowly missing giant saw blades that slice over his head.

Penitent is another word for humble. When you hear the word *humble*, what's your first thought or reaction? What's the purpose of humility? Why is humility often pictured by a person kneeling in prayer? Humility is an attitude that recognizes God is infinitely greater than you are. The truly humble don't need to put themselves down. Instead, they submit to God and focus on lifting Him up. This means being willing to repent of sin and recognize that God loves you even though you aren't perfect. When you approach God humbly, He is able to teach you to do what's right so you can avoid sin and its destructive consequences. Take a few moments and confess any sin in your life. Ask God to give you a spirit of humility so He can teach you to do right.

41

I Hear You

*"You will call to Me and come and pray to Me, and I will
listen to you. You will seek Me and find Me when you
search for Me with all your heart." (Jeremiah 29:12–13)*

Read Hebrews 4:15–16. About whom are these verses written? (Hint:
see verse 14.) In the time when the Bible was written, a high priest would
act as a liaison between the people and God. How would it feel to depend
on another human being for your relationship with God? Would you feel
confident in this system? Why or why not? How does Jesus serve as your
High Priest? Because of Christ's death, believers have a direct line of
communication with God. He understands all your weaknesses, and He
promises to meet you where you are and give you what you need. So you
can, and should, come to Him confidently, expecting Him to meet with you
and reveal Himself to you.

Describe a time in your life when you approached God and He came
through for you. Thank Him for being faithful to you. God promises to listen to you when you pray and to reveal Himself to you when you seek Him
humbly and with your whole heart. With that in mind, ask Him to help you
approach Him with confidence in your quiet time. He hears you!

42

Tell The Truth

The LORD is near all who call out to Him, all who call out to Him with integrity. (Psalm 145:18)

You have probably been in a relationship where the other person wasn't completely honest with you. Were you able to grow very close to that individual? Why? To what type of person does God draw near? What does *integrity* mean to you? This verse presents a picture of God responding to an invitation—your invitation. He promises to draw near to you when you come to Him with an honest heart—a heart of integrity.

In your view, what is *honesty*? How would you rate your honesty with God? Is it okay to ask God questions or admit that you don't understand something? Why or why not? God does not expect you to hide how you feel. You can be open with Him because He already knows everything about you. Truthfulness with Him is for your benefit, so you can receive His presence and blessing in your life. Dishonesty or incomplete honesty creates a barrier between you and God. He can never be as close to you as He desires without your honesty. Is there an area of your life where you haven't been completely truthful with God? Confess that to Him and ask His forgiveness and help.

43

Volume Control

*Yet He often withdrew to deserted places
and prayed. (Luke 5:16)*

Let's try an experiment. Turn up the volume on an MP3 player or other electronic device so that you can clearly hear it without wearing the headphones. Now turn on a TV and crank up the volume. Do the same with a stereo system. Can you still hear the audio from the headphones? Can you distinguish the sounds coming from them? Okay, enough already. Turn everything off. Sometimes life is a lot like that—loud! Media, activities, and people seem to get in a screaming match for your attention. Like the sound from the headphones, it can be hard to hear God's voice through all of the other "noise" in our lives. What are some things that compete for your time and attention? What does today's verse tell you about Christ? Why do you think it was important for Jesus to do this? If Jesus—God Himself—thought it was important to have quiet time away, don't you think it's important for you too? You need periods of silence and solitude so you can recognize the voice of God speaking to you and then respond to Him. If you want to have an effective time alone with God, you must first turn down the volume of life.

44
Can We Talk?

Trust in Him at all times, you people; pour out your hearts before Him. God is our refuge. (Psalm 62:8)

Mrs. White was the study hall tyrant. Study hall was supposed to be quiet time. Nobody, absolutely nobody, talked in Mrs. Smith's study hall. Get caught whispering even a word and you were signing demerit slips or sitting in the principal's office before you could blink. How would it feel if your quiet time with God were like study hall with Mrs. White? Do you think you'd grow as a Christian? Why? Would you even want to? Why?

What two words of instruction are we given in today's verse? What does it mean to you to pour out your heart to God? Quiet time with God is about having a conversation with the One who loves you unconditionally. He wants you to tell Him everything that is going on in your life and to hear what He has to say in response. What word did the psalmist use to describe God? When you think of a refuge, what images come to mind? You can rest assured, God can handle your joy and your pain; He offers a safe place to pour out your heartaches, questions, and silent longings. He can handle the tough stuff no one else can. Take some time right now to share your heart with Him.

45

Listen Up

*Be silent before the LORD and wait
expectantly for Him. (Psalm 37:7)*

Are you ready for a tough truth? Here goes: It's not all about you. If you want a healthy relationship with God, sometimes it needs to just be about listening to God. Read Mark 9:2–7. What did God tell the disciples? When Peter was in God's presence, he wasn't sure what to do—so he started talking. Can you identify? How do you think you would have responded had you been there with the disciples?

Time with God isn't always about talking, you have to listen too. God won't always speak in the same way or about the same things. He may speak through His Word, through the voice of others, or through events in your daily life. Sometimes He'll teach you general words of truth or truths that apply to particular situations. He may give you commands, counsel, comfort, encouragement, reprimands, or guidance. At times, He may simply reveal more of His nature.

Bottom line: If you do all the talking, you'll miss what He really wants to show you. Learn to listen. Now is a good time to start. Take a minute to ask God what He wants to show you today, then listen to whatever He has to say.

46

Keep Your Eyes on the Road

Let us run with endurance the race that lies before us,
keeping our eyes on Jesus. (Hebrews 12:1–2)

In driver's education courses, one thing they always teach you is to keep your eyes on the road. Whatever direction you look is the direction toward which you will tend to move. Can you think of some other areas of life where this is true? How could this principle apply to your spiritual life as well? What does Hebrews 12:1–4 suggest? The only way to move toward Christ in your daily life is to remain focused on Him—to fix your eyes on Him—no matter what distractions come your way. If you place your focus on avoiding temptation, you'll soon find yourself moving toward it. According to verse 3, what happens as a result of focusing on Jesus? Discouragement comes easily when it seems no one can identify with your struggle. Hebrews 12:1–4 helps you understand that it doesn't have to be that way. Jesus knows how hard life can be, and He will help you navigate it successfully. Choose one thought about Christ from these verses, and think about it as you go throughout your day. Remember, keep your eyes on the road!

47

Capture The Moment

*Tie them to your fingers; write them on
the tablet of your heart. (Proverbs 7:3)*

These days it's pretty hard to find a cell phone without a camera in it. Some of the most popular sites on the Web are those where anyone can upload and share their photos or videos. It's pretty handy to have so many ways to remember the special moments of your life. Actually, that is not a bad idea when it comes to your spiritual life either!

Read Proverbs 7:1–3. What six terms identify what you are to do with God's Word? (Hint—the first is "Obey.") What's the point of these verses? One way to help keep your focus on Christ throughout the day is to take a tangible memento of your quiet time with you. When you're tempted or need encouragement, you'll have an instant reminder!

Here are some ideas for reminders: write Scripture verses on index cards; use self-stick notes as reminders in your locker; put an inspiring phrase on your cell phone banner; load worship music on your MP3 player; carry a journal of prayers, Scriptures, and God-moments. Can you think of at least three other ways to take God's truth with you? Be creative. Now capture a moment from today's time with God—and take it with you!

48

Inside-Out

He said, "Even more, those who hear the word of God and keep it are blessed!" (Luke 11:28)

Think for a moment on some of the things you've learned about having a personal time alone with God. What stands out most to you? What actions have you put into action in your life? What does today's verse mean to you? We have discussed talking with God and listening to God. Today, it is important for you to understand that your faith in Christ should lead you to action. You need to put into practice what you are reading and learning. So how do you go about that?

There are two primary ways to apply what God teaches you. Read Mark 12:30–31. What are the two ways? Let truth change you internally. As you discover new truths, apply them to your life. Let them affect who you are. It boils down to knowing God and owning your faith. The changes that take place on the inside naturally will become apparent on the outside. Let what you learn change what you do, how you act, talk, and treat others. In other words, make your faith in Christ known to others. Make a point to devote part of your time with God to planning ways to put into action what you learn each day. Start today!

49

The Boss

He is also the head of the body, the church; He is the beginning,
the firstborn from the dead, so that He might come
to have first place in everything. (Colossians 1:18)

What are some titles that are given to people in top positions in a corporate office of a company? What are some titles of Christ mentioned in today's verse? Which title jumps out at you? Why? One title given to Christ is "the beginning"—it means that Christ is the beginning of everything, including the church.

Read Ephesians 1:22–23. What does this passage tell you about Christ and the church? To whom does the church belong? Why? You might feel or think that you have part ownership of the church or church building. You really don't; none of us do, because it's by God's grace that we are accepted into His church in the first place. The reason Christ is called "the beginning," "the firstborn from the dead," and "the first place in everything" is because the church belongs to Christ. Take a moment and think of all the ideas you have about the church. Write them down. What do you see? Pray to the Lord for help in developing the correct idea about His church—and your part in it.

50

The Cornerstone

> So honor will come to you who believe, but for the
> unbelieving, The stone that the builders rejected—
> this One has become the cornerstone. (1 Peter 2:7)

What is your definition of *cornerstone*? Who is the cornerstone of the church? The word *cornerstone* means "binding together the sides of the building." This tells us that Christ binds the church together in order for us to be whole. We are bound together with believers all around the world, even though we may never meet them until we get to heaven.

Read 1 Corinthians 1:2. How does it make you feel to know you are a part of something this big? This verse is part of the introduction in Paul's letter to the church at Corinth. He addressed it that way on purpose. It was addressed to the Corinthian church because they were the first to receive it. They were a local body of believers. They most likely met in someone's home. The local church isn't just a building—more importantly, a church is a local group of people who believe in Christ as their personal Savior and Lord.

How often do you attend your local church? In what areas of church ministry do you participate? In what way is Christ the cornerstone, or foundation, of all that you do at church? The cornerstone is the most important part of any building—it sets the angles, directions, and depth for the foundation. When you think about your relationship with Jesus, is He setting the direction for your life? Is there depth in your relationship with Him? Give careful thought to your cornerstone this week.

51

Promote Love

*And let us be concerned about one another in order
to promote love and good works. (Hebrews 10:24)*

Who are the top ten people you love? Why is each person on your list? What are you supposed to do as a Christian and a church member? Today's verse encourages us to promote love to others. In fact, it encourages us to be concerned as we promote love. The word *promote* means "to stimulate." This verse is telling us we should stimulate each other in godly love through our actions. How can you promote godly love?

Read 1 Thessalonians 3:12. We should encourage the body of Christ. We need encouragement from each other. We need to tell each other as fellow believers, "I love you." How do you feel when a fellow believer tells you, "I love you"? We need to show those who are not Christians what Christ's love is all about. If we can't show love to people without Christ in their lives, they may never see who Christ is. Where can you show Christian love to other people? Ask God to help you overcome these difficult areas through His love. Ask Him to help you promote love to others as you draw near to Him.

52

Distribution Center

They sold their possessions and property and distributed
the proceeds to all, as anyone had a need. (Acts 2:45)

What are some different types of distribution centers in your area? Why do those distribution centers exist? What product do they distribute? To whom? Today's verse tells us how the first century church was a distribution center. They sold their possessions and property and distributed the money they made to everyone who was in need. The word *distributed* means "parted thoroughly" or "parted equally." There was no one left out. One of the best ways to show people you love them is by helping provide their needs through sacrifice. How can meeting someone's needs help show them God's love?

Read Acts 4:34. What was the result of the sacrifice? This verse tells us there was no one in need. They even sold land and homes in order to allow the needy ones to have an equal amount. They were definitely thinking of the common-good of the church. They were showing God's love for all. What are some ways your church shows God's love for others? What are some ways you show God's love to others? Ask God to show you new ways to show His love to others.

53

Loving Others

Dear friends, let us love one another, because love is from God, and everyone who loves has been born of God and knows God. (1 John 4:7)

What is the command in this verse? Loving others is not a suggestion from God but a command. When you love others, you let them know you are in a personal relationship with Christ. According to this verse, who are you supposed to love? Why are you supposed to show love to others? Loving everyone isn't always easy. You might allow the way a person looks, dresses, or talks determine whether or not you like that person. Liking a person is different than loving a person. Loving a person doesn't mean you necessarily like everything about that person. When you show love to others, you care enough to share the Gospel with them. You even go to the extent of inviting them to your next student ministry function. Ask God to give you the courage to invite people to your church or next student ministry function.

54

Expression of Love

We always thank God for all of you, remembering
you constantly in our prayers. (1 Thessalonians 1:2)

List the ways your parents share expressions of love toward you. For whom was Paul thankful? Paul began his letter to the Thessalonians by saying that he was thankful to God for the church. He didn't thank God for them occasionally, but he said "always." It was a regular expression of thanks he had for the church because of their faith in God. Paul also did another thing in this verse. He remembered them in his prayers. This is one of the highest forms of expressing your love toward someone—praying for them. Do you love your student minister? If so, you should pray for him or her on a daily basis. Who are some others for whom you could pray? Commit to pray for your family, pastor, pastor's family, student minister, student minister's family, and your friends on a daily basis. As you pray, thank God for something specific for each person.

55

Peace

*"Peace I leave with you. My peace I give to you.
I do not give to you as the world gives. Your heart
must not be troubled or fearful." (John 14:27)*

In the sixties and seventies, the word *peace* was used quite frequently. What are some thoughts that come to your mind when you hear that word? What kind of peace does Jesus give? Christ gave His disciples the promise to leave them with peace once He was gone from the earth. In the verse prior to this one, Christ informed His disciples that the Holy Spirit will take His place. Why is peace so important? The peace we receive from Christ calms us and gives us the knowledge of how we can get along with others. True peace can't be demonstrated through a symbol or sign but only through the way we get along with other people. We can only receive true peace from Christ.

When the world thinks of peace, or portrays peace in the media, what images are used? How is this different from the peace that Christ offers? Pray that God will help you improve on getting along with other Christians and showing peace.

56

Humble Pie

Do nothing out of rivalry or conceit, but in humility consider others as more important than yourselves. (Philippians 2:3)

How does a person demonstrate humility? Read Philippians 2:1–4. What is the key to being able to demonstrate humility? Humility is one of the hardest characteristics to find in the college and professional level of sports. Humility is a characteristic that all Christians should work on. In fact, Paul, urged us not to have rivals or be conceited. You shouldn't make others look bad just so you can look good. All that does is cause friction, and it makes you look conceited. Paul said that being humble means that you make other people feel more important than yourself. That's hard, but when you do this, it makes you feel so good. What makes it hard to put the interests of others above your own interests? Ask God to help you grow in your humility.

57

The Focal Point

Now may the God who gives endurance and encouragement allow you to live in harmony with one another, according to the command of Christ Jesus, so that you may glorify the God and Father of our Lord Jesus Christ with a united mind and voice. (Romans 15:5–6)

What would you paint if you were painting a mural? There is a term used among artists called the focal point. It is a point in the painting around which everything is focused. It is the center of attention. Based on today's passage, what is to be your focal point? Your focal point should be Christ. When your focus is on Christ, you bring glory to God. You might have disagreements or differences of opinion at times, but you should always focus on Christ. When you focus on Christ, you aren't concerned with your own agenda as much as you are concerned for His kingdom and His plans. What are some things that can help you focus on Christ? Commit to reading your Bible every day this week to help you keep a focal point for all you do.

58

Parts Are Parts

For as the body is one and has many parts, and all the parts of that body, though many, are one body— so also is Christ. (1 Corinthians 12:12)

When does your team, choir, or band perform the best? Why does your team, choir, or band need so many different people doing different things? Read Romans 12:4–8. Why are there so many different people in the church? Your team does its best when each member does his/her individual job that makes the overall performance good. The idea of being on a team goes along with being a Christian who is involved with a local church. Your mission, as a Christian, is to use your abilities and spiritual gifts to serve God in the local church. You need other Christians for camaraderie. You also need other Christians because you can accomplish more as a team than as an individual. What does today's verse indicate about the make-up of the local church? What do you think is your role in the body of Christ? Take a moment to ask God to help improve on your teamwork within your church.

59

Important People

*But even more, those parts of the body that seem
to be weaker are necessary. (1 Corinthians 12:22)*

VIP stands for Very Important Person. Who are some people you know personally whom you feel are VIPs? Read 1 Corinthians 12:21–23. Who is the most important person in your church? Believe it or not, you are a VIP. Without you, the body of Christ would be missing a part. Even though you might not consider yourself a VIP, you are because of your relationship with Christ. Jesus cares so much for each one of us that He gives each believer a function (part) in the ministry of His kingdom. What experiences have you had through your church that have been the most meaningful to you? Why? If you weren't an important person, Christ wouldn't have put Himself on the cross for your sin. That's how important you are to Him—and to the ministry of your church. Each believer is given at least one spiritual gift to use in ministry and service through the church. You should be serving in at least one ministry in your church. How does it make you feel knowing that you are very important to Christ and His ministry? Give thanks to God for giving you a part in His ministry work.

60

Support Group

*So if one member suffers, all the members suffer with it;
if one member is honored, all the members
rejoice with it. (1 Corinthians 12:26)*

There are many support groups found in most communities. Think of a few support groups found in your community and their purpose. What happens when someone suffers? Did you know that being a Christian gives you membership to a support group? Paul told us that if a member is suffering, we should all suffer with that member of the body of Christ. The word *suffers* means "endures pain." Paul meant we should sympathize with a person when he or she is in a painful situation. When has someone showed you sympathy? Paul also mentioned that we should rejoice within the body of Christ. We should be glad or joyful when a fellow believer rejoices because of a situation. How has someone rejoiced with you? How does it make you feel knowing that believers will give you support? Pray that God will bless them for giving you and others support.

61

When Good Is Not Enough

But everything that was a gain to me, I have considered to be a loss because of Christ. (Philippians 3:7)

You have probably found yourself in one of two places. You may have been the teacher's pet that everyone referred to as "the kiss-up" or "the brownnoser," or you may have been one of the kids who were calling the names. Which kind of student were/are you? Have you ever tried to be "God's pet" instead of the teacher's pet? Read Philippians 3:4–7. What did Paul do that he thought would earn God's approval? Paul was more religious than you may ever be, yet after having an encounter with Jesus, he realized that none of the "good" that he was doing really mattered. Have you ever found yourself doing religious activities just because they make you feel better about yourself? Do you sometimes get caught in the trap of thinking that God likes you more because of all the good things that you do? Take time to ask God's forgiveness for finding your value in your own actions rather than in Him. Pray that God will help you seek to please Him simply because you love Him, rather than out of obligation or so that others will pat you on the back.

62

The Pursuit of Happiness

*When I considered all that I had accomplished
and what I had labored to achieve, I found everything
to be futile and a pursuit of the wind. There was
nothing to be gained under the sun. (Ecclesiastes 2:11)*

Have you ever invested a lot of time in something to later find that it didn't really matter that much? When I was in high school, our boys' basketball team was pretty good. We were expected to make it to the state basketball tournament, which hadn't been done in a while. The team went through the playoffs and made it to the point that if they won, they would play at state, but if they lost, the season was over. Our team lost, and the whole town was devastated. I remember wondering how life as we knew it would go on. Amazingly enough, the sun still rose the next day, and life went on.

What is your "thing"? It could be sports, art, competitive speech, voice, band, dance, cheerleading, or any number of activities. While these things are good, whether you succeed or fail in these activities, you often feel dissatisfied. What is the problem with accomplishments? (Hint: read Ecclesiastes 2:4–10 to discover some of King Solomon's accomplishments.) Did Solomon feel satisfied? Why? As you recognize that your accomplishments can't fulfill you, you must turn to the One who can— Jesus. Pray something like this today: "God, help me find peace and fulfillment in You alone today."

63

Created for Good

For you are saved by grace through faith, and this is not from yourselves; it is God's gift—not from works, so that no one can boast. (Ephesians 2:8–9)

When I was in high school, I took part in a Bible study that helped us learn to share our faith. We were led to memorize Ephesians 2:8–9. In your own words, what do these verses mean? If salvation is a gift and there is nothing that you can do to earn it, why should you do good things? Now read Ephesians 2:10. Why were you created? Although your good works don't define you, don't save you, and don't earn you favor with God, He created you to do good things. You might have obvious abilities (like singing or playing an instrument), or you might have skills and abilities that are less obvious (such as encouraging others or good organizational skills). What are some gifts, talents, and abilities that God has given to you? How might He want to use those in His kingdom? Thank God for His grace and for creating you uniquely to serve Him. Ask Him to show you how He wants to use you to further His kingdom.

64

Great Job

*And the world with its lust is passing away, but the one
who does God's will remains forever. (1 John 2:17)*

Whether it be a "great job" at the top of a test or getting credit in the local newspaper for an accomplishment, you probably enjoy a good pat on the back for a job well done. If you could receive attention or a meaningful compliment from any five people in your life, who would you choose? Why? There's nothing wrong with enjoying a compliment, but you have to be careful whose compliments you seek. Sometimes you can get consumed by seeking the approval of the world. What is John's warning in 1 John 2:15–16? John challenged us not to love the world or anything in the world. Do you think that finding worth in the approval of others could be considered loving something in the world? Why? What is the promise in today's verse? God desires that you find your worth in Him, not in the applause of people. God alone sees your heart and knows whether or not you are pleasing to Him. Start today by praying something like this: "Dear God, help me to find my worth in You and not what others say about me—whether it be good or bad."

65

Who Are You Trying to Fool?

*"The heart is more deceitful than anything else, and incurable—
who can understand it? I, Yahweh, examine the mind, I test
the heart to give to each according to his way, according
to what his actions deserve." (Jeremiah 17:9–10)*

Have you ever thought about how easy it can be to fool people? For example, some people might let their parents think that they were doing homework on-line while they were really chatting with friends or catching up on social media. Others might take credit in a group project even though they did little or no work to help. While it may be easy to fool people, you can't fool God.

How does today's passage contradict the popular idea in our society today that most people are really "good at heart"? Is their anything that we can do on our own to give us pure hearts? Why? God alone, through the shed blood of Jesus Christ, can make us pure. While we may fool people into thinking we're good or we may hear them point out our flaws, God alone can see what's inside. Take time now to thank God for allowing Jesus to die on the cross so that you might have a clean heart. Ask God to help you be real with people today.

66

Riding The Fence

For am I now trying to win the favor of people, or God?
Or am I striving to please people? If I were still trying to
please people, I would not be a slave of Christ. (Galatians 1:10)

Jeremy is a youth minister. He often shares with students how as a high school student he tried to "ride the fence." His dad was a preacher, so Jeremy was good at playing the church game on Sundays and then trying to please the crowd at school Monday through Friday. Like Jeremy, we all struggle with pleasing God versus pleasing man.

Paul had made up his mind about whom he would seek to please. What is the problem with trying to win the favor of people? Paul was facing pressure from some well-intentioned people, but he realized that he had to choose whether he would please God or people. He could not please both.

Reflect on a time when you have chosen to please people (this could even include yourself) rather than God. What were the consequences? Why do you think that we should seek to please God rather than other people? Since God alone can see your heart, shouldn't He be the one you strive to please? Pray that God will give you a passion to live in a way that honors Him.

67

For The Birds

"This is why I tell you: Don't worry about your life, what you will eat or what you will drink; or about your body, what you will wear. Isn't life more than food and the body more than clothing?" (Matthew 6:25)

My daughter is three years old, and she loves to try to argue with just about anyone. Last week, we were sitting at the table talking about who loves us. Although we have tried to teach her that God loves her more than we ever could, she started arguing with me telling me that God doesn't love us. While you or I might not say that out loud, sometimes our actions fail to show that we believe that God loves us no matter what. Read Matthew 6:25–26. Do you really believe that God loves us more than the birds? How does God show that He cares for the birds? If God takes care of the birds, do you think that He will take care of you? Why? God loves you no matter who you are or what you've done—or even failed to do. How should being reminded of God's love change how you live? While you may not always feel like God loves you, His Word says that He does. You are loved and valued by God. Remember that every time you see a bird today. Ask God to help you feel His love today—and then share it with others.

68

Wonderfully Created

*I will praise You because I have been remarkably
and wonderfully made. Your works are wonderful,
and I know this very well. (Psalm 139:14)*

Have you ever heard the saying "Beauty is in the eye of the beholder"? What do you think it means? It basically means that the person looking at or holding an object determines its beauty or value. This means that an item that some might consider worthless can be full of value to the one who owns it. Think about this saying in terms of your relationship with God. If you are His, then who determines your beauty or worth? Read Psalm 139:13–16. How do you know you are valuable to God? God not only holds you; He created you. What word did David use to describe the works of God in verse 14? Because you are wonderfully made and God has a plan for you, you can live knowing that God values you. Not only does He value you, He wants to use you in His kingdom for good. He made you uniquely to fill a specific role in His kingdom and to minister to specific people. Pray and ask God to help you remember that you are wonderfully made. Remind others of His love for them.

69

I Love You

Give thanks to the Lord, for He is good.
His love is eternal. (Psalm 136:1)

What phrases do you and your friends repeat over and over? Maybe you are all fans of a particular movie and love to quote it. There are some phrases that make me think of particular friends from college every time I hear them. In these cases, memories come flooding back to my mind just from hearing certain words. If God repeats something in the Bible, it is definitely worth noting. If you skim the rest of Psalm 136, how many times are the words *His love is eternal* repeated? God didn't just tell us about His love once or twice in His Word. In this chapter alone He reminds you of His everlasting love twenty-six times. His love endures forever! What does that tell you about the importance of God's love? God's great love for all people is a theme throughout the Bible. He showed His love when He sent Jesus to earth to die on the cross so that you might have eternal life. Psalm 136 reminds you that God's love lasts forever. Pause now and thank God that His love lasts forever no matter who you are or what you'vo done.

70

Courageous or Crazy?

For I am not ashamed of the gospel, because it is
God's power for salvation to everyone who believes,
first to the Jew, and also to the Greek. (Romans 1:16)

I know a guy who will do just about anything without thinking twice. We went to a minor league baseball game once and dared him to go strike up a conversation with a girl. Although she looked about his age from the back, when he got closer he realized that she was probably in her mid-thirties, and she was with a man who was her husband, not her dad. In spite of the circumstances, he still started talking to her. Several rows back, we could not contain our laughter; but Clay still showed courage. While most of us might not have the courage of Clay, we can still be bold because we belong to God.

Why do you think Paul was not ashamed? What was the source of his courage? Even the most outgoing person can get a knot in his or her stomach when it comes time to share Christ with someone. In my experience, the knot goes away, and the Holy Spirit takes over as soon as you initiate the conversation. Read Romans 1:17. How are you to live your life? Living a life of faith can open doors for opportunities to share your faith. Who is one person with whom you could share Christ? Pray that God will give you boldness in sharing His love.

71

Live with Confidence

*I am not ashamed, because I know the One I have
believed in and am persuaded that He is able to guard
what has been entrusted to me until that day. (2 Timothy 1:12)*

Are you a person that others would describe as confident? Why? I have to admit that while I might give the appearance of confidence, even now as an adult there are times when a war is waging in my heart. During my inner struggle, I have to turn to God's Word. Many years ago, God gave me great reason to be confident in my relationship with Him, and this gives me boldness in living. Why could Paul live with courage? How can this verse give you confidence and boldness in your life? I actually learned this verse as part of an old hymn, but it reminds me that I know God personally—the God who created the universe. If you are a Christian then you, too, know God, and He knows you. This fact should give us boldness in our daily lives. What are some areas in which you struggle with being bold? Witnessing? Choosing not to gossip, cheat, or drink? Loving others? Being consistent? Pray something like this today: "God help me to live boldly today, remembering that I know You personally and that You know and love me."

72

Evidence of Love

If anyone says, "I love God," yet hates his brother, he is a liar. For the person who does not love his brother he has seen cannot love the God he has not seen. (1 John 4:20)

What do you think loving God looks like in the life of the average middle school or high school student? How might a "God-lover" be different from his or her peers? Read 1 John 4:19–21. What is the evidence that we love God? Loving others is difficult at any age. As a teenager the temptations to be mean to others are around every corner. If you have seen the movie *Mean Girls*, you know that even those who seem the nicest or have the most going for them can get caught up in hurting others in order to feel better about themselves. Because you belong to God and God loves you more than you'll ever know, you can be different from those around you. Imagine for a minute how your school would be different if just the students in your youth group chose to love others with God's type of love. While you don't have control over the actions of others, you do have to choose whether or not you will love others. Pray that God will help you to be bold in loving others at school, at home, and at church, even if it means being different.

73

Don't Be Served . . . Serve

"The Son of Man did not come to be served, but to serve, and to give His life—a ransom for many." (Matthew 20:28)

Read Matthew 20:24–28. What did the rulers of the Gentiles do? How did the men of high position treat them? What two words did Jesus use to define greatness? The Greek word for servant is *diakonos* which means "an attendant or waiter"; the Greek word for slave is *doulos* which can mean a "voluntary slave." What do these words have to do with serving others? What's the difference between the attitudes of the rulers or men of high position and the attitude of a servant or slave? What did Jesus come to do? The sinful nature in each of us desires power over others. We want others to serve us, or we want to be popular instead of being servants. Instead, as a believer in Jesus, you are to follow His humble example and choose to serve others. In what situations do you desire others to serve you? How could God use you to serve others in these same situations? Confess your desire for power to God. Ask God to help you choose to serve the people in your life.

74

The Cup

*Going a little farther, He fell facedown and prayed, "My Father!
If it is possible, let this cup pass from Me. Yet not as I will,
but as You will."(Matthew 26:39)*

The greatest obstacle of service most often is pride. Read Matthew 20:20–23. What did this mother ask Jesus? In biblical times, the seat at the right and left were seats of highest honor. Knowing this, what specifically was this mother asking Jesus? How did Jesus answer? Read Matthew 26:36–39. What "cup" was Jesus talking about? In Scripture, the image of a cup is symbolic for fate or lot in life. Jesus knew it was His fate to suffer on the cross. Knowing this, what was Jesus' conclusion? Jesus reminded James and John—and all His disciples—that service requires sacrifice. Jesus loves you and all humanity enough to make the ultimate sacrifice—death on the cross. As you look for ways to serve others, you will need to be prepared to make some sacrifices of your own. How does pride make it hard to sacrifice and serve? Don't give in to pride! Ask Jesus to give you the ability to serve Him by sacrificing and serving others—just like He did! And when it gets hard—and it will—remember, Jesus knows how you feel.

75

The King's Lesson

Now I, Nebuchadnezzar, praise, exalt, and glorify the King
of heaven, because all His works are true and His ways are just.
He is able to humble those who walk in pride. (Daniel 4:37)

Pride is thinking mostly about "I," "my," "me," or "mine." You know, kind of like "It's all about me," "Have you seen my car? It is incredible!" or "I don't think so; it's my way or the highway." Read Daniel 4:28–30. In verse 30, how many times does King Nebuchadnezzar say "I" or "my"? What's wrong with his comments? Read Daniel 4:31–33. King Nebuchadnezzar would be driven away until when? Read Daniel 4:34–37. How are these comments from the king different from verse 30? What was the result of this attitude in verse 36? In what area of your life can you easily take too much credit, stealing God's glory? Maybe your grades? Your athletic accomplishments? Your musical talent? Your looks? Your popularity? You can serve yourself or you can serve God. You cannot do both. The moral of this story is found at the end of verse 37. What does God do to those who walk in pride? Choose to humble yourself, or God will do it for you! Ask God to forgive you for any pride. Recognize that your life is a gift from Him. Humbly choose to serve Him.

76

Dirty Jobs

He poured water into a basin and began to wash His disciples'
feet and to dry them with the towel tied around Him. (John 13:5)

Jesus did not just tell the disciples to serve—Jesus served them. Jesus provided them, and us, the perfect example. Imagine a coach telling his team to run laps and then lacing up his shoes and running with them. Read John 13:1–5. What did Jesus do that shocked the disciples? The task of washing dusty, dirty feet was a lowly servant's job. Why did Jesus—the Son of God—choose to do this dirty job? If Jesus is not above choosing to do the dirty jobs, neither are His followers! There are dirty jobs all around you. Toilets have to be cleaned, diapers changed, trash taken out, dishes washed, and weeds pulled. Think of a dirty job, a humble way you can serve someone. Before you go to bed tonight, do it! You just followed Jesus' perfect example. Ask Him to help you choose to tackle dirty jobs—just like He did.

77

God Sees

Whatever you do, do it enthusiastically, as something done for the Lord and not for men. (Colossians 3:23)

Read Colossians 3:22–24. For a moment, consider yourself a slave. What instruction is given to slaves? Who are your earthly masters? Who tells you what to do? When are you to obey? When you obey your parents, teachers, and coaches, who are you really serving? "Whatever you do" means whatever you do! The small tasks, the dirty jobs, the anonymous behind-the-scenes services aren't done for your own recognition. Have confidence that you do it for an audience of one—the Lord Himself!

There's a story of a prominent man who went to visit a cathedral that was being built. He stopped to watch one of the workers. He saw the worker carving a tiny bird into the inside of a beam that would eventually be covered over by the stone roof. The man asked the worker why he was spending so much time and giving so much attention to something that no one would ever see. The builder never looked up. He never stopped carving as he replied, "Because God sees." Praise the Lord for the opportunities to serve Him! Ask Him to help you work at whatever you do with all your heart!

78

Simple Service

Therefore, confess your sins to one another and pray for one another, so that you may be healed. The urgent request of a righteous person is very powerful in its effect. (James 5:16)

What is the most powerful thing you can do to serve someone? When you don't know what else to do, you can always pray! When you feel helpless, you can pray! When you have done everything you can think of, pray! The humblest, simplest, yet most powerful act of service is to pray! Why is prayer so powerful? Prayer acknowledges your total dependence upon God and His total ability to work. When you doubt your ability to serve, remember the power of prayer! Stop now and think of someone who needs prayer more than anything else you could do. Right now, stop and pray for that person. Ask God to work in their life in a way only He can. Ask God to use you to serve that person. This week, tell that person face-to-face that you are praying for them. If you can, take the time to pray out loud for them. Don't stop! Pray!

79

Living Sacrifice

*Therefore, brothers, by the mercies of God, I urge you to present
your bodies as a living sacrifice, holy and pleasing to God;
this is your spiritual worship. (Romans 12:1)*

You are to present your body as a living sacrifice. What thoughts come
to mind when you hear that phrase? In the Old Testament, a sacrifice was
presented at the Temple. Sacrifices were usually animals (bulls, sheep,
goats, or birds); but they could also be food, such as grain. Sacrifices
were given for various reasons. The fellowship sacrifice was given as an
expression of thanksgiving for God's blessings. A sin offering was given
for cleansing from sin. A burnt offering was given in connection with
worship or seeking God's favor. Each sacrifice cost something. The Jews
either brought them from home or purchased them at the Temple. With
all of these images in mind, what do you think it means for you to be a
living sacrifice?

Now read 1 Corinthians 6:19–20. You are not your own! What is your
body? How can you "glorify God in your body"? Out of thanksgiving for
the price that Jesus paid for you, offer your body to God for His service.
Your hands become His hands. Your mouth becomes His mouth. Your
feet become His feet. Are you glorifying God in your body as a living
sacrifice—or are you only glorifying yourself?

80

One Part

For by the grace given to me, I tell everyone among you not to think of himself more highly than he should think. Instead, think sensibly, as God has distributed a measure of faith to each one. (Romans 12:3)

Think about all the parts of your body. In an average body:

—It takes about 1 minute for a red blood cell to circulate through your entire body.

—At rest, you usually breathe between 12 and 15 times a minute.

—You use 200 muscles to take one step.

—You blink over 6,000,000 times per year.

—Your heart beats around 100,000 times per day or 35,000,000 times per year.

You could not survive without all the parts of your body working together.

Read Romans 12:3–5. What does verse 3 have to do with Paul's comparison to the body? You have many parts working together as one body. Like the heart is one part of an amazing body, you are one part of Christ's amazing body! Your gifts, while important to the body, are only one part. Your gifts would be useless without the other parts of Christ's body working too. When each part does what it should, together we are Christ to the world. What is your part? Paul gives some suggestions in Romans 12:6–8. Prayerfully consider your role in Christ's body. Don't just consider your gift—use it! Look around for other people that you can work with to be Christ to the world.

81

The List

*Do not be conquered by evil, but
conquer evil with good. (Romans 12:21)*

Not sure how to serve? Not sure exactly what you're supposed to do? Don't worry! Paul gave us a list! Read Romans 12:9–19. How would your world be different if you obeyed this list?

Of all the instructions Paul gave, which three seem the hardest for you? Which instruction would make the biggest difference in your family? at your school? at your church? Grocery lists, packing lists, to-do lists—lists are nice, but they are only helpful when you actually do what is on the list! While some of these instructions sound short and simple, actually doing them is challenging. You cannot do any of these by your own power! With the power of the Holy Spirit, God can do them through you and change your world! Spend a few moments prayerfully reading the passage again. Ask God specifically how you can apply each instruction. Confess your own failure to serve others, and ask the Holy Spirit to strengthen you and serve through you!

82

Do Something!

*But a Samaritan on his journey came up to him, and
when he saw the man, he had compassion. (Luke 10:33)*

Read Luke 10:25–37. What one word explains why the Samaritan stopped? *Splagchnizomai* is the Greek word for compassion. That crazy looking word means "to have the bowels or stomach yearn." In English we'd say gut-wrenching. Picture this: the Samaritan sees the man stripped, beaten, and half-dead. The gut-wrenching sight turns his stomach. The Samaritan knows he cannot just walk past the man—he has to do something. When have you felt this kind of physical reaction to a situation? Refugees, starving children, the AIDS pandemic, genocide, tsunamis, earthquakes, hurricanes, and floods—there are incredible overwhelming needs all around us. It is easy to feel overwhelmed and helpless. Instead, feel compassion—that gut-wrenching reaction that you have to do something to make a difference. Begin with one person. Who's someone you know with a need that you can meet? What specifically can you do? Jesus felt compassion for us—for you. He saw you hopelessly lost in your sin, and He had to do something. He died on the cross to offer you the hope of salvation. Ask God to help you feel compassion to the point that you must do something. Do something, however small, in response to God's leading.

83

Least of These

"'I assure you: Whatever you did for one of the least of these brothers of Mine, you did for Me.'" (Matthew 25:40)

Read Matthew 25:35–40. Who comes to mind when you think of the "least of these"?

—Every year 15 million children around the world die of hunger.

—1.4 million children worldwide die each year from lack of access to safe drinking water and adequate sanitation.

—National Law Center on Homelessness and Poverty estimates in the US there are 700,000 homeless people per night; or 2 million per year.

—Half the world—nearly three billion people—live on less than two dollars a day.

—Worldwide, nearly 10 million children every year die of totally preventable diseases (UNICEF).

—According to the US Department of Justice, 2,299,116 prisoners were held in federal or state prisons or in local jails.

Gut-wrenching? These figures are staggering. When you consider these statistics, are they just numbers, or do they represent millions of opportunities to serve Jesus Himself? What will you do? What you do for one of the least of these, you do for Jesus.

84

God's Economy

*At the present time your surplus is available for their need,
so their abundance may also become available for
our need, so there may be equality. (2 Corinthians 8:14)*

Read 2 Corinthians 8:13–15. The quote in verse 15 is taken from Exodus 16:18. The Israelites were wandering in the wilderness. God fed them with mystery flakes that appeared on the ground after the dew evaporated. God gave the Israelites clear instructions for collecting it—gather only what you need. Some people gathered more, some less. Incredibly, when they measured it, each person had only what they needed. Why in the world did Paul use this illustration? In the present time, who are you? What do you have surplus of? What do you have a need for? How can you use the abundance God has given you to serve someone else's need? How has someone else's surplus served your need? Praise God that in His economy, there is abundance for everyone! Ask Him to open your eyes to the surplus in your life and the need in someone else's. Follow the Holy Spirit's direction to serve someone, or allow others to serve you!

85

Elohim

In the beginning God created the heavens and the earth. (Genesis 1:1)

What are some names of God? If you can't think of any names off the top of your head, make a list of some characteristics of God that help you understand Him. Names are a pretty big deal. When's the last time you talked to someone and didn't know their name? Sure, it happens every once in a while, but we tend not to talk to people when we don't know their names. That's why you introduce yourself, so others feel comfortable enough to make conversation. What is your favorite movie? Who's your favorite character? How are they introduced in the movie? What name of God do you discover at the beginning of your Bible? Wow! Did you get that? This is Elohim! This is God our Creator! In the grand scheme of things, does it get any bigger than the One who created everything? God comes into the picture first thing, and He reveals something about Himself. He is the Creator of all things, so He has all authority.

Take some time to think about all the things God has created. If God created all these things, isn't it natural God would have all authority? Do a Google search for "Names of God" to discover more incredible names for God.

86

Control

*"Where were you when I established the earth?
Tell Me, if you have understanding." (Job 38:4)*

When was the last time you were in a good battle of Tug-of-War? I don't really know if there has ever been a good battle because it always seems one side ends up on the ground while others fall on top of someone. Sometimes we get in a battle with God. We question His actions or motives. It's easy for us to say that God is in control, but it's hard for us let go of the over-sized rope.

Job needed to be reminded of that as well. (If you don't know the story of Job, this may be a great time for you to sit down and read his story. If you don't have time right now, come back and read it in sections.) Read Job 38:1–5. Who is in control? How do you know? Get the picture? Sometimes we need to be reminded that we are not the ones in control. When Job began to question, God reminded him that he wasn't there when God created the universe. When we question God, we should ask the same question. Where were we when it all started? You may want to take this time to tell God you're sorry for continuing to tug on the rope. List some things that will remind you God has all authority.

87

Under His Authority

God replied to Moses, "I AM WHO I AM. This is what you are to say to the Israelites: I AM has sent me to you." (Exodus 3:14)

Many people think *I'm kind of a big deal.* You may have even said it. I think we all like to think we're bigger than we really are. In our own world, we are a big deal, because it's all about us. We're the president, senator, and governor on our own little planet in our head. Read Exodus 3. Who did Moses discover really is a big deal? Now that you've read it, count how many "I" statements God makes. There are upward of seventeen "I" statements in these twenty-two verses. Why does God talk about Himself so much? Because He's God! When Moses asked what he was to say to the people, God replied, "I AM WHO I AM." This is what you are to say to the Israelites: "I AM has sent me to you." Moses was to tell them it's all about God. In case you didn't know it, God is a big deal. He speaks with all authority because He has all authority. We may be a big deal in our own little world, but God's world is bigger, and He created it. How big of a deal is God to you? Take these next few minutes to thank God for being so big.

88

I'm My Own Boss

"Get up! Go to the great city of Nineveh and preach the message that I tell you." (Jonah 3:2)

I used to love playing hide-and-go-seek. There's just something about finding a place where no one can find you. Was there ever a place you could hide and just laugh (in a villain like manner) because you knew no one would find you there? The truth is, sooner or later you would be found. It's all part of the game. When it comes to the will of God, we sometimes run and hide from it because we know it's going to mess up our plans for life.

Read Jonah 1–3. Why did Jonah run from God? Why Tarshish? Well, Tarshish, in Jonah's day, was thought to be the end of the earth. He wanted to get as far away from God as he could. Plus it was in the opposite direction of where God wanted him to go. He didn't want to do what God wanted Him to do.

When God is leading you to do something, where do you run? Do you run away because you think you've got it under control, or do you run toward the will of God? In what way is God leading you to obey Him? Maybe it's talking to the person who sits alone at lunch. Maybe God is calling you to the ministry or maybe even missions. My suggestion to you is don't run!

89

Me, Myself, and I

He must increase, but I must decrease.
(John 3:30)

Here's a math test for you: What is it that makes one number greater than the other? It's simply because the other number is bigger. Sometimes we think we're of greater value than we really are. We think more highly of ourselves and our ways than we probably should. That's what's great about John; he understood his role in God's will.

Read John 3:25–30. Where did John see himself? Sure, John had been doing a lot of great things, but now it was time for him to step back. He didn't want there to be any confusion of who the people were to follow. His words were simple, but they were also words that revealed his willingness to be follower. Jesus must become greater than you, and you must become less than Him. When's the last time you saw the ways of Christ as greater than your ways? Take these next few minutes to ask God to make His ways greater in your life and your ways less.

90

I Am The Way

Jesus told him, "I am the way, the truth, and the life.
No one comes to the Father except through Me." (John 14:6)

If you were to create the greatest burger in the world, what would it have on it? What about a sibling or a friend, what would theirs have on it? Chances are their burger wouldn't look or taste like yours. There's more than one way to make a burger.

How many ways are there to get to heaven? There's not more than one way to get to heaven. In our pluralistic society, we've tried to come up with our own ways to make it there, but in doing so we've only produced a cornucopia of ways not to get there. We, as well as others, think our way is best; but truthfully, all human ways lead to disappointment. There is only one way to get to heaven—and all the roads don't get you there. Read Matthew 19:16–22. What did Jesus say? This young man thought he knew the way, but when he learned what he really must do, he left disappointed. He was disappointed because it wasn't by his doing. Read Isaiah 55:8. How are God's ways different? It's good that our ways aren't God's ways. We can really mess some stuff up. Take some time to thank God for providing the way to Him. Thank Him for not leaving it up to us.

91

To Obey or Not to Obey

Children, obey your parents as you would the Lord,
because this is right. (Ephesians 6:1)

What are some things your parents ask you to do on a daily basis—such as chores or errands? Better yet, what are some things your parents ask you to do which you don't gripe about? It seems like parents always need you to do something. Maybe it's taking out the trash or going to pick up your brother or sister from soccer practice. It always seems you're being asked to do something. Parents don't seem to understand. The truth is they understand all too well. It's easy to forget they used to be your age going through some of the same things you are going through. They probably have a really good idea of the pressures you face. That should make it easier for you to honor them.

Read Ephesians 6:1–3. Why should you honor your parents? Honoring your parents is not only a command from God, but it also comes with a promise. What does the promise mean to you? Wow. That's a pretty good reason to honor your parents. If you hold your parents in high regard and obey them, God will bless your life. What an amazing promise. Spend the next few minutes thanking God for your parents. Ask God to show you ways you can honor them.

92

Obedience During Insanity

*"For now I know that you fear God, since you have
not withheld your only son from Me." (Genesis 22:12)*

If you're a fan of social networking sites, then you've probably wasted a bunch of time filling out one of those surveys letting others know some very unimportant information about yourself. On almost every one of those surveys you will find a question that goes something like this: "Have you ever done anything crazy? If so, what?" We all do crazy things, and parents are no different. Your parents will do things you don't agree with. They may even do something that embarrasses you a great deal, but how can you honor your parents when they're acting a little whack?

Read Genesis 22:1–14. What did Abraham do that would be considered crazy? Isaac probably thought his dad was about to do something crazy, but if you look at the attitude of Isaac, there's a lot of trust. Even in the midst of what seemed like insanity, Isaac honored his father. Parents can act crazy sometimes, but that doesn't mean we love, honor, or obey them any less. Pray that God would give you the same understanding as Isaac.

93

24/7

*But be doers of the word and not hearers only,
deceiving yourselves. (James 1:22)*

Is listening worth anything if there's no action involved afterward? Explain. Read Deuteronomy 6:4–9. What did God command His people to do? Two things are involved here—teaching and listening. Your parents are to teach you daily the ways of God, and you are to listen. But you're supposed to do more than listen; you're supposed to do—to put some action to what you hear and learn. James reminds us we are supposed to be doers of the Word, not just hearers of the Word.

On a scale of 1 (terrible) to 10 (great), how would you rate yourself on being a doer of God's Word? Why? The words in Deuteronomy are challenging. You're supposed to listen to God's Word when you rise, sleep, sit, and walk around. That's pretty much all day. You're supposed to actually listen to the spiritual guidance of your parents. And yes, dating advice can be spiritual guidance. Another great lesson to be learned from this passage is the fact that God is to be the center of your relationship with your parents. When you take God out of your conversation with your parents, it's no wonder why it's hard to understand why you are to honor them.

Spend a minute thinking about the topic that dominates your conversations with your parents. What can you do to put God in the center of your relationship with them? In doing this, understanding them and honoring them will become easier.

94

Follow The Leader

Remind them to be submissive to rulers and authorities,
to obey, to be ready for every good work. (Titus 3:1)

Make a list of individuals who have positions of authority. On this list, who has direct authority over you? We have an inauguration ceremony for our new president. On that day, he or she takes over as the President of the United States of America. That's a pretty important role. Another pretty important fact about our new President is he or she was appointed by God to be in this role. Really.

Read Romans 13:1–7. What instructions are given in these verses? When was the last time you prayed for the President? He's not usually on the top of our prayer list, but if he's been appointed by God, then he is deserving of your prayers. It's the same for your parents, principal, teacher, mayor, or pastor. They all have positions of authority, and they've all been appointed by God. So based on what you have read, what needs to change about your attitude toward those in authority? Spend the next few minutes praying for the list of people who have been appointed by God to have a position of authority.

95

Simon Says

The king was overjoyed and gave orders to take Daniel
out of the den. So Daniel was taken out of the den,
uninjured, for he trusted in his God. (Daniel 6:23)

When was the last time you played a game of Simon Says? Those were the days! I'm sure you were always happy when you finally got to be Simon. You had to be a little devious in this game because you wanted to trick people. The goal was to get everyone to follow "Simon," but if Simon didn't say it then it was time for them to go. Sometimes that's probably how you feel about the authorities over you. They want you to do what they say, and if you do something out of their authority then you're out! But is it ever okay to disobey authority?

Review the story in Daniel 6:1–26. What stands out most to you? How would you describe Daniel's view of those in authority over him? Daniel got thrown into a lion's den because he disobeyed his authority. But the true question is: why did he disobey? Answer: Because he wanted to honor God.

There's a difference between rebellion and disobedience. Daniel did not rebel against his authority. (As a matter of fact, it appears Daniel didn't even put up a fight.) Daniel disobeyed in order to honor God. Whether it's obedience or disobedience, we do one or the other to bring glory and honor to God. If you live your life as a pleasing aroma to God (Ephesians 5:1), then you are living under the authority of God. Spend the next few minutes asking God to help you submit to authority. Ask Him to help you bring Him glory and honor in the way you live your life.

96

Following a Follower

The One who descended is also the One who ascended far above
all the heavens, that He might fill all things. (Ephesians 6:10)

Do you like to read directions? If you go out and buy a new video game system or computer, do you plug it in and go, or do you stop to read all the directions? If you don't stop to read the directions, then chances are you are not getting everything out of your new purchase. The directions are placed in the box to help you out. They're there to help you get everything you can out of your game system or computer.

Think about your youth pastor (or your pastor or Bible study leader). Did you know that person has been placed in your life for spiritual guidance? Read Ephesians 4:10–13. Why did God place pastors and ministers in positions of authority? In the same way directions are placed in a box, God has placed someone who has spiritual authority in your life to equip you for ministry. God has placed people in your life to help you grow. Believe it or not, those people want to help you reach your full potential—because that's what they've been called to do.

Take some time to pray for the person you named earlier. Pray that God would grant them godly wisdom to impart to you and your student ministry. Pray for them to have the strength to minister.

97

Higher Than I

"For as heaven is higher than earth, so My ways are higher than your ways, and My thoughts than your thoughts." (Isaiah 55:9)

Think of your favorite band. What does their music (especially the lyrics) reveal about them? Songwriters write about what moves them. Artists portray life as they see it. Writers highlight what's important to them. Our worldview—how we see life—dictates our actions. Now there's nothing wrong with that. However, Proverbs cautions us that we may think our way is right, but we'll find out later that it leads to death (Proverbs 14:12).

So what do we do? What does it mean to you that God's ways and thoughts are different than yours? God is omniscient—that means He knows everything. It also means that sticking close to God will keep you on the right track. Do you agree? Why? As you study God's Word, your worldview is reshaped. You develop a biblical worldview—viewing life through the lens of Scripture. Let's go back to your favorite band. You choose to listen to their music. Now what does that reveal about you? Perhaps a change is needed. Pray about it.

98

It's Not About Me

When all has been heard, the conclusion of the matter is:
fear God and keep His commands, because this is for all
humanity. For God will bring every act to judgment, including
every hidden thing, whether good or evil. (Ecclesiastes 12:13–14)

Who was the wisest man that ever lived? Need help? Check out 1 Kings 3:12. Who found everything to be meaningless? Right again, our friend Solomon did. After much reflection, however, he finally figured it out. What did Solomon conclude? Yes, it's all about God. It's never been about us—about you. We'd like to think it is, but Solomon, the wisest man that ever lived, told us otherwise. So now what do you need to do?

Paul told us to stop conforming to this world, and to be transformed by the renewing of our minds (Romans 12:2). Your mind is where your worldview is formed. Your worldview controls your attitudes, thoughts, feelings, and actions. If your mind is renewed by God's Word, your worldview becomes Christ-centered. How can you be transformed? Commit to an intimate walk with God—daily. Immerse yourself in His Word—daily. Think of the difference a transformed and renewed you would make.

99

Make a Difference

The God who made the world and everything in it—
He is Lord of heaven and earth and does not
live in shrines made by hands. (Acts 17:24)

What did it feel like when you first met God? We all have different stories, but there is one thing that we can all agree on. God met us where we were. Some of us were just cruising through life. Some were actively seeking God. Others had given up on Him. Wherever we were, God met us there. Before knowing God, you may have been convinced that you knew best. You most likely saw life through a selfish lens and acted accordingly. Then God stepped in and showed you that there is so much more to life. The same thing happened in Acts 17:22–31. What was Paul's main argument? Paul engaged his listeners by using their own worldviews. He affirmed their belief in an unknown God and then introduced them to the real God. Paul said that in Jesus Christ we live, move, and have our being. How we see life has been radically transformed to reflect Jesus to others. Thank God for your new life. Live to bring others to a place where they, too, can meet God.

100

Masterpiece

*Your works are wonderful, and I know
this very well. (Psalm 139:14)*

What would you consider to be your latest masterpiece? A song or poem you wrote or a cool art or science project? How about a sports trophy or good grades? When God finished creating the heavens and the earth—and us—He looked and saw that "it was very good" (Genesis 1:31). Despite the wondrous splendor of the heavens and earth, however, we (including you) are God's masterpiece. Read Psalm 139:13–14. What image is presented here?

Imagine someone knitting, paying attention to every detail. God did the same. He carefully put you together in your mother's womb. Imagine that! God personally fashioned you and put you on this earth for a reason. Can you believe that? You were specially made and given dominion over the rest of creation. More than that, you were made to have an intimate relationship with your Creator. We alone, as humans, can call Him Father. What does this mean to you? God treasures you above anything else He created. Reflect on Revelations 4:11. Pray and let Him know how much He means to you.

101

It's Your Story

For we are His creation, created in Christ Jesus
for good works, which God prepared ahead of time
so that we should walk in them. (Ephesians 2:10)

Creation. It's the story of how you came into being. It's the story of God's workmanship and devotion. We know the story well. God created us. God redeemed us. God is actively seeking to be involved in our lives. What's your response? God deserves your faithfulness. He deserves your best effort. Think about the plans you have for your life. What are your dreams made of? Where is God in all these? God has a plan for your life. He wants you to actively serve Him somewhere. Walking closely with Him will help you see where that somewhere is. Be faithful in your daily walk. It will bring you to the big picture God is painting. It's a painting called "My Story." Your faithfulness will determine how the finished product will look. We know God is up to something. Jump in and join Him. Thank God for creating you. Thank Him for taking the first step in loving you.

102

Adopted into the Kingdom

He predestined us to be adopted through Jesus Christ for Himself, according to His favor and will. (Ephesians 1:5)

Describe yourself in one sentence. Now read Ephesians 1:3–6. Paul described himself as being in Christ, as having been blessed even before the creation of the world with eternal blessings. What was he talking about? Paul described his adoption into God's kingdom, his relationship with God, who through Jesus became his Father. It is the same relationship you can have. Can you grasp what this means? You were created by God, for God. You were created to have an intimate relationship with Him. You have been adopted as His child. What does it mean to you that you are adopted into God's family? You are unbelievably rich! Because of Jesus, you have every spiritual resource for the asking. The eternal blessings that will never fade are now available to you. Not only do you have the promise of heaven, you can experience a close walk with God while on earth. That's what the abundant life really looks like. So ask away, keeping in mind that your Father knows what's best for you.

103

My Life, His Pleasure

For Yahweh takes pleasure in His people;
He adorns the humble with salvation. (Psalm 139:4)

It's true. We are driven by our desire for pleasure, and sadly most of our regrets can be traced back to this. But pleasure is not necessarily bad. What makes God happy? God created you to bring Him pleasure. Hard to believe, isn't it? God sees more than what you see when you look in the mirror. He takes pleasure in you. Wow! Turn to Philippians 2:13. Stop for a moment and think about how God has been working in your life. Do you see a pattern? That's just God showing you His will for you. And don't worry, He will give you the strength to "act for His good purpose." He just needs your commitment. Think about it. The Creator of all, your Father, is working in you to enable you to achieve your mission. He wants you to do His will, and He even empowers you to do it, so walk closely with Him. Allow Him to reveal His purpose for you. Then live to obey. You are created to bring God pleasure. Make it your goal to accomplish this.

104

Be His Glory

*Therefore, whether you eat or drink, or whatever you do,
do everything for God's glory. (1 Corinthians 10:31)*

Have you ever been caught in a thunderstorm? They are so incredible! The searing flashes of bright light. The booming thunder. The strong, sweeping rain. Creation never ceases to bring God glory. It doesn't matter how hard people deny God, the works of His hands will always testify to His existence. And what about His children? What about you? How can you bring God glory? God expects you to do the same thing the rest of creation does—you are to bring God glory. Paul gave the Corinthian church some great advice. What is the challenge? Doing everything for God's glory seems like an impossible task, but there's something you need to know: you don't have to rely on yourself to carry this out. God will be with you. He promised. So return the compliment to the One who made eternity a joyful prospect for you. Demand great things of yourself, expecting God to be there for you. And don't forget to give all the glory back to Him.

105

The Final Cut

*Nothing profane will ever enter it: no one who
does what is vile or false, but only those written
in the Lamb's book of life. (Revelation 21:27)*

Have you ever tried out for anything? Did you make the list? One thing about these lists—there's always a next time. But have you heard about that other list? It's called the Book of Life. When it's brought up, it'll be too late for second chances. Who gets into heaven? If you haven't made your mind up yet, now is the time. God created you to be with Him forever. Jesus died on the cross to save all those who would believe in Him. Jesus' work is finished. There is nothing more to be done. But that doesn't mean you don't have to make a choice. If you are convinced Jesus died for your sins, you need to choose to act on that belief. All you need to do is confess your sins and accept all that Jesus did. If you've already made that choice, and you've been walking with God, take this as a reminder of how much God really loves you. If you have not made the choice, would you do it today? There are so many things to worry about. But thank God that eternity is no longer one of them. Live a grateful life in response to everything God's done for you.

106

In The Meantime

*Therefore, dear friends, while you wait for these things,
make every effort to be found at peace with Him
without spot or blemish. (2 Peter 3:14)*

Ever tried one of those crazy, jaw-dropping roller coasters? They're a lot of fun—once you get past the long lines. The truth is the waiting part is no fun. But didn't you want to tell others about the great experience? Unfortunately, there's a lot of waiting to be done this side of heaven. In fact, if you've put your faith in Jesus, life is just one long wait to meet Him face to face. Read Philippians 3:20–21. What are we waiting for? It's a done deal. You're heaven-bound. But you don't have to sit back and do nothing. What should you be doing right now? *Spotless. Blameless. At peace with God.* God wants you to live a life that brings honor to His name. In doing so, you can be His own personal invitation to those with whom you come in contact. You (if you are a Christian) have the promise of eternity with God. Don't you want others to have that too? Who in particular? Reflect on how you can share Christ with those you know. The wait is shorter than you might think. Make sure you bring as many people with you as you can.

107

Running to Win

Let us run with endurance the race that lies before us, keeping our eyes on Jesus, the source and perfecter of our faith, who for the joy that lay before Him endured a cross and despised the shame and has sat down at the right hand of God's throne. (Hebrews 12:1–2)

A race—that's how the Bible describes our time here on earth. The writer of Hebrews tells us that the race is marked out for us (Hebrews 12:1), and Paul encouraged us to run hard enough to win the race (1 Corinthians 9:24). God will be there when you reach the end of the track. Will He be pleased with how you ran the race? Why? It's tempting to get lazy and fall back. Sometimes we even rationalize things—"I'm saved, I will always be saved." We start taking Christ for granted. There's an answer for this. What should you do in this race? Fix your eyes on Jesus. Look to Him and follow the path of faith that He shows you. Imitate His perseverance. Be encouraged by His example. Reflect on what prevents you from giving this race your best shot. What doubts, insecurities, or favorite sins keep you from focusing on Jesus? Give them all to Jesus. He is waiting. He'll help you get in shape. Then get in position. Ready? Set? Run!

108

Your Loving Father

"If you then, who are evil, know how to give good gifts to your children, how much more will your Father in heaven give good things to those who ask Him!" (Matthew 7:11)

Have you ever talked to someone whom you didn't know very well? What was the conversation like? It probably wasn't very personal. Sometimes it can be kind of awkward. Do you know that God wants to have a personal, ongoing relationship with you? Read Matthew 7:7–11. How do these verses describe God—your heavenly Father—and His relationship to you? When was the last time you stopped praying because it didn't seem to make any difference? Jesus said to keep asking, searching, and knocking. But He didn't stop there. Jesus explained that you couldn't go wrong asking because you are talking to your heavenly Father who loves you and cares about you. Do you ever worry that God will not answer your prayers the way you want? Could it be because your trust in Him is lacking? God may not answer the way you want, but He will always give you what is best. What would make you truly believe that God wants the best for your life? Society makes God out to be boring, outdated, and out of touch, but nothing is further from the truth. God truly understands you and what is happening in your life. Start getting to know God by having a simple, regular conversation with Him.

109

Other-Centered

First of all, then, I urge that petitions, prayers, intercessions, and thanksgivings be made for everyone. (1 Timothy 2:1)

In 2000, a movie called *Pay It Forward* depicted the story of a 12-year-old boy who wanted to change the world. His idea, "When someone does you a big favor, don't pay it back . . . pay it forward." It demonstrated the same selflessness that Jesus has called us to show. Read 1 Timothy 2:1–6. What instructions do you read here? What are most of your prayers about? Do you pray for others? Are you praying for something bigger than yourself? You are called to expand the borders of your prayer life. This is the kind of selflessness that God wants you to have in your prayer life. Think about the heart and nature of God. What do you think He wants to do in the world around you? When you think of prayer in terms that it is bigger than yourself, you are more in line with the genuine purpose of prayer. How can you commit to pray for others around you and even those who are in the world? Realize that Christ died for all—that includes you (and even people whom you don't know or may not like). Pray as if you are God's representative to the world—because you are.

110

Pray Big

*I pray that the perception of your mind may be
enlightened so you may know what is the hope
of His calling, what are the glorious riches of
His inheritance among the saints. (Ephesians 1:18)*

If you had one million dollars, what are the top five things you would spend the money on? What about one hundred million? A billion? It seems unimaginable to think of how you could spend that much money. To spend a billion dollars, you would have to spend thirty thousand dollars every day for the rest of your life.

Read Ephesians 1:18–19. Who are you to God? Do you know that God has ultimate resources at His disposal? Do you realize that all He is waiting for is for you to ask? Of course, you can't ask for a billion dollars if you have selfish motives. In fact, you can't ask for anything with selfish motives. But if you ask for things that are according to His will, He will give you His glorious riches, His power, and His vast strength. Why have you not asked for great things from God? If you really believe that you have access to the God of the universe, you can ask for all things, large and small. Examine what you ask for from God this week. Pray about some big things that you believe God wants to see happen. Pray about those things and ask for God to do great things.

111

God Knows

*LORD, You have searched me
and known me. (Psalm 139:1)*

Think of your library. How many books are stored there? Of all those books, how many have you read? Ten? Twenty? Maybe more? Think about this—God knows every single bit of all the information that is in every book in that library and in every book ever written—and even in those that are not written yet. His knowledge is infinite. The dictionary definition of *infinite* uses phrases such as "subject to no limitation; immeasurably great." Read Psalm 139:1–6. What does God know about you? God knows everything you want to ask before you even ask it. God knows everything about everything—and everything about you. Imagine you were talking to a friend who had the ability to see every desire you have, all the things in your past, and every reason for thinking, saying, or doing everything. What would your conversation sound like? Wouldn't you feel a little vulnerable—or embarrassed? Now think about your prayer with God. He does see all of these things in you, and He loves you. Based on this, in what ways should your prayers change? God sees you for everything you are and still loves you and wants to have an ongoing relationship with you. Relationships need conversation to grow. Talk to God. Then let Him talk to you.

112

Power and Responsibility

Now we have this treasure in clay jars, so that this extraordinary power may be from God and not from us. (2 Corinthians 4:7)

In one Spiderman movie, the timid and awkward Peter Parker was bitten by a "super spider." The next morning, he noticed something different. He didn't need glasses, his body was built like an athlete, and he had extraordinary agility and senses. He experimented with this newfound power with great excitement and boldness. It completely changed his perspective. But Peter's uncle Ben reminded him, "with great power, comes great responsibility." What would you do if you woke up and found that you had extraordinary abilities?

Read 2 Corinthians 4:7–11. What is your treasure? Are you experiencing extraordinary power in your life? Why or why not? Life can get you down and be very painful, but one of the promises of God is that no matter what happens, you will not be crushed, you will not be in despair, you will not be abandoned, and you will not be destroyed. What kinds of things in your life make you feel defeated or powerless? What things are hurting you? Knowing that God is completely for you, what kinds of things would you pray for now? Live in such a way that others will see the power of Christ working through you.

113

In Sync

Now this is the confidence we have before Him: Whenever we ask anything according to His will, He hears us. (1 John 5:14)

Firefighters have a tough job. One firefighter, the apparatus engineer, has the job of making sure that the truck is close to a water source and can pump the water through the truck to provide the needed water to the fire hose to aid the fire-fighters as they enter the building. This is their lifeline. Without it they would face eminent danger and likely death. Firefighters entering the building go through countless hours of training to be in sync with the fire apparatus engineer to make sure they can safely and effectively enter the burning building to save lives.

When we are in sync with God's will, our prayers are most effective. What is one way you can know the will of God? Understanding the character of God by studying Him in the Bible is a good way to know His will. What are some of the characteristics of God? Are there some things in your life that you know are part of God's will? Pray for that right now. What kinds of things have you been afraid to ask God for? This verse says that you can pray for it confidently if it is in His will. Pray to God with confidence today.

114

It's All About Me

"I tell you, this one went down to his house justified rather than the other; because everyone who exalts himself will be humbled, but the one who humbles himself will be exalted." (Luke 18:14)

Almost every time my pastor preaches, he wisely warns people in the church about the subtlety of sin. Sin sneaks into your life, usually without you knowing. And before you recognize it, it catches you in its grip. That's the point of the Casting Crowns song "Slow Fade." My preacher says that the heart of all sin is pride. And at the center of pride is the letter *I*. Putting yourself in the center is pride that God despises. It is saying to God that you don't need Him, but nothing is further from the truth. Until you understand how much you need God, your prayers are ineffective.

Jesus told a parable about humility and pride. Read Luke 18:9–13. Pharisees were the religious leaders of the day. In the passage, how did the Pharisee approach the temple to pray? Tax collectors were among the most despised people in society. How did the tax collector approach the temple to pray? Jesus praised the tax collector in his prayer because of his humility. What is your humility like? Do you think too highly of yourself? Are your prayers about God's will? The needs of others? Or is it all about your will? Humble prayer is about understanding that God is God and you are not.

115

Humble Prayer

My people who are called by My name humble themselves, pray and seek My face, and turn from their evil ways, then I will hear from heaven, forgive their sin, and heal their land. (2 Chronicles 7:14)

There was an artist who created a statue for a church. It was a statue of Jesus kneeling before a basin with a towel in his hand. Jesus is looking downward as if He is about to wash someone's feet. When asked why she created a statue of Jesus in such an unusual posture, the artist replied, "You have to kneel down, or be down already, in order to look into the face of Jesus." Are you humble? Have you confessed your sin? What does God want from you? One of the biggest obstacles to prayer is sin in your life. What kinds of sin do you need to turn from? Could it be the sin of things that you are looking at? Perhaps you are sinning in the things that you think about. What about your attitude? What about the way you treat people? Know that your sin hinders your prayers to God. He loves you and wants an intimate relationship with you, but the perfect and holy God of heaven can have no part of sin and evil. God will help you get rid of the sin, but you need to choose to let Him and turn away from it.

116

Faith Movers

"If you believe, you will receive whatever you ask for in prayer." (Matthew 21:22)

Go outside and look at a tree. Now try something: tell the tree to uproot and move over twenty feet. Impossible? Not really. If you told someone that you could do that, you would probably be committed to a mental institution, yet that's exactly what Jesus said you can do. In fact you can do more than that; Jesus said that you can move mountains—if you have faith. Read Matthew 21:18–22. What is faith? Do you have faith? You may have faith, but in what do you have your faith? Are you dependent on your skill, your abilities, your social status, or your knowledge? Jesus taught His disciples not just to have faith but to realize it is important in what they place their faith. If you have faith in things with no power, you will be left with no power. If you have faith in unlimited power, you can accomplish anything. Are you dependent on the power of God? When you have faith in God, your prayers, no matter how impossible, can and will be answered. Isn't that amazing? You can do anything—anything! What do you depend on? Do you doubt? Confess that to God right now, and pray that He will help your doubt.

117

I Loved You First

We love because He first loved us.
(1 John 4:19)

Do you sometimes feel that you need to pray to earn God's love? Do you feel like your prayer has to have the right words or the right "feel?" The way you say the prayer has much less to do than the heart of your prayer. When you go to God in prayer with the right heart and right motives, realize that God loves you and will supply your needs. Read 1 John 4:15–19. What do you read in these verses? God is love, and He is the initiator of love to you. In what ways do you feel God's love? What is going on in your life right now that is making it hard to feel His love? The truth is that it is hard to pray if you don't believe that God loves you with a perfect love and that He wants the best for you. The reality is, however, that no matter how you feel, God does love you, and He wants the best for you. It can be discouraging sometimes if you don't get an answer to your prayers, even if you feel like you are praying with the right heart. Take some quiet time to examine your heart. Now acknowledge that God loves you. Keep praying to Him, and don't lose heart.

118

Which Way?

*"For I know the plans I have for you"—this is the
Lord's declaration—"plans for your welfare, not for disaster,
to give you a future and a hope." (Jeremiah 29:11)*

Have you ever been lost? What did it feel like? How did you find your way again? How did you feel once you knew where you were and knew where you were going? Are there times when you feel lost in life? In what areas of your life do you feel lost? In Jeremiah 29:11–13, Israel received a promise from God that He had plans already in place to give them a future and a hope. What things are stressing you out right now? Have you lost hope about some things? How can you apply the promise of verses 12 and 13 to your life? God says that you will call upon Him and pray to Him, and He will listen to you. You will seek Him, and you will find Him when you search with all your heart. What an amazing promise! Even if you feel like you are praying and praying and no one is listening, God says that He is listening. You will find Him. And guess what? He offers you a future and hope. Don't get discouraged—keep praying and keep trusting. He hears every word and doesn't forget.

119

Constant Communication

He then told them a parable on the need for them
to pray always and not become discouraged. (Luke 18:1)

Have you ever had to go through something that occupied your mind so much that no matter what happened all day you couldn't think of anything else? Jesus emphasized to the disciples that they needed to "pray always and not become discouraged." Does God occupy your mind enough that you "pray always?" Read the rest of the story in Luke 18:2–8. Prayer is a habit, a continuing conversation. It can be short—like conversations throughout the day; or it can be long—like a time to share and connect with God. What is your prayer like? E.M. Bounds wrote that "always" doesn't mean that you drop everything that you do in life. What it means is that you are always in touch with God throughout the day. You complete what you need to do and then rest naturally back to a place where you are talking with God (*Purpose in Prayer*). When is the last time you spent more than five minutes in prayer? Did you pour your heart out to Him? Did you spend some time in silence to let God speak to you? Try this. Pray when you wake up. Pray when you walk to school. Pray in between classes. Pray before meals. Pray before you study. Pray before you sleep. Pray frequently. Pray deeply. Pray always.

120

Like No Other

There is no one holy like the Lord. There is no one besides You!
And there is no rock like our God. (1 Samuel 2:2)

People do all sorts of things to make them stand out from the rest of the crowd. They wear different clothes, wear wild hairstyles, or behave in really unique ways. What do you do to separate yourself? God separates Himself from everyone else too. He is holy. That means He is pure, untainted, and sinless—completely unlike any other person in the world. Hannah was a woman blessed by God. She prayed and thanked God by describing who He is. Read 1 Samuel 2:1–3. If you were to describe God's characteristics, what words would you use? Most would describe things God can do or how powerful God is. We often forget how the very core nature of God is completely opposite of our foundation. Take some time to reflect on what makes God so special. Hannah knew God defines holiness. He sets the standard of what is good and right—and holy. No one can measure up to God's holiness. Hannah rightfully compares God to a rock. He is unyielding and unchanging. He can never stop being holy, and He will always be set apart from us. Thank God that Jesus is the bridge between God and us.

121

Defining Moment

The living creatures give glory, honor, and thanks to the One seated on the throne, the One who lives forever and ever. (Revelation 4:9)

What comes to your mind when you think about the end of the world? Many people get caught up with all the wondrous and terrifying events that will signify Jesus' return to earth. What is often forgotten is the defining moment when God's holiness is trumpeted and glorified throughout the universe. Imagine these incredible creatures doing only one thing: calling God holy. Read Revelations 4:8–11. What words stand out most to you? Why? At the center of the world's ending is God. It's easy to get distracted by the whirlwind of activity, but God's holiness is the sole reason why the world is separate from Him. It is too easy to get caught up with exciting—but ultimately less important—creatures and people. Before we can even begin to understand the complexity of the end times, we must connect to God and His holiness. We must understand why He is holy, and we must acknowledge His holiness. When was the last time you praised God for being holy? Honor God's holiness today with a prayer or a song.

122

Above It All

For all have sinned and fall short of
the glory of God. (Romans 3:23)

Did you ever get a report card comment that read something like "tries hard to do well, but still needs improvement?" Or have you ever felt that sinking sensation in class that no matter how much you study, you still won't pass? Sin and holiness are like that. No matter how hard you try to be good, you can never be as holy as God. Read Psalm 14:2–3. How do these verses compare to Romans 3:23? Our sin separates us from God. All of us. No one even comes close to God's holiness. Read Isaiah 59:1–4. The word *barriers* in verse 2 describes our condition perfectly. Sin is a wall. What are some "bricks" in your wall right now? You might say that your hands are not "defiled with blood" (v. 3) or you don't "conceive trouble" (v. 4). Find a newspaper and skim through it. Read about the death and injustice rampant in the world. We live in a sin-drenched world, but in His holiness, God is separate from it all. God's beauty lies in His purity. Praise Him because He is holy and separate.

123

Five Words

Then I heard the voice of the Lord saying: Who should I send?
Who will go for Us? I said: Here I am. Send me. (Isaiah 6:8)

Isaiah was a prophet who saw tremendous visions. But Isaiah did more than talk about the future; he was a man of action and deeds. Read Isaiah 6:1–8. What jumps out at you in these verses? When Isaiah saw the holiness of God and the immense divide between himself and God, he immediately confessed that he was unclean and sinful (v. 5). After Isaiah's confession, God removed his sin (v. 7). When you contemplate God's holiness (and your lack of holiness), does that make you want to confess your sin? Have you trusted in Jesus to cleanse you? What do you need to confess to God right now? When Isaiah finally stood before the Lord purified and forgiven by His love, God asked a simple question (v. 8). Isaiah's wonderful response is five words. Like a child in a classroom, frantically waving his hand to answer a question, Isaiah boldly and simply said, "Here I am. Send me." There was no hesitation. There was no long debate or dialogue. Isaiah completely surrendered himself to God. Will you give yourself to God? Tell God that you surrender to Him.

124

A Grand Act

May He make your hearts blameless in holiness
before our God and Father at the coming of our
Lord Jesus with all His saints. (1 Thessalonians 3:13)

When was a time with family or friends where you felt warm, secure, and genuinely happy and free? When you search your memories for special relationships, are you able to come up with a particular event or gathering that signifies the joy of those relationships? Paul, Silas, and Timothy had that special connection with the believers in Thessalonica. Read 1 Thessalonians 3:6–13. Review these key phrases: *good memories*, *encouraged about you*, and *joy we experience*. Those words underscore the strong bond between these two groups of people. In turn, that bond became the basis for this prayer that their hearts would be blameless in holiness. To be holy before God means to be set apart by God—and for God. Recognizing God's holiness is a vital step in getting to know God. Will you acknowledge God's holiness? Since God is holy, do you believe He wants you to change? Perhaps God wants you to help others become holy too. It is a grand act for believers to help each other to become holy and true. Pray now for your loved ones to be blameless and holy before God.

125

The Pursuit

Pursue peace with everyone, and holiness—
without it no one will see the Lord. (Hebrews 12:14)

Sometimes life really is black and white. For example, assume you have a test in school next week. You can study or not study. You may get away with not studying a few times, but ultimately bad habits catch up with you. The results of your work, or lack of it, will show up on your report cards and your evaluations. Esau was a man who made a bad decision. He gained in the short term but lost out on something deeper in the long run—a blessing. Read Hebrews 12:14–17. What should we pursue? Why? Esau is an example about pursuit. In this case, he didn't pursue a desire to be holy before God. Holiness is not an option. This pursuit of holiness isn't a one day, one event, or one act kind of thing. Pursuing holiness requires a daily dedication and a moment-by-moment desire. Pursuing other things might be easier and even appear beneficial in the very short-term, but ultimately holiness helps us see the Lord. It's a blessing we shouldn't be selling away. Admit to God your desire to pursue other things and commit to pursue holiness.

126

Our Superpower

For it is written, Be holy,
because I am holy. (1 Peter 1:16)

It would be really cool to have a superpower where you could change into anything you want to be. Imagine turning yourself into something fast, like a car, or something tiny, like a needle. The prophet Isaiah tells us we all have this power but in a bad way. Read Isaiah 64:6. Where did the change come from? We are all unclean, and even the good things we do are no good at all. We can't control this change. It happens because of who we are. Holiness isn't something we can achieve on our own. So can we be holy or is it hopeless trying? Why? Read 1 Peter 1:13–16. Why should we strive to be holy? Our only hope for holiness rests on the grace of Jesus Christ. That's the good part of this power to change. Jesus helps us change into holiness. Are you willing to talk to Jesus about becoming holy? Will you take His offer to change you into holiness? Do you desire to be holy because He is holy? What can you do this week to strive for holiness? Get your mind ready for action—spiritual action—this week.

127

As Good as We Can Get

He also told this parable to some who trusted in themselves that they were righteous and looked down on everyone else. (Luke 18:9)

What is your opinion about the following types of people you might see at your school? Bully. Drug addict. Copying/cheating/selfish student. Atheist. Egotistic athlete. Pornography viewer. Would your opinion change if these people humbled themselves before God and admitted they were sinners? Why? What is your opinion about the following types of people you might see at your church? Someone who gives a lot of money to the church. Someone who tries to act righteous. Someone who fasts a lot. Someone who knows all the different church rules. Would your opinion change if these people thought of themselves as really great? Why? Read Luke 18:9–14. What is the difference between the two men? Jesus gave us an example of what holiness doesn't look like. In this case, holiness doesn't mean doing a collection of good acts and then bragging about it. Jesus pointed out that the sinner who is humble before God is the one who will be exalted. Holiness is a blessing from God. Holiness is a result of God's mercy. Think about your opinions about who acts holy. Then think about how you view yourself.

128

Looks Like Holiness

Therefore I, the prisoner for the Lord, urge you to walk worthy of the calling you have received. (Ephesians 4:1)

What does a holy person look like? What words or phrases would you use to describe one? *Frequently says wise things; walks around in simple clothes and sandals; meditates; nods head a lot; speaks quietly; gives away all their possessions; always pursues peace?* Some of these actions may be holy actions, but Paul gave some simple guidelines about what holiness looks like. Read Ephesians 4:1–6. How would you summarize what he said? Paul's themes of a kind and gentle spirit in the unity of the Lord identify the heart of holiness. Sometimes we focus so much on actions or image that we begin to think holiness can be broken into a large to-do list. Or perhaps we think of holiness in terms of personality or age. It is too easy to get distracted by trying to impress people with good behavior and exaggerated acts of giving. Instead, are we willing to patiently put aside our egos and our own desires and goals and walk with our faith communities and churches in joining God in His work? Holiness isn't about things we have done. Ask God to forgive you for trying to achieve holiness on your own.

129

New Glasses

Therefore, I say this and testify in the Lord: You should no longer walk as the Gentiles walk, in the futility of their thoughts. (Ephesians 4:17)

Some kids go through a long period of time without realizing they need glasses. After someone notices and sends them to the optometrist, they put on glasses for the first time. Suddenly, the world becomes clearer, and things that were impossible to see now appear in sharp focus. Paul wrote about a complete switch from an old life to a new life. He used this metaphor to talk about transforming the way we think, behave, and grow. Read Ephesians 4:17–24. What is the key to a focused life? The pursuit of holiness involves a complete 180-degree turn. There needs to be a complete and utter rejection of all that is against God. To what are you still clinging that represents your "old life?" Why? If you looked up the word *renewal* in a thesaurus, you would get these suggestions: *revitalization, rejuvenation, rebirth, replenishment,* and *restoration.* Those are wonderful ways to describe what happens when you seek to renew the "spirit of your minds" (v. 23). It's like putting on glasses for the first time, and realizing there is more to this world than you have ever dreamed or imagined. There is no magic. There is no illusion. It is a real and personal relationship with God that creates your new self.

130

Passionate Pursuit

And walk in love, as the Messiah also loved us and gave Himself for us, a sacrificial and fragrant offering to God. (Ephesians 5:2)

When laws are created, people do not automatically begin obeying them. For example, imagine a new speed limit was being introduced in your neighborhood. Drivers, cyclists, and pedestrians need to be taught about the new limit. Drivers need to see the new signs and slow down. They need to practice obeying the new law. Others need to bike or walk safely and watch for and encourage drivers. Pursuing holiness works in much the same way. Read Ephesians 4:25–5:5. What does it mean to imitate God? Being angry when you go to sleep, coarse and crude joking, and sexual immorality are not easily stopped just because you read it in the Bible. Pursuing the opposite of these sins can require you to learn about the temptations and warning signs that lead you to them. It requires the practice of holiness—developing characteristics through living life and making consistent godly choices. It requires the support of faithful people willing to watch out for you. It also requires a first step. Do you have the deep desire to pursue holiness with all your heart and passion? What will you do this week to demonstrate that desire? Practice walking in imitation of Christ this week.

131

Yadda Yadda Yadda

*The Spirit's law of life in Christ Jesus has set you free
from the law of sin and of death. (Romans 8:2)*

All your life it seems like someone is always telling you what to do. Parents, teachers, coaches, and other adults seem to always be lecturing, "Do this, do that, and don't do any of that." Even when you get to church, it feels like pastors or deacons or Sunday school teachers add their voices to the chorus of imperative instructions. What do you do when you don't feel like doing what you've been told—even if you know it's good for you? Paul felt the same way. He knew what was right. He wanted to do the right things, but he struggled with sin. He couldn't help himself. Read Romans 7:24–8:11. With what did Paul struggle? The Holy Spirit lives in us (vv. 9, 11). Since the Spirit is all about peace and life, you can depend on the Spirit to help you when you don't feel like following through with what is right. We aren't perfect people, and we don't need to put a mask on in front of others to try and pretend we are perfect. Do you ever feel pressure to look good and say all the right things in church? When? Free yourself, tear off your mask, and work with the Holy Spirit to pursue holiness in your life.

132

Herd Mentality

*Then Jacob tore his clothes, put sackcloth around his waist,
and mourned for his son many days. (Genesis 37:34)*

Are you "rolling deep," hanging out with your friends, doing things, and making decisions with friends? When a group of folks go along with the same idea/action without giving much thought to how it will affect the group or individual persons, it's called a herd mentality. Read Genesis 37:19–20. How is herd mentality illustrated in this story? Sometimes a herd mentality, or rolling deep, can hurt someone. Can you think of a time when you and your friends were "rolling deep?" What were you doing? What kind of decisions were you making? How do the decisions of your group affect you? Others? What was the result of the actions of the group? Maybe stepping away from the crowd, if just for one moment, will give you a chance to make a better choice. You never know whose life you may affect when you decide to think on your own without the help of the crowd. You have the power to break away from the crowd and make the best choice. Read Genesis 37:21. What choice did Reuben face? What choice did he make? Thank God for giving you a sound mind to make decisions based on His Word and not the decisions of others.

133

Standing Up and Standing Out

Joseph said to his brothers, "I am Joseph! Is my father still living?" But they could not answer him because they were terrified in his presence. (Genesis 45:3)

Use your own mind; make your own decisions. Don't follow the herd. What are some possible things you might sacrifice by going with the crowd? Read Genesis 42:17–21. What did the brothers sacrifice? All of the heartache that the brothers experienced reminded them of how cruel they were to Joseph. They felt distress because they hurt Joseph. Sometimes following the crowd has lasting results. If you follow your friends down the wrong path, you may have to deal with several consequences. You may watch someone else get hurt. Read Genesis 37:29. You may feel guilt because you didn't stand up for what was right. How do you think you would have reacted to Joseph? Joseph's own brothers were afraid of him because they knew they'd been horrible toward Joseph. Because of their jealousy, they plotted against him. Now they were forced to deal with the consequences of their decisions. Have you been in a tight spot this week? What kind of consequences could you face if you find yourself following the crowd? Thank God for giving you opportunities to make the right choice so you can glorify Him.

134

What Can I Do?

Joseph kissed each of his brothers as he wept, and afterward his brothers talked with him. (Genesis 45:15)

It's hard to step out when pressure is all around. You feel uncomfortable, hemmed in, squeezed. You may even cave in to the pressure. How do you feel when you give in to peer pressure? What should you do when it's all over? Read Genesis 45:14–15. Joseph and his brothers talked to each other. They had a lot to talk about. The relationships between the brothers needed to be restored. Who do you need to talk with this week? What relationship do you need to restore? Read Genesis 50:15–18. Jacob asked that Joseph forgive his brothers. When Joseph received this message from Jacob, he wept. Joseph's brothers felt so bad about what they'd done to him that they offered to be his slaves. Read Genesis 50:19. Even though his brothers wronged him, Joseph loved them and cared for them all the more. Jesus died for us so that we could be forgiven of all our sins. We first have to confess and agree that we have sinned against God and others.

135

Which Way Should I Go?

Listen, my son, to your father's instruction, and don't reject your mother's teaching, for they will be a garland of grace on your head and a gold chain around your neck. (Proverbs 1:8–9)

When was the last time you were encouraged to do the right thing? Peer pressure isn't all bad. A great help in making good decisions is to listen to people who make good decisions. A great way to grow wise is to listen to wise counsel. Whose opinion do you value most? Why? On the flip side, if you hang around people who consistently make poor choices, eventually, you will make poor choices too. With which group would you rather be associated? Read 1 Kings 12:6–8. King Rehoboam got advice from two sets of people—his young friends and the wise elders. Who gave the best advice? Why? Most times, the advice of older people is wise advice. This is so because older people have lived through a lot. They have a voice of experience. Who do you know who gives good advice? Solomon urged his son to listen to older people and follow the advice of both his mother and father. There are rewards for listening to wise counsel. Ask God to lead you to those people who can give wise counsel.

136

Watch and Learn

My son, if sinners entice you,
don't be persuaded. (Proverbs 1:10)

Everybody wants you on his or her side. So which way should you go? You can always tell when you're getting bad advice, because eventually bad things happen. What was the last bit of bad advice you received? Who gave it to you? Would you go back to them again for advice? In what area are you most enticed to sin? When the pressure is on, several things should be going on in your head: prayer; discernment; listening; watching. Yeah, that's a lot, but it can make the difference between a good day and a bad day. Doing those four things will keep you from giving in to bad peer pressure. They will also help you accept good peer pressure. Read 1 Kings 12:7, 10–11. To whom did Rehoboam listen? The elders gave Rehoboam advice based on their experience with King Solomon. The elders knew the people, walked among the people. The younger men gave foolish advice; they knew nothing about running a kingdom. What would you do? How can you use Rehoboam's experience in deciding to whom you will listen? Ask God to open your eyes and ears to wisdom so that you will know who is looking out for your best interest.

137

Stay on Track

The one who walks with the wise will become wise,
but a companion of fools will suffer harm. (Proverbs 13:20)

Don't trip, just listen. Clear your mind and heart to really understand what's best to do. Sometimes advice is in your best interest as well as the best interest of others. Read 1 Kings 12:7. For Rehoboam, a favorable answer to the people would give him a peaceful reign, but Rehoboam decided to take the advice of his foolish friends. Read 1 King 12:19. What was the result of Rehoboam's choice? The result of Rehoboam's decision left Israel in rebellion against the house of David. Rehoboam found himself at war with his own people. He suffered harm because he kept companion with fools. How would others describe your companions? Following wise counsel yields positive results; you will become wise. Be sure to keep company with wise people. What is the most foolish thing you have been persuaded to do? What do you think about that decision now? Read Galatians 5:7–8. Why is the matter of whom you hang out with such a big deal? People who see you on the right path may try to trip you up. They are not doing God's will. Watch out for those who try to change your direction. Aren't you glad God puts wise people in your life? Take some time to thank Him for your wise counselors.

138

Two Are Better Than One

Two are better than one because they have a good reward for their efforts. For if either falls, his companion can lift him up; but pity the one who falls without another to lift him up. (Ecclesiastes 4:9–10)

We say "don't leave me hanging" when we want to be sure someone is on our side, sharing our views, and meeting us where we need to be met. We all need assurance that we're not alone. It's hard breaking away from the crowd. You question your decision and wonder if you've done the right thing by separating yourself from negative peer pressure. You never know, your decision to stand for what is right may lead someone else your way. Why are two better than one? To whom can you turn for help? You're never alone. The Holy Spirit is always there to comfort you. And often He will send a brother or sister in Christ to encourage you when you suffer. You must do the same thing when you see someone in need of encouragement: pray for them; acknowledge their hurt; minister to them; exhort them; remind them that God is still with them. They will be thankful that there is someone to help through hard times. So will you. Friendship and like-mindedness are powerful. Thank God for the wonderful friends He's given you to keep you strong and lifted up in hard times.

139

Take a Stand

*Even if He does not rescue us, we want you as king
to know that we will not serve your gods or worship
the gold statue you set up. (Daniel 3:18)*

"Is it me, or is it hot in here?" You've probably asked this of your friends or people around you when you're not sure if you are sharing an experience or having a moment all by yourself. Once you realize that others are feeling what you feel, you sigh in relief. There is comfort in knowing that someone else shares a common experience with you. Read Daniel 3:12. Why was it easier for these three guys to take a stand together? Setting yourself apart may set you up for some heated situations. Just know there are others that will stand with you. This collective of Christians reaffirms your faith and keeps you strong. Shadrach, Meshach, and Abednego were high officials in Nebuchadnezzar's kingdom, but they did not let their status keep them from holding to their true beliefs. Read Daniel 3:16–18. What stands out most to you about their statement? Even in answering King Nebuchadnezzar regarding their refusal to bow, they remained respectful to the kings' authority. They did not deny or defend. They stood up for what they believed in. They respected the king's authority. They accepted the king's consequences. They exercised their faith in God. Value the friends that support and encourage you.

140

Three-Strand Chord

And if someone overpowers one person, two can resist him.
A cord of three strands is not easily broken. (Ecclesiastes 4:12)

When you find yourself in a sticky situation, who's got your back? When it is time for you to face opposition, who's there to stand with you? Who comforts you when you feel like you are all by yourself? The Holy Spirit is the true Comforter, but God also places friends in our lives to minister to us when we feel all alone in a situation. What gave the guys—Shadrach, Meshach, and Abednego—strength to stand? Who are two friends on whom you can always depend? You should look for friends who have the same ideals and ethics that you have. You will become support for each other. Solomon in Ecclesiastes urged close friendships. Two or more people facing adversity will be able to defend themselves better than just one. Why is a cord of three strands not easily broken? Whom do you trust to guard your friendship? What friend can you support with your encouragement? Do you have a friend who can "pick you up" when you fall? Who? Take a moment to pray for your friends and thank God you have them.

141

Turn On The Light, Please

*"No one lights a lamp and puts it under a basket,
but rather on a lampstand, and it gives light for
all who are in the house." (Matthew 5:15)*

What kind of influence do you have on others? When did you realize that you had influence? Even if you don't think so, you have the light of influence, which is given to you by God. Read Matthew 5:13–14. Jesus says that you are light and salt. What does that mean to you? How does salt help others? How does light help others? When you become a part of God's family, you are given a light. That means you are to stand out so others can be helped by your influence. A lot of responsibility comes with leadership. Sometimes we end up being leaders when we don't want to be. Sometimes we may try to hide our influence or light so that others won't expect so much. As a light for God, what are you not supposed to do? What are you supposed to do? Your influence or light shouldn't be hidden. The power of your influence is needed to minister to others. As the classic Newsboys song states: Shine!

142

Shine On

*"In the same way, let your light shine before men,
so that they may see your good works and give
glory to your Father in heaven." (Matthew 5:16)*

Influence is hard to hide. When we become a part of God's family it is almost impossible to hide God, who lives in us. It is hard to hide that we are followers of Jesus Christ. God intended it that way so people will be drawn to Him. Read Matthew 5:14. Try as you might, if you possess the glory of God, and if He has set you apart for His plan, you will always shine. Own your light; don't be afraid. Get your shine on! Your friends should see you shining. They need to see you choosing the right path and making the right choices. In your own special way, you can turn peer pressure into a good thing. What are people supposed to see when they look at your life? Shining before people doesn't mean bringing attention to yourself by showing off; it is the complete opposite. You should let your light shine to bring glory to God. Use the wisdom and influence God gave you to make choices that glorify and lead others to Him. Ask God to help others see Him in you so much that they will want to become a part of the family of God.

143

Be an Influencer

For the Lord's message rang out from you . . . in every place that your faith in God has gone out. Therefore, we don't need to say anything. (1 Thessalonians 1:8)

Influence spreads. The wonderful thing about God and His Word is that if you follow the teachings of the Bible and let His light shine in you, the word about your service will spread. "Who is the person of influence I've heard so much about?" That person is you. Once others hear and see your influence, they will be all abuzz about the wonderful things you are doing. People will not be able to stop talking about how God is working in your life. What type of influence is identified in today's verse? You won't have to do much, just be the positive influence in your own circle of friends. They will spread the word about how God's love has influenced your life. Words are powerful, but the Word of God is even more powerful. When you allow the teachings of the Bible to work in and through your life, you are exhibiting the power of God. Read 1 Thessalonians 1:5–6. What does it mean to imitate Jesus? What's the point of that? Even when you feel down and out, God is there with His Word to pick you up. Thank God for His Word.

144

Word Became Flesh

*The Word became flesh and took up residence among us.
We observed His glory, the glory as the One and Only
Son from the Father, full of grace and truth. (John 1:14)*

Have you ever gotten so involved in a book or a series of books that the characters felt real to you? It was like you could almost touch them or talk with them. Perhaps you even felt like you knew those characters better than you knew your family or friends. Read John 1:1 and John 1:14. Who are these passages referring to as the Word? Jesus isn't just some character in a book that seems real, He is real! Jesus has many names in the Bible: the Almighty, I AM, Counselor, and Savior—to name a few. But the very first name in the book of John by which He was called was the Word. Why do you think He was called the Word? The Word became flesh and made His dwelling among us. Jesus lived on the earth as a living, breathing human. He lived as you live. He ate, slept, and worked. Now He lives within you if you are Christian! How awesome is that? Why is it important that Jesus lived as you live? If Jesus hadn't lived as you live, He couldn't have died in your place. The Word became flesh to be your Savior.

145

In His Image

He is the image of the invisible God, the
firstborn over all creation. (Colossians 1:15)

Ever been told you look like your mom? Someone probably even said that you are the spitting image of your mother when she was young. What do you think Jesus looked like when He was a teenager? How does today's verse describe Jesus? We see pictures of Jesus everywhere—in Bibles, on walls, and even in stores. Have you ever wondered if He really looked like that? We don't know exactly what He looked like. What we know from the passage today is that He was "the image of the invisible God." What do you think that means? If you want to know what God looks like, look at Jesus. His life and ministry give us a very revealing look into the heart of God. What does your life look like? How are you revealing the heart of God? It's kind of a cool thing to look like your physical parent. It's even better to look like your heavenly One.

146

Who Do You Say I Am?

"But you," He asked them, "who do you say that I am?"
Simon Peter answered, "You are the Messiah,
the Son of the living God!" (Matthew 16:15–16)

How embarrassing is it to forget someone's name? It's especially embarrassing when they ask if you remember them, and you can't answer. Don't you hate that feeling? When Jesus asked Peter, "Who do you say that I am?" how did Peter respond? How would you respond? Who do you say Jesus is? Sometimes you can spend a lot of time with someone and not truly know who they are. The disciples spent many days and nights with Jesus, and it still took them time to understand who Jesus really was. The best way to truly know someone is by spending time with that person. How much time do you spend time with Jesus? How could you get to know Him better? Learning about Jesus at church or in Sunday school is great, but the best way to really know Jesus is to spend time with Him through prayer, worship, reading the Bible, and spending time alone with Him. In your prayer this week, ask Jesus to reveal Himself to you. Then the next time someone asks you who Jesus is, you will have an answer.

147

Jesus, The Tour

*So many people gathered together that there was
no more room, not even in the doorway, and He
was speaking the message to them. (Mark 2:2)*

Where do most people want to be at a concert? At the front. They maneuver to the stage and reach out their hands, hoping that the lead singer will touch them. Perhaps you have been a part of that group, wanting to get closer to your favorite singer. Read Mark 2:1–4. How did these four guys deal with the crowds? Jesus was famous too. He "toured" from town to town. But He didn't do it for money. He didn't even get paid. He did it because He loved everyone. He wanted everyone to know who He was and who God was. The people were hungry to hear His message. The crowd in the house that day was so packed in that these guys realized there was no way to work their way to Jesus. They had to go a different route. Why did they work so hard to get their friend to Jesus? Those guys were willing to do whatever it took. They knew Jesus was his only hope. What are you doing to get your unsaved friends to Jesus? You don't have to push through the crowd or tear open a roof; just introduce them to Christ. He's their only hope.

148

Hangin' with the "Out" Crowd

*While He was reclining at the table in the house,
many tax collectors and sinners came as guests
to eat with Jesus and His disciples. (Matthew 9:10)*

People say, "You become who you hang out with." Maybe you've also heard the phrase *guilty by association.* Read Matthew 9:10–11. With whom was Jesus associating? What do you think the Pharisees were thinking? Jesus loved everyone so much that He didn't care what people thought of Him. He wanted to visit with anyone who wanted to hear Him. He especially wanted to visit with the sinners, the people who needed Him most. Are there certain people with whom you don't associate? Why? It is not in our nature to associate with people who are different from us. We find all kinds of reasons not to regardless of their spiritual condition. Who are some people in your school that need to hear about Jesus the most? What are you doing to tell them? You are called to share the good news of Jesus with everyone. Not just people who look or act like you. With whom do you need to share Jesus this week? Reach out this week to someone who is different from your group of friends, someone you know who desperately needs Christ.

149

Compassion in Action

Moved with compassion, Jesus reached out
His hand and touched him. (Mark 1:41)

How do you feel when you hear about or meet a person who is in pain or hurting? Read Mark 1:40–42. How did Jesus feel about the man? What is compassion? Jesus didn't heal people for the publicity. He wasn't trying to put on a show or raise a bunch of money. He healed them because He hurt for them. He felt compassion and acted on that feeling. Jesus traveled from town to town—healing people. He cured persons with diseases and ailments. He even brought a couple of people back to life. All that time, His heart ached for those people. Does your heart ache for people today? Why or why not? There are lots of people around us who are sick and hurting. Too often we are so busy with our lives that we pass them by without a single glance. Or if we happen to notice, we may feel a pang of sympathy then rush on to what's next on our agenda. However, just as Jesus felt compassion, so we must also, and that compassion must move us to action. Who do you know that is going through a difficult situation right now? How is your compassion moving you to help? You are now the hands and feet of Jesus. Don't let your agenda or anything else blind you to the people who are hurting.

150

He Suffered

Going a little farther, He fell facedown and prayed,
"My Father! If it is possible, let this cup pass from Me.
Yet not as I will, but as You will." (Matthew 26:39)

Have you ever gone to the doctor or dentist knowing something was going to happen that was going to cause you some pain? Maybe you were getting shots? Maybe you were getting teeth pulled? The point is you knew it was going to cause you pain. Did you want to go through the pain? Probably not. Would you have avoided it if you could? Probably so, but you did it because it had to be done. Read Matthew 26:38–39. How do you think Jesus felt at this time? Jesus knew exactly what was going to happen. He knew He was going to suffer. He knew He would die, yet He did it anyway—for you. History is full of heroes who died saving someone. Perhaps they knew there was a chance to die, but do you think they would have completed the rescue knowing pain and death was a certainty? Jesus knew what was about to happen. He did it anyway. Why? First, He wanted to follow God's will. Second, because of His never-ending love for you. He wanted to save you. Next time you read about Jesus' crucifixion, think about what He must have felt. Consider His struggle, knowing the pain He would suffer. Take time to thank Him for enduring to the end just for you.

151

He Took It All

Even the criminals who were crucified with
Him kept taunting Him. (Matthew 27:44)

It hurts to disappoint people, especially your parents. What's something you've done to disappoint your parents? How did they express their disappointment? How did it make you feel? Read Matthew 27:33–46. Why did Jesus cry out to God? God is so pure and holy that He cannot look upon sin. When Jesus became sin for us, God turned away. He turned His back on His own Son. Do you think that must have been difficult for God? I'm sure it was. All parents hurt when their child does something wrong, but Jesus didn't do anything wrong. He lived a pure and sinless life. He didn't deserve His punishment. Wow, think about the billions of people who have lived since Jesus. He took on all of that sin, the sin of every person who has ever lived or will live. That must have been an ugly sight for God to see. Take some time and think about all the sins you have committed. Thank Jesus for taking them off you and wiping your slate clean.

152

Like New

But now He has reconciled you by His physical body through His death, to present you holy, faultless, and blameless before Him. (Colossians 1:22)

There is nothing like a nice, long shower after a workout or after working outside. What a great feeling to get all the sweat and grime off of you. Why were you alienated from God? How did Jesus' death change you? The death of Jesus made you brand new. The grime and ugliness of your sin has been washed away. Do you feel spiritually clean? Why or why not? Sometimes we think that God can wash away some of our sins but not all of them—that there may be a couple of sins, really bad ones, that are beyond forgiveness. Ever felt this way? Paul said that we are presented "holy, faultless, and blameless," basically using three words to say the same thing. He was emphasizing that all of our sins are gone . . . even the bad ones. There is no sin you've committed that God can't forgive, no grime He can't wash away. Open your heart, confess all your sins, and receive the shower of His grace and forgiveness. There is no other feeling like it!

153

Doubters Anonymous

Jesus said, "Because you have seen Me, you have believed. Those who believe without seeing are blessed." (John 20:29)

Missouri is called the "Show Me State." Why? Because Missourians have the reputation of not believing something until you show them the proof. Many of us would make good Missourians. Read John 20:25, 27–29. What did Thomas doubt? Why? Thomas was typical of most humans. Until we see something, we won't believe it. We have a hard time accepting something we didn't witness for ourselves. However, you weren't there when Jesus was resurrected, yet you believe. You weren't there to see and touch the holes in Jesus' hands and feet, yet you believe. Because you believe and did not see, you are blessed. How do you know that Jesus was resurrected? You read about Jesus' resurrection in the Bible, but it is also likely that someone shared that good news with you. Just like the disciples shared the news with Thomas. Yet you didn't have to see to believe. This week, make an effort to share that good news with someone else, perhaps even with someone who has a hard time believing. Explain to them that you don't have to see to believe. Hang in there with them through their doubts. Keep sharing with them and showing them Christ. Pray that soon their doubt will become belief.

154

Inheritance

According to His great mercy, He has given us a new birth into a living hope through the resurrection of Jesus Christ from the dead and into an inheritance that is imperishable, uncorrupted, and unfading, kept in heaven for you. (1 Peter 1:3–4)

The dictionary defines *inheritance* as a portion, birthright, or heritage. Being born into a family gives you a certain birthright. Have you or your family ever received an earthly inheritance? Someone you loved had to die before you could receive that inheritance. Read 1 Peter 1:3–5. What kind of inheritance is being spoken of here? Jesus' death and resurrection gives us a hope for our future. When you accept Jesus as your Lord and Savior, you are born again. But this time, you are born into a different family. You are born into a Christian family—a family in which all of us will share a future home in Heaven. Your new inheritance doesn't have anything to do with money. You can't buy a house with it. It's not heirlooms to be passed down. This inheritance is worth so much more. Are you excited about your heavenly inheritance? Why or why not? Because of Christ's death and resurrection, you have the best inheritance in the world waiting for you in Heaven. Because of Him, there is hope for your future.

155

Waiting

*This Jesus, who has been taken from you
into heaven, will come in the same way that
you have seen Him going into heaven. (Acts 1:11)*

The night before Christmas is an exciting time for children. Do you remember how excited you were anticipating Santa's return? You couldn't wait! Read Acts 1:1–11. Why were the people still looking into the sky? How were the angel's words comforting to them? Those who had spent the most time with Jesus were at a loss when He left. They were confused, not sure where to go or what to do. But after the angels spoke there was a cause for celebration. Jesus would return someday. As a child you really didn't think about Santa much throughout the year. It was the few days leading up to Christmas when you really started preparing. You put in your request. You were on your best behavior. You even planned what treats you would leave for Santa. Unfortunately, most people prepare for Jesus the same way. They don't think about Him until they need Him. They think they have plenty of time to prepare for Jesus' return. Even if Jesus returns in your lifetime you won't know it until it happens. Don't be like a child waiting on Santa. Don't wait to prepare until you think we are in the final days. Prepare now . . . and help prepare others by telling them about Christ.

156

Blind Jump

Then the woman saw that the tree was good for food and delightful to look at, and that it was desirable for obtaining wisdom. So she took some of its fruit and ate it; she also gave some to her husband, who was with her, and he ate it. (Genesis 3:6)

Skydiving is a sport that has been around for many years. People that have experienced the thrill of jumping out of a plane at 10,000–15,000 feet say it is exhilarating. If the parachute fails to open then the person will surely crash to the ground. Have you ever felt like you were about to crash to the ground? There are many families who have figuratively jumped out of a plane, but their parachutes have not opened. They are racing to the ground at a very high rate of speed, and they are very close to disaster. Temptation can enter the life of a family in very subtle but devastating ways. However, if the family will trust God to be their parachute, He can save them. Read Genesis 3:1–6. How has temptation devastated your family? God made Adam and Eve perfectly and gave them a world where they could perfectly obey him, but they chose to walk their own way. God has revealed the way he wants you and your family to live. Families that stay focused on God and close to Him are families who are able to stand together when temptation strikes. Seek God as your family's parachute.

157

Family Feud

"If you do what is right, won't you be accepted? But if you do not do what is right, sin is crouching at the door. Its desire is for you, but you must rule over it." (Genesis 4:7)

Chances are if you have a sibling, you probably think your parents love and pamper your sibling more than you. In most situations that is not the case. Parents will tell you they love their children equally but differently. Many children think this means they show favoritism to the other sibling. This can be a dangerous thought because it can lead to bad decision making. Read Genesis 4:3–8. Have you ever felt like God was blessing someone more than He was blessing you? When? God always shows us a greater amount of love than we show Him. It is important to understand that God does not bless you by what you have to offer Him materially. He blesses you when all you have to offer Him is your heart. Do you trust God with every aspect of your life? How do you demonstrate that? Abel gave the very best he had, and he made a sacrifice to give it to God. Cain, on the other hand, tried to take the easy way out and refused to offer a heartfelt sacrifice. When God rejected it, Cain became angry and killed his brother. Commit yourself to giving God your very best.

158

Undercover Brothers

*Eli's sons were wicked men; they had
no regard for the Lord. (1 Samuel 2:12)*

It appeared that Robert Hanssen was serving his country faithfully. He had been an FBI agent for more than twenty years and had climbed the corporate ladder. He was known in the Bureau as a computer expert. He was given one promotion after another, and it seemed like he had a promising career in law enforcement. It wasn't revealed until years later that Hanssen had been selling secrets to the Soviet Union. Because of his espionage, many CIA and KGB agents were killed. Special Agent Robert Hanssen appeared to be serving his country. In reality, he was selling out his country for a profit.

Read 1 Samuel 2:12–17. How do you think the father felt about the way his sons were acting? In a way, Eli's sons were a lot like Robert Hanssen. They were appearing to be godly men, but they were actually looking out for their own interests. They made a profit by pretending to be something they were not. Eli's sons knew God's desire, and they also knew what their father desired, but they chose to disobey both. God would later punish this entire family because of their rebellious hearts. How faithful are you to God's commands and to the commands of your parents? Are you pretending to be a godly teenager when you're really something else? Commit to faithfully serve God and to represent Him well to others who are watching you.

159

Fishing Fanatic

*"Follow Me," He told them, "and I will
make you fish for people!" (Matthew 4:19)*

Alton Jones from Waco, Texas won the Bassmaster Classic Championship in 2008. At the end of the day, the angler weighed in with a total fish weight of 49 pounds, 7 ounces. Later that day, Jones picked up his check for $500,000 for winning the tournament. He was crowned the greatest fishermen in 2008. Pretty exciting! Yet, there are more important things to catch than fish.

Read Matthew 4:18–22. What did Jesus ask these men? How hard would it be for you to leave everything and follow Jesus? Simon came from a very interesting home life. His father died when he was young, and he lived with Zebedee, the father of James and John. His name, Simon, means unstable and untrustworthy. He had to live with the humiliation of his name and his family for many years. Simon was a professional fisherman on the Sea of Galilee. However, when Jesus called him to fish for men, he dropped his nets and followed Jesus. Do you know how Jesus is calling you to live? It doesn't matter what kind of background or family life you come from, Jesus has the power to do great things in your life. Trust Him with your life and your future today.

160

Blind Faith

Then Saul got up from the ground, and though his eyes were open, he could see nothing. So they took him by the hand and led him into Damascus. (Acts 9:8)

Ginny Owens has been blind since she was two years old. Despite her lack of sight, Ginny has become a leading Christian singer in her generation. She has won three Dove awards, and every tour date in 2008 was completely booked. It is through her testimony that thousands of blind people continue to strive to reach their full potential for Christ. Have you ever met anyone who was blind? Read Acts 9:1–9. What do you think Saul was thinking when he was blinded by the light? Saul was educated and trained to be a Pharisee. His job was to ensure that everyone kept the Law. Saul hated Christians and had been given orders to kill as many as he could find. Because of his background, Saul thought he was doing what he was created to do. God had other plans for him. Does what your family thinks of you determine what you will become in life? God took Saul out of his misguided background and used him in a powerful way for the kingdom of God. His name would later be changed to Paul, and he would be considered one of the greatest men who ever lived. If you are willing to be used, God will do something very special and very powerful in your life. Make sure your heart is ready for Him to speak to you.

161

Born To Matter

There will be joy and delight for you, and
many will rejoice at his birth. (Luke 1:14)

Just before her pregnancy, Pam Tebow fell into a coma caused by drinking contaminated water. Pam and Bob Tebow were Christian missionaries in Manila, Philippines at the time and did not have any idea that she was expecting a baby. When the doctors discovered that she was pregnant, they told the parents the baby had already been affected by the contaminated water, and there was no way he would ever survive. When have you witnessed one of God's miracles? Pam refused to believe that her baby would die. She and her husband began to pray for the baby every day. On August 14, 1987, a beautiful but skinny baby boy was born to the Tebow's. They named him Timmy. Twenty years later, Tim Tebow would lead the Florida Gators to an SEC and National Football Championship—a living example of God at work around us.

Read Luke 1:11–14. Do you realize that you are a blessing to your parents? In what way are you a blessing? Zechariah was happy that God was going to bless him with a son. However, he couldn't imagine all the ways God was going to use John. John the Baptist had been created by God for a specific purpose. It is important to understand that you were created by God for a specific purpose. God created you to do something very special for Him. Pray that God will give you a clear direction in your life.

162

Smart Choices

A wise son brings joy to his father, but a foolish son, heartache to his mother. (Proverbs 10:1)

May 5, 1994, was a day of embarrassment for our nation. It was the day 18-year-old Michael Fay was to be punished for the crime he had committed. The entire nation had been watching his trial, and now they would see his punishment. Fay had pleaded guilty to spray painting several cars in Singapore. His punishment would consist of four hits with a wooden cane and a $2,200 fine. Fay received his four hard hits and then was released from prison. Michael Fay paid his debt to society, but the humiliation he brought upon his family would never fade away.

What is an incident that caused your parents embarrassment? How did you feel when you realized your parents had been humiliated? The Bible teaches us to obey and honor our parents. There will be times when you think they don't understand, accept, or even love you, but they do. Your parents love you more than you will ever know. Your responsibility is to love and respect them. Commit today to respecting your family. This week, consider any changes you might need to make in your life to love and respect your family.

163

Total Trust

*Abraham answered, "God Himself will provide
the lamb for the burnt offering, my son." Then
the two of them walked on together. (Genesis 22:8)*

Firefighters never stop training. They are constantly running, lifting weights, and climbing ladders. These are all very important aspects of their job. But the most important aspect is trusting one another in a burning building. Firefighters will practice entering a burning home by putting tape over their mask. If they can't see where they are going, then they are forced to stay together and follow the lead firefighter. This increases the trust factor within the group. Following someone blindly can be a scary thought. Have you ever trusted someone with a "blind faith"? Explain. Are you comfortable putting your life in the hands of other people? Why?

Read Genesis 22:6–12. How did Isaac demonstrate his trust in his father? Abraham knew what was best for his son—and Isaac was obedient enough to follow his father wherever he went. Your parents have probably made some decisions in the past with which you did not agree or understand at the time. Those decisions were probably made to benefit you in some way. If you can't commit to obeying your earthly father and/or mother, you will never be able to commit to obeying your heavenly Father. God knows where He wants to lead you. Trust Him.

164

Faithful Follower

Children, obey your parents in everything,
for this pleases the Lord. (Colossians 3:20)

The Alaskan Husky is an amazing dog. It only weighs about fifty pounds but is capable of pulling twice its body weight. The animal is bred with just one purpose in mind, and that is to pull a sled. They are the best sled dogs in the world. An Alaskan Husky will run for hours and hundreds of miles at the command of his master. They are faithful to run because they want to please the one leading them. As God's children we should want to please Him in everything we do. What are some of the areas in your life that are not pleasing to God? What command does God's Word give you about your parents? Sometimes it is hard for teenagers and parents to see eye-to-eye on certain issues. Your job is not to agree or disagree with your parents but to obey their leadership. God is glorified when you honor and obey your parents. Do you and your parents struggle to communicate? In what ways? How does this make it hard to follow and trust them? Have you talked to God about obeying your parents? Spend some time this week thanking God for your parents and asking Him to help you please Him by honoring and obeying your parents this week.

165

Bad Choices

*David responded to Nathan, "I have sinned against the Lord."
Then Nathan replied to David, "The Lord has taken
away your sin; you will not die." (2 Samuel 12:13)*

Have you ever made a bad decision and then realized you would have to live with the consequences of that decision? There are many people who have made ungodly decisions in their lives. Because of their choices, their entire lives have been changed forever. Sometimes the choices we make and what God has planned for our lives are different. Read 2 Samuel 12:13–15. Do you think David knew he had been disobedient to God? Why? Every decision that is made in a family affects the entire family. It doesn't matter if it is made by an adult or a child. It is important for you to make very wise choices in your life. If you don't, your family could suffer the consequences. When was the last time you asked God for His opinion before making a decision? Do you understand that God has a perfect plan for your life? If you will trust God with your life and your decisions, He will bless you in a powerful way. God knows what is best for you, and He is waiting for you to ask Him for guidance and direction. Don't wait. Trust Him today.

166

Good Genes

*Clearly recalling your sincere faith that first lived in
your grandmother Lois, then in your mother Eunice,
and that I am convinced is in you also. (2 Timothy 1:5)*

Billy Graham is one of the best known evangelists in the world. He has been preaching the gospel for almost seventy years and has helped lead thousands of people to a saving knowledge of Jesus Christ. After becoming very ill, Billy Graham passed the reigns of the Billy Graham Evangelistic Association to his son, Franklin Graham. Because of the Christian model he saw in his father, Franklin has been able to accept and continue this great ministry. Who do you have in your life whom you admire? Have you ever had anyone help you grow spiritually? Who? It sounds like Timothy's mother and grandmother were his spiritual leaders. How did their Christian example help shape Timothy's life? Everyone has someone to whom they look up and want to be like. There is at least one person in your life whom has been a role model for you. Who is that person (or persons) in your life? Does that person know how much you appreciate him or her? Have you ever told that person how important he or she is in your life? The choices your spiritual models made could be the reason for your success. Take some time to write a letter or message to that person and express how their influence has changed your life.

167

Deadly Decisions

Then Peter said to her, "Why did you agree to test the Spirit of the Lord? Look! The feet of those who have buried your husband are at the door, and they will carry you out!" (Acts 5:9)

We all know people who appear to be one way but are really living another type of life. These are the people who will laugh with you and then laugh at you. They can't be trusted because they have hurt you in the past. Somewhere along the way, they made a conscious decision to treat everyone badly. Have you been hurt by a friend or another person who has made some bad decisions? How did that affect your friendship? Read Acts 5:1–10. How would you describe these two people? Bad decisions can be deadly. Sometimes people try so hard to be something they aren't. You may have people in your family or in your church who act this way. God does not want you to pretend to love Him. He wants you to love Him with all of your heart, mind, soul, and strength. You will never fool God into thinking you are something you are not. Maybe you are guilty of pretending to love God and your friends. Have you evaluated how you treat others and how you worship God? What do you recognize? Commit today to becoming a genuine worshiper of God. Commit to loving people unconditionally and without any hidden agendas.

168

My Heart's Desire

Rejoice in the Lord always.
I will say it again: Rejoice! (Philippians 4:4)

What does your heart desire? What is the one thing you wish for more than anything else? Pretend for a moment that your wish came true today. What words would express your feelings? What did Paul say we should always do? How difficult is it to rejoice when you don't feel happy? Happiness comes from our circumstances. Joy comes from within. It is often impossible to change our circumstances, but joy can still be present even in those situations we cannot control. How long does the new of a new car last? How about the new in a new relationship? You can work to achieve great financial wealth and acquire many things in your lifetime, but the happiness those things bring is short-lived. The new begins to fade, and your desire moves on to bigger and better things. When you focus your attention on your relationship with Christ, you will find your focus begins to move away from all the things you can gain and instead toward the One you can glorify. Ask God to help you to desire more of Him. This is where you will find true joy.

169

The Problem with Happiness

*That day Haman left full of joy and in good spirits.
But when Haman saw Mordecai at the King's Gate, and
Mordecai didn't rise or tremble in fear at his presence,
Haman was filled with rage toward Mordecai. (Esther 5:9)*

What made you happy as a child? Was it a new toy or a new puppy? Or maybe it was simply Grandma's homemade cookies? What about when you were a pre-teen? Did you find happiness in your new bike or skateboard? Would those same things make you happy today? Why? Read Esther 5:8–10. Verse 9 states Haman's "happiness" as he left the king. What caused his change of heart? Why was his happiness quickly gone? Happiness is an emotion. Like anger, sadness, and excitement, the state of being happy is brought about by things and situations. The problem with depending on our circumstances and material possessions to bring us happiness is evident. What might bring happiness today, will change swiftly with the passing of time. Our wants and desires change. Our first crush from elementary school is long forgotten. That new bike we rode with excitement rusts and loses its luster. What was the last thing that you thought would really make you happy but then discovered the happiness faded quickly? Depending on anything to make you happy will fail without exception. True happiness is found in the Lord. The joy He brings gives abundant life and never ceases. Seek God and His joy this week.

170

Joy Is a Decision

"No one lights a lamp and puts it under a basket, but rather on a lampstand, and it gives light for all who are in the house." (Matthew 5:15)

Have you ever been mistreated or bullied? What is your initial reaction when someone is cruel to you? It may take much restraint to not lash out verbally or physically. Read Matthew 5:15–16. What are we commanded to do as Christians? Who is praised when you let your light shine? True joy is the lamp that we must shine for the entire world to see. Joy is a fruit of the Holy Spirit. It isn't something we can grow and maintain on our own, but rather it comes from the Spirit. The qualities of God's character come alive within us when we foster our relationship with Him. Joy—like love, patience, kindness, and goodness—is a decision. We make a choice to love. We make a choice to be patient and kind to others. We make a choice to be joyful, because we make the choice to grow in our relationship with Christ. To what are you turning for happiness? What can you do to grow in your relationship with Christ? Let your good deeds done out of your love for Christ shine into the lives of others this week.

171

What Is Joy?

"He who has the bride is the groom. But the groom's friend, who stands by and listens for him, rejoices greatly at the groom's voice. So this joy of mine is complete." (John 3:29)

If I had an iPod, I'd be happy. If I had her looks, I'd be happy. If I had her boyfriend, I'd be happy. Sound familiar? An online dating site advertises, "What makes you happy? Visit us to find it." A car rental business states, "Happiness is renting our cars." Will any of these things really make you happy? Why?

Read John 3:27–30. Who is the bridegroom to whom John is referring? What causes the friend great joy? Never before has there been a time of greater technological advances than now. Just take a look at what's in your pockets. More than likely, you will find a cell phone, mp3 player or iPod, and maybe even a USB jump drive. Do you have your "stuff" and find there is still no contentment? Do you find yourself constantly desiring more? Why? John said in these verses the real source of his joy was in listening for the voice of Christ. His joy was complete when he was with Him. Joy comes from learning to love the Savior's voice and being in His presence. Do you find yourself longing for more? What more do you want? Spend time with Jesus today and ask Him to be the Source of your joy.

172

Are You Satisfied?

*I know both how to have a little, and I know how to have a lot.
In any and all circumstances I have learned the secret of
being content—whether well fed or hungry, whether
in abundance or in need. (Philippians 4:12)*

Have you spent much time thinking about what you want to do when you finish high school? The possibilities are endless. Just trying to narrow down colleges or technical schools can be mind-boggling. Decisions are difficult, but being satisfied with the decision you make is usually the hardest part. Read Philippians 4:12–14. What was the source of Paul's contentment? From where did Paul say his strength came? Take a walk through a grocery store or department store. For any single item, there are typically several choices. I recently went to the store to purchase cans of tomatoes and found half an aisle devoted solely to different types of tomatoes. One choice of tomatoes would have been easier. After deciding on the brand and the type of tomato, I couldn't help but wonder if another kind might have been better. It is human nature to want what we don't have. One of the Ten Commandments tells us not to lust after our neighbor's belongings. We see something bigger and better and desire it. How can you learn to be content in your present situation? True contentment and joy comes from learning to be content with what you have.

173

Learn from Solomon

*The Lord was angry with Solomon, because his heart
had turned away from Yahweh, the God of Israel,
who had appeared to him twice. (1 Kings 11:9)*

Have you wanted something only after you saw someone else enjoying it? Children will often find a particular toy appealing once they see someone else playing with it. Has a certain pair of jeans looked so good on your friend that you felt you must have them too? Those are normal human feelings. Read 1 Kings 11:1–15. What did Solomon desire? Why? Solomon had it all: wisdom, power, and wealth. But there was something he desired that he placed above God. What was the result after he obtained it? Did he find lasting contentment? It is difficult to be satisfied. Finding contentment in life and in our circumstances is difficult when we are looking to gratify ourselves. The wants are endless and never fulfilling. Like Solomon, we must learn to listen to the Father and find contentment in Him alone. Our difficulties and adversaries in life often come because we, like Solomon, do not learn to be still in the Lord and be thankful for the blessings we have. Instead, we seek to please others and gratify our own fleshly desires. What are you seeking that will not bring glory to the Lord?

174

It Is Good for Me to Be Afflicted

*It was good for me to be afflicted so that
I could learn Your statutes. (Psalm 119:71)*

Why me? Ever ask that question? Let's face it. Some things in life are just not fair. But that doesn't make it easy to swallow when someone tells you to "get over it, life isn't fair," does it? Read Psalm 119:67–71. What did the author of this psalm say was good for him? What was the result of his suffering? Psychologists say there are two methods people use when facing challenges. It's called the "fight or flight" response. Do you run from your trials and cower, or do you stay there and fight? Both of these options can be dangerous. Of the former, it is easy to pretend the challenges don't exist; and of the latter, it is tempting to manipulate your resources to try to make things turn out your way. How do you typically face challenges in your life? The Bible shows us a different way. The Bible says it is good for us to face suffering and sorrow because through these difficulties we learn to depend on the One true God, and we learn to find joy in Him. Before we are faced with pain, we go astray; but through it, we can know true joy. Life may not be fair, but God is fair and just. Trust Him.

175

Consider Joseph

Pharaoh also said to Joseph, "See, I am placing you over all the land of Egypt." (Genesis 41:41)

When was the last time you were treated unfairly, and it caused you great pain? Read Genesis 41. What do you learn about Joseph? Joseph was sold by his brothers into slavery. Then he interpreted the cupbearer's dream and asked to be remembered when he got out of prison, and even then he was forgotten. The Bible says that "after two years had passed" Pharaoh had a dream, and the cupbearer suddenly remembered Joseph. Two years. Can you imagine what he was thinking? Perhaps it was *God has forgotten me* or *God doesn't love me* or maybe just simply *why me?* But read the words of Pharaoh after Joseph interprets Pharaoh's dream. It is obvious Joseph wasn't sulking over his misery while in prison. He was growing in his love and his devotion to the Almighty. God will turn your pain and heartache into a desire within you to really know Him. I love what Joseph said to his brothers at the end of Genesis, "You planned evil against me; God planned it for good to bring about the present result—the survival of many people" (Genesis 50:20). Look for God's hand at work around you this week.

176

I Want It All

"We have heard of Moab's pride, great pride, indeed—his insolence, arrogance, pride, and haughty heart." (Jeremiah 48:29)

Have you ever known anyone who seemed to have it all? The newest clothes, the nicest car, the biggest house? Have you ever been confronted by the guy or girl who wanted it and got it? What was his or her personality like? Was he or she demanding, controlling, or mean-spirited? Read Jeremiah 48:11, 29–30. What stands out to you in these verses? The Bible describes that these people "had it made." But look carefully at verses 29 and 30. As a result of the easy life, they also were full of pride and conceit. The Bible says that in their hearts they were arrogant. These people would learn the hard way that life wasn't about them. They would quickly learn the holiness of God, and it would come through suffering. The Bible promises we will face suffering in this life. No one will escape it. But the great news is in another promise Jesus made, and that is found in John 17. Jesus, referring to Himself, said that we would have "My joy completed in them." Live in that joy this week.

177

Who Has the Reins in Your Life?

*Now if you faithfully obey the LORD your God and are
careful to follow all His commands I am giving you today,
the LORD your God will put you far above all the
nations of the earth. (Deuteronomy 28:1)*

Have you ever tried to house-train a puppy? How challenging was that? It is easy to get frustrated when puppies, dogs, horses, or even children don't obey and do what we expect them to do. How about you? Do you always do what you know God wants? How do you think God feels about your answer? Read Deuteronomy 28. What is the commandment found there? What is the blessing promised for obedience? Recently I attended a professional horse show. A certain horse caught my attention. The moment the animal went to jump, something happened. He stopped. The rider tried to turn the stubborn horse and force him to go; yet he remained. Time was up. The competition was over for this animal. Then something happened. The rider rode him around the ring again. This time, as he led the horse to the jump that had caused his demise moments earlier, the horse cleared it cleanly. It was a test of wills between the horse and the rider. The horse must be made to submit his will to the rider. It is the same with us. We find joy in our life when we obey the Lord.

178

The Lord Is in All Things

But David found strength in
the Lord his God. (1 Samuel 30:6)

Have you ever felt alone and abandoned? An outcast? You are not alone. At least thirty percent of teenagers report feeling alone or left out. Read 1 Samuel 30. What verses indicate the men may have felt abandoned? David found himself in battle against the Amalekites. He came upon a town called Ziklag, but when he and his army arrived, it was not a joyous welcome home. Instead the men found their families gone, taken captive by the Amalekites. David was so angered that he consulted Abiathar, the priest, to see if he should pursue the offenders. He was told to go, and he would be victorious. Then David found an Egyptian slave in a field. The Bible says he wasn't just any slave, but he was a slave of an Amalekite. He had fallen ill, and three days earlier his master had abandoned him. David found the Amalekites, and they were reveling in their victory. David's men attacked and defeated the Amalekites, and David and his men were joyous at the reunion with their families. It is so easy to overlook just how mighty God is and how we never know how our trials are going to turn out. Only God can turn our weeping into dancing. God tests our faith in the valleys and not on the mountains. Find joy in the Lord today.

179

Put Off The Old Self

You took off your former way of life, the old self that is corrupted by deceitful desires. (Ephesians 4:22)

Have you ever had your feelings hurt? Have you ever known the pain of a broken heart? What about the opposite? Have you ever caused someone else to hurt? When was the last time you apologized for saying a hurtful word to another? Read Ephesians 4:17–32. What was the reason for the Gentiles' hardening of their hearts? When we belong to Christ, our hearts become His. Our old self becomes new. Because of this, we do not act the way we once did. Our lives change after we meet Jesus. Paul said that when we continue on in the old self we are causing the Holy Spirit grief. How does it make you feel to know you are causing God grief? The world has become so confused in its quest for true joy. We are searching for love and happiness in all the wrong places. It is easy to dispose of others when they don't continue to satisfy. We use others for our pleasure and then toss them away when they are no longer needed or valuable. We have become a society of self-satisfying and cold-hearted people. Christians must be different. Remember, it is through a relationship with Christ that our hearts are changed and our attitudes toward mankind become more like Him.

180

What Do You Talk About?

*I wrote the first narrative, Theophilus, about
all that Jesus began to do and teach. (Acts 1:1)*

How can you tell what is most important to a person? The best way is to listen to someone talk. Most people talk about what is important to them. Based on what you talk about, what would your friends say is important to you? Luke wrote the Gospel of Luke (big surprise) and the book of Acts to someone named Theophilus. You can't listen to Luke talk, but you can read what he wrote to his friend. Read Acts 1:1–3. Based on what Luke wrote to his friend, what would you say was most important to him? Luke was not an eyewitness to the life of Jesus. He didn't get to see Jesus walk on water. But Luke had heard the stories from eyewitnesses, and he had come to know Jesus through their testimony. Jesus Christ became the most important thing to Luke. (His two books account for almost a quarter of the New Testament.) What is the most important thing to you? If Jesus is the most important thing to you, how much time do you spend talking about Him? This week, look for opportunities to talk about what Jesus has done in your life. Let others know that Jesus is important to you.

181

What We Have Touched

We are writing these things so that
our joy may be complete. (1 John 1:4)

SeaWorld has these dolphin petting tanks. You pat the water. If a dolphin feels friendly, it will come to you, and you can rub its back. You might think dolphins feel soft, but they feel more like car tires. If you have touched a dolphin, you know firsthand. Read 1 John 1:1–4. What are the ways John experienced Jesus firsthand? John had actually spent time with Jesus, had seen Him face-to-face, had leaned against Him, and had heard His voice. He wrote about someone whom he knew personally. You can't see Jesus with your eyes or touch Him with your hands, but you can experience Jesus. In what ways have you experienced Jesus? Witnessing is telling people what you have experienced of Jesus. John mentioned two reasons why he told others what he knew of Jesus. What are John's two reasons for sharing Christ in verses 2 and 4? John wanted his readers to experience eternal life, which is found only in Jesus. Plus, John knew that sharing Christ brings joy. Touching a dolphin is fun, but it is nothing like the joy of introducing someone to Jesus. Think about your experience with Jesus. What has He done that you could share with someone this week? Talk about your experience with Jesus.

182

This Is Your Time

For we did not follow cleverly contrived myths when we made known to you the power and coming of our Lord Jesus Christ; instead, we were eyewitnesses of His majesty. (2 Peter 1:16)

Imagine what your high school graduation might be like. You look around and see friends you have spent years with—in classes, in the hallways, at ball games, and at concerts. You have spent time laughing and maybe even crying with these friends. The time you have spent with these students is coming to an end. You will never see many of them again. What do you want them to remember because of your influence? Read 2 Peter 1:12–18. What did Peter want others to remember about him? The Apostle Peter knew his death was drawing near. Peter wasn't concerned about how people thought of him when he was gone. Peter wanted people to remember the things of Christ. What do you think Peter meant when he said, "We were eyewitnesses of His majesty"? Peter was an eyewitness to Jesus. He had heard the words God spoke about Jesus. He was there when Jesus walked on the water. He knew that nothing in the world was as important or as amazing as Jesus Christ. Look around your school. Think about all of the people you see every day. You have an incredible opportunity to have an impact on them. Like Peter, you need to share what you have seen and what you know of Jesus while you have the opportunity.

183

Humanity-Sick

But when He heard this, He said, "Those who are well don't need a doctor, but the sick do." (Matthew 9:12)

A museum in London has recreated the medieval streets on which the Black Plague took place. As you walk through the museum, you can hear the cries of those afflicted with the disease. Modern medicine is much better at fighting disease, but pandemics like the H1N1 can still sweep through a community, causing pain and death. Jesus said that He came to care for people because humanity is sick. Read Matthew 9:10–13. How is sin like a disease? The picture that the Bible paints of people without Christ is harsh. They are even worse off than having a plague eat at them. They are spiritually dead and separated from God. If they physically die like that, they will be eternally separated from God. The people around you look healthy enough, don't they? When was the last time you realized they had the disease of sin? What can you do for them? Spiritually, the human race is born dead in sin. Because people are spiritually dead, they need the Holy Spirit to make their souls alive and accept Jesus. People are dying, and only the touch of Jesus Christ can bring healing to their souls. You may feel scared to talk with people about Jesus. However, when you see people as Jesus does, you realize how badly they need Christ. Begin to view people without Christ as people who are spiritually dead and need to be made alive. God has compassion on them, and He wants you to feel that same compassion for them.

184

Humanity - Orphaned

"I will not leave you as orphans;
I am coming to you." (John 14:18)

Jen Gash leads a ministry called Sweet Sleep. On a mission trip to an orphanage in Moldova, the awful mats the children slept on broke Jen's heart. She decided to take a team back to build beds for the children. Sweet Sleep now builds beds for orphans in countries in Africa, Eastern Europe, and the Caribbean. Being an orphan is a terrible thing. Think about the things you enjoy as a member of your family. What do you think you would miss most if you had no family? Read John 14:15–21, and underline the promise Jesus made to His disciples in verse 18. People without Christ are like orphans. They are lost without a Heavenly Father to love them and care for their needs. Jesus promised His disciples He would never leave them as orphans. Today, pay attention to people around you. Do they need the love of a Father? The best thing you can do for them is to introduce them to God.

185

Humanity-Enslaved

*"You will know the truth, and
the truth will set you free." (John 8:32)*

You probably know about the Underground Railroad of the 1800s. The railroad consisted of a trail of people who helped slaves escape to freedom. Escaped slaves on the Underground Railroad—and those who helped them—were under constant threat. But something in the human spirit does not want to be enslaved—we all desire freedom. Read John 8:31–36. Mark the word *slave* each time it is used. You may feel like a slave at times—to your parents, your teachers, or the boss at your part-time job. But what would it really be like to be owned by someone else? From where does freedom—real freedom—come, according to these verses? Jesus said people are enslaved by their own sin. A person may believe he or she is free, but Jesus said sin is bondage. What do you think Jesus meant about our sin keeping us enslaved? It is a strange paradox, but when you choose to be obedient to Christ, you become free. Christ makes us free from the fear of punishment, free from the need to prove yourself, free from guilt, and free to follow Christ. Begin to notice the bonds of people around you. Their only hope for freedom is to know Jesus.

186

The Past Is Forgiven

"She will give birth to a son, and you are to name Him Jesus, because He will save His people from their sins." (Matthew 1:21)

Have you ever done something so stupid that your family and friends will never let you forget it? Wouldn't it be awful if your whole life were defined by your worst moment? Most people will only remember Larry Walters for the time he tied forty-five weather balloons to his lawn chair. He shot up to 16,000 feet in the air. When Lawn Chair Larry finally got down, he was placed in handcuffs and hauled off to jail. All of us have done things we wish we hadn't. We have hurt people. We have defied the commands of God. We are sinners. We are guilty because of the darkness in our hearts, and we stand condemned by God. That would be terrible news if the only thing God knew of you was your sinfulness. But in Jesus, your past is forgiven. Read Matthew 1:18–21. What was the prophesy about Jesus at the end of verse 21? The story of Jesus is the central point of all history, and the story of Jesus is about forgiveness of sin. Think about how you talk about sin. If you treat it like a joke, consider how you can take the problem of sin more seriously. To God, it is a serious thing.

187

The Present Is Empowered

I baptize you with water for repentance, but the One who is coming after me is more powerful than I. I am not worthy to remove His sandals. He Himself will baptize you with the Holy Spirit and fire. (Matthew 3:11)

Most people coast through life without really considering their purpose. Get a job. Get a car. Graduate from high school. Go to college. Get a better job. Get a better car. Get married. Get a house. Have kids. Get a mini-van. Get a better house. Go to little league. Get old. Play dominos. Die. Not much to invest your life in—is there? Read Matthew 3:11–12. What did John the Baptist say Jesus would do in verse 11? In Jesus, your present life is empowered. Life without Christ is all about you. You decide what is good for you and do what makes you feel good. When Christ comes into your life, everything changes. The Holy Spirit empowers you to live out God's calling for your life. Think about your life since you came to know Christ. How has Jesus used you to make a difference for His kingdom in the world? Many of the people around you are living without purpose. They need the power and direction of the Holy Spirit to give their lives meaning. How can you make that truth clear to them? Think of someone with whom you can talk about the meaning of life this week.

188

The Future Is in Heaven

*"For the Son of Man is going to come with His angels
in the glory of His Father, and then He will reward
each according to what he has done." (Matthew 16:27)*

How do you picture heaven? Read Matthew 16:21–28. What was the promise Jesus made in verse 27? Jesus' arrest was coming soon. He told His disciples about His coming crucifixion, but He also told them He would be raised to life again on the third day. Jesus' resurrection is full of meaning. Because Jesus rose from the dead, He proved that He can raise you to eternal life too. Those who are in Christ will spend eternity with Him in heaven. In Jesus, your future is in heaven. Think for a minute: Do you know anyone who would be better off without Christ? The people around you may not think much about eternity, but everyone will face it. Everyone will stand before God. Everyone will spend eternity either in heaven or in hell. Everyone needs the promise of eternal life with Jesus. How can you help them to understand what God has in store for those who love Him? Try to engage someone in a conversation about heaven this week. Ask them what they think it will be like. Look for an opportunity to tell them what the Bible says it takes to go to heaven.

189

Overcoming the Jitters

*Summoning the Twelve, He gave them power and authority
over all the demons, and power to heal diseases. (Luke 9:1)*

Just the idea of witnessing can make people nervous or upset. Do you get a queasy stomach just thinking about talking to a non-Christian about Jesus? Read Luke 9:1–6 and mark the words *power* and *authority* in your Bible. What type of power and authority are described in these verses? During His earthly ministry, Jesus sent His disciples into the various villages to preach the good news of the kingdom of God and to do miracles. The words in this passage are His instructions to the Twelve as they were on missions. Guess what—you are also on a mission for Christ. As a believer in Christ, God expects you to tell others about His Son. Jesus never told us it would be easy to tell people about Him. Some people will reject us. Some people will ignore us. Some people may even abuse us. Jesus did promise that He would provide the power for us to witness. How does knowing that Christ will empower you affect the way you approach witnessing? What do you need to do to talk to others about Christ? Ask Jesus to empower you to be His witness—then start talking. Trust Him to strengthen you as you share.

190

What To Pack

"Take nothing for the road," He told them,
"no walking stick, no traveling bag, no bread,
no money; and don't take an extra shirt." (Luke 9:3)

Let's do a little "fast forward" thinking for a moment:

—Youth camp is next week. What are you doing this week to get ready to go?

—After your last summer at home, you head off to college. What do you pack for your first semester in the dorm?

—You are going to witness to people. What do you need to take with you?

Read Luke 9:1–6. Underline the instructions Jesus gave His disciples in verse 3. It seems strange that Jesus didn't let His disciples pack a duffle bag as they went from town to town to witness about Him. Can you imagine going on a mission trip when no one has made plans for food? Why do you think Jesus told His disciples to take nothing with them? Jesus wanted His disciples to depend on God. You can do a lot of things to get ready to witness: take witnessing classes, gather gospel tracts, mark your Bible. These are all good things. However, the key to witnessing is opening your mouth and talking about Jesus. Don't wait until you feel you have everything you need to witness. Just go and witness.

191

Shake the Dust

"If they do not welcome you, when you leave that town, shake off the dust from your feet as a testimony against them." (Luke 9:5)

Read Luke 9:1–6. When you witness, eternity is at stake. If your friend rejects Christ, it can be a huge frustration. How do you deal with the feeling of failure? Do you ever really fail when you witness for Jesus? Explain. What did Jesus instruct His followers to do if rejected? First, realize you have not failed. You shared Christ. That is a huge success. Second, understand that the Holy Spirit has to act in a person's life to convict them of their sins and move them to forgiveness and salvation. People don't always respond the first time they feel this. Your friend may respond the next time. You may have paved the way for your friend to come to know Christ in another week or another year. It is easy to become discouraged when people don't respond, but it is not your fault if another person rejects Christ. Jesus called His disciples to let go of the rejection and go talk to the next person. Don't take rejection personally. Continue to share. Kick up your feet and keep going.

192

Worthy of Worship

Yahweh is great and is highly praised;
His greatness is unsearchable. (Psalm 145:3)

Think about the things you value most in life. Why are these things valuable to you? Many different things have value to us—certain possessions, favorite hobbies and activities, special relationships. But none of these things even come close to the incomparable value or worth of our amazing God! Look at Revelation 4:9–11. What is happening? What is God worthy to receive? Why? God is holy and all-powerful. He created all things. Let that sink in. Absolutely nothing in all creation—nothing on earth and nothing in heaven—is more awesome and worthy of praise than God!

Today's verse is one of many verses in the Bible that affirm the idea that God is great and therefore worthy of worship. Actually, the word *worship* comes from two old English words that mean "to declare worth" or "to attribute worth." When you worship God, you are declaring that God—and God only—is worthy of your worship. Worship is recognizing and responding to God's worth. Take a moment to reflect on God's incredible worth. Think about what makes God great. Let this lead you into a genuine expression of praise and adoration. God is worthy of your worship!

193

Expression of The Heart

*I will thank Yahweh with all my heart; I will
declare all Your wonderful works. (Psalm 9:1)*

God loves you and desires a personal relationship with you. The Bible makes this clear from beginning to end. You were created to know and respond to God's love, and that's exactly what happens in genuine worship. True worship is a heartfelt expression of your love and gratitude for all God is and all God has done. Let's say that someone you love has just done something wonderful for you. How would this person feel if you expressed your love and appreciation in a half-hearted, indifferent way? Imagine what that might look like. Now how would the scene be different if you expressed yourself with all your heart? Read Psalm 9:1–2. The psalmist said that he was going to thank God with all his heart. What does it mean to thank God with all your heart? Worship is an expression of your love relationship with God. That's why it is important for worship to involve your heart as well as your mind. What are some ways you can involve your heart in worship? God isn't honored by half-hearted expressions of worship, so let your worship be an all-out expression of your heart.

194

The Right Attitude

Let us enter His presence with thanksgiving;
let us shout triumphantly to Him in song. (Psalm 95:2)

Are you enthusiastic when you worship, or do you just go through the motions? Do you enjoy praising God, or are you distracted and anxious to move on to the next thing? What's your attitude when you worship? Psalm 95:1–7 gives us some clues about the right attitude for worship. Read verse 1. How did the psalmist describe what our singing or shouting should be like? Note that he didn't say we should be joyful in worship only when we are happy or feel good. We are to be joyful whenever we worship—at all times. How can we do that? To check your answer, look at verse 2. How are we to enter God's presence? Being thankful for who God is and what God has done is the key to joyful worship. Recognizing God's greatness and goodness to us fills us with joy—regardless of our circumstances. Now check out verses 3–7. Acknowledging God's greatness also makes us humble. Why is humility necessary in order to have the right attitude for worship? Next time you worship, think about all God is and all God has done for you, and humbly give thanks and praise to God. As you do, your worship will overflow with joy!

195

The Right Focus

"God is spirit, and those who worship Him must worship in spirit and truth." (John 4:24)

What is the best way to worship God? Ask that question of several people, and you'll probably get several different answers! Most people will think of music when they think of worship. Some will say traditional worship—with an organ and hymns—is the best way to worship. Others say contemporary worship—with a band and praise music—is the way to go. Some like a combination of the two. What is your preferred style of music in worship? Did you catch the word *preferred*? Most of the time, worship style is a preference (although God is not honored by worship that violates His commands). The important thing isn't whether you use organs or guitars, but instead it is to keep the focus on honoring God. Read John 4:19–21. What was the woman's concern? What did Jesus tell her is more important? In other words, focusing on God is more important than being concerned about where we worship or how we worship. Look at verses 22–24. What do you think it means to worship God in spirit and truth? To put it simply, worshiping in spirit and truth is genuine, heartfelt worship that's focused on the truth. According to John 14:6, truth has a name. What is it? Don't get caught up in the how of worship. Stay focused on the why—Jesus—and your worship will be pleasing to God!

196

The Right Response

Do not harden your hearts as at Meribah, as on
that day at Massah in the wilderness. (Psalm 95:8)

Choose the right response: Your friend hurts your feelings but later apologizes.

—Forgive your friend.

—Say something hurtful to "settle the score."

Someone gives you a compliment.

—Explain why you don't think it's true.

—Smile and say, "Thank you!"

Okay, the answers are obvious! Still, sometimes we don't respond as we should—and that includes when God reveals Himself to us. Read Psalm 95:7–9. How did the Israelites respond to God in the wilderness? What does it mean to "harden your heart"? When God reveals Himself to you—such as through creation, the Bible, family and friends, or other demonstrations of His love—the right response is always to worship Him. That's what worship is: responding to God with gratitude, praise, and love. When you're indifferent to God, or your response is ungrateful or unloving, you're hardening your heart. The more you harden your heart, the more unresponsive it becomes. That's what happened to the Israelites. They saw the mighty things God did, but they stopped responding with gratitude, praise, and love. Don't harden your heart like the Israelites. Choose the right response. Worship God by responding to Him with gratitude, praise, and love!

197

Worship with Your Voice

*Therefore, through Him let us continually offer up
to God a sacrifice of praise, that is, the fruit
of our lips that confess His name. (Hebrews 13:15)*

"Keep it down." "Don't raise your voice." Ever hear those words? Well, God actually wants you to raise your voice . . . in worship! Read Psalm 150. The psalmist talked about praising God with different instruments. Then he instructed everything that has breath to praise the Lord. You—along with all living things—were given breath to praise the Lord. Your voice is an instrument of worship! Read Psalm 40:10 and Psalm 98:4. These verses name three ways you can worship God with your voice. What are they? Again and again the Scriptures tell us that we are to sing, shout, and speak God's praise. There are more than 220 biblical references to singing as an expression of worship and more than 50 references to speaking or shouting God's praise. Why do you think God places such emphasis on praising Him with your voice? Have you ever thought of your words—whether spoken, sung, or shouted—as a sacrifice or offering to God? How often are you to offer this sacrifice of praise? Your voice is meant to be an instrument of praise. Use it to worship God—and don't be afraid to raise your voice!

198

Worship with Your Talents

*Let them praise His name with dancing and make
music to Him with tambourine and lyre. (Psalm 149:3)*

In the movie *Napoleon Dynamite*, Napoleon and Pedro talked about the school dance. Napoleon said no one would go out with him because he didn't have any skills. Then he named several things he couldn't do. Pedro asked, "Aren't you pretty good at drawing?" Napoleon answered, "Yes. Probably the best that I know of."

Are you ever like Napoleon, focusing on what you can't do rather than on what you can? God has given you specific skills and talents, and He wants you to use them to worship Him. Worshiping with your talents is simply doing what you're good at with the purpose of glorifying God. Read Psalm 149:1–3. What ways of worshiping God are mentioned? Now read Exodus 31:1–11. What talent or skill did God give to Bezalel and Oholiab? Why? Do you sing or play an instrument? Can you dance or act? Do you enjoy crafts or decorating? Are you good at working with tools? Do you have computer, sound, lighting, or other technical skills? Maybe you're friendly and could welcome people to worship. Whatever you're good at, you can find a way to use it to worship God! Name something you're good at. Find a way to use this talent to worship God!

199

Worship with Abandon

You are never to bow down to another god because Yahweh, being jealous by nature, is a jealous God. (Exodus 34:14)

It's all about me. At least that's what popular culture says. From TV to movies to magazines to the Internet, the message is the same: "Life is all about you and what you want." Often we bring this same mind-set to worship—*I'm not enjoying worship today; This sermon is boring; Finally! A good song!; I hope someone notices my new clothes.* Thoughts like these focus on me and what I want. God says worship should be all about Him, what He does, and what He wants. What does God command? The word *jealous* means zealous, or passionate. God wants all of your worship. He wants you to worship Him with abandon—to forget about everything else and focus only on Him. Is it possible to worship God with all your heart if your focus is on anything other than God? In the song "The Heart of Worship," Matt Redman talks about coming back to the heart of worship. He writes, "It's all about You, Jesus." Focus on Jesus and let your worship be all about Him!

200

Worship Together

Let us be concerned about one another in order to promote love and good works. (Hebrews 10:24)

God designed us to live and worship in a community. We're a family of believers. Worshiping together is like a joyful family gathering. It's a time to remember and reflect; celebrate our Father and enjoy His presence together; share hope, encouragement, and instruction; be renewed; and be a witness to those outside the family. In worship we remember and reflect on all God is and has done. That gives us reason to celebrate! Read Psalm 22:3. What happens when we praise God together? God actually sits in our presence when we worship together! Read Hebrews 10:23–25. Why are we not to neglect meeting together? (Hint: The answer has to do with the things we're told to do!) Worshiping together allows us to give and receive hope, encouragement, and instruction. Colossians 3:16 names one way this happens. What are others? Worship also is a time of renewal. Read Romans 12:2. What happens when our minds are renewed? How have you been transformed—changed—by worship? Finally, worship is a way to witness. When those outside the family of God see His power in our worship and our transformed lives, they're drawn to God—and the "family" grows! Think of worshiping together as a family celebration, and look forward to it with anticipation!

201

Worship by Yourself

He often withdrew to deserted
places and prayed. (Luke 5:16)

Think about your best friend. How did you become close? By spending time together, right? The same is true of your relationship with God. The more one-on-one time you have with God, the more you will know and love Him. When you spend time alone with God, praying and reading God's Word, you are worshiping God. Worshiping God in this way is just as important as worshiping with other believers. Read Psalm 42:1–2. What did the psalmist long for? Whether you're a new Christian or you've been a Christian for years, you need time alone with God. Even Jesus needed it! Read Mark 1:35, Luke 5:16, and Matthew 14:22–23. What did Jesus do? Was it an occasional practice or a habit? What kind of place did He choose for these times? When you spend time alone with God, why is it important to find a place where you won't be distracted? Where can you find such a place? Jesus knew how important it was to spend time alone with God, and He set the example for us. Find a quiet place where you can read God's Word and pray. He's waiting to meet with you.

202

Worship with Your Life

Therefore, brothers, by the mercies of God, I urge you to present your bodies as a living sacrifice, holy and pleasing to God; this is your spiritual worship. (Romans 12:1)

It's important to worship with other believers and to worship on your own, but did you know that all of your life is meant to be an act of worship? What does it mean to be a "living sacrifice?" In the Old Testament, worshipers offered animal sacrifices to God for their sins. After Jesus made the final sacrifice for all sins with His death on the cross, those sacrifices were no longer necessary. Now the sacrifices that are pleasing to God are our very lives. Being a living sacrifice is giving all of your life to God—every moment of every day. Living in this way is an act of worship. Read 1 Corinthians 10:31. How can you do everything for God's glory? Whenever you direct attention to God's greatness, goodness, and love, you're glorifying God. You can glorify God in anything you do by doing it in a way that pleases God and reflects Jesus. Helping others, spending money wisely, studying diligently—these are all ways to glorify and worship God. What else can you do to bring glory to God? Every moment is an opportunity to worship God. Do something to bring God glory today!

203

Smooth as Glass

But He said to them, "Why are you fearful, you of little faith?"
Then He got up and rebuked the winds and the sea.
And there was a great calm. (Matthew 8:26)

Have you ever had the opportunity to stand on the shore of a lake when the water was incredibly still? It's especially impressive when you have gone to sleep the night before with the water all churned up from a strong wind or storm. It's like you go to sleep with one lake and wake up with an entirely different one. What was once kind of scary and wild becomes calm and quiet. Life can be that way too. Read Matthew 8:23–26. Jesus and the disciples were out on a lake when a severe storm developed. The terrified disciples woke Jesus, who calmed the storm. The sea became smooth as glass. What's interesting is that they were at the same exact place in the same body of water before and after. What made the difference was the removal of the influence that had things all stirred up. What was once chaos became quiet. As the disciples learned to trust Jesus more following that experience, you can learn to trust Him as the storms in your life settle and you discover the peace that can follow those storms. When was there a time that your life seemed a hopeless storm, and then, in the blink of an eye, all was quiet? Thank God that He is always there for you and that He can bring peace into the storms of your life.

204

Passing Words

"Beware of the scribes, who want to go around in long robes and who love greetings in the marketplaces, the front seats in the synagogues, and the places of honor at banquets." (Luke 20:46)

Almost everyone has said it. *What's up?* How do you respond when a passer-by asks how your day is going? In Jesus' day, the Pharisees had turned greetings on the street into showy opportunities for people to exclaim the religious leaders' own accomplishments. Instead, those who followed Jesus came to greet one another by saying "shalom" or "peace." And not just any peace but the peace that came from knowing their long-awaited Messiah had arrived on the scene. This was kind of like that moment of relief when the story you've been watching or reading reaches the climax to which it has been building. Whether it's a love story, one of suspense, or maybe a mystery, it's the point when the anticipation is reached, and you let out that big sigh as your heart and breathing begin to return to normal rhythm. Why do you think the Christ followers made it a point to greet one another in this manner? Do your greetings with fellow believers reflect anything different about you or them? Today, look those you meet in the eye and say something like "Excellent!" or "Blessed!" when greeted—and think about the amazing place Jesus is preparing for you at that moment.

205

Clearing The Air

If we confess our sins, He is faithful and righteous to forgive us our sins and to cleanse us from all unrighteousness. (1 John 1:9)

Read 1 John 1:7–9. Have you ever done something you weren't supposed to do? Even if mom and/or dad don't know what you did, you just don't feel comfortable sitting in the same room with them, much less talking with them. When have you had this scenario happen to you? Then it comes out. Your parents heard from a friend of a friend. Here comes "the talk." Debate. Discipline. And then, well, then something amazing happens. Shortly thereafter, though uncomfortable, the fear to be in the same room with your parents is gone. You know you've disappointed them, but the relationship is restored. You are at peace with your parents. What would being at peace with your parents feel like? How does this situation relate to the Scripture passage for today and your relationship with God? Coming to terms with God about your sinfulness is similar. While your salvation is secure, falling into sin again (and again and again) can make it uncomfortable to pray or read your Bible. That's why we confess even after being saved—to ensure a right relationship with the Father. If there's anything you've not talked to the Father about (any sin that you need to confess), pause right now and talk to Him about it.

206

Peace Seeker

*Happy is a man who finds wisdom and who
acquires understanding. (Proverbs 3:13)*

When have you found yourself in a situation where you had to make a difficult choice and couldn't figure out which choice would bring about peace? Sometimes in order to find peace you must look for something else first. Read Proverbs 3:13–19. What does God say about wisdom? What is one of the benefits of obtaining wisdom? Wisdom leads to peace. When was the last time you made a decision that caused you all sorts of trouble? Think back to right before you made that decision. Did you have another option? One that might not have been as much fun but would have kept you out of all that trouble? That would have been the wise choice—the one that ended in a peaceful situation. Wisdom—discerning what is the right choice based on God's Word—will lead you to make the right choices. When you make the right choices, peace will naturally follow. The writer of these verses even describes this peace as more valuable than gold or silver. How are you going to face today? Will you be wise and peaceful? Or will you be reckless and troubled? It really is up to you. Peace is just around the corner—so wise up.

207

Peace Out

Watch the blameless and observe the upright,
for the man of peace will have a future. (Psalm 37:37)

Are you aware that your future is being formed right now, today, by you and only you? What are you told to do in today's verse? What does "the man of peace will have a future" mean to you? Yeah, I know. Sometimes things happen that are out of your control, but how do you react to those situations? Do you react with anger, deceit, or arrogance? You are instructed in this verse to watch those who live for Christ. You can learn a lot about how to live for God by watching those who are following Christ. Remember, every action you take today will have an impact on your future—and somebody else is probably watching how you will respond. Peace isn't just a cool word to throw out when you leave a room. It's a lifestyle that's vital to the health of your future. How are you going to respond to tough situations today? Peace out—literally.

208

Think About It

*For the mind-set of the flesh is death, but the
mind-set of the Spirit is life and peace. (Romans 8:6)*

People like reality shows because they are "live"—well, at least we think so. No script. No do-overs. Just pure reality and live action. What would it be like to actually be in a reality show that is able to reveal every word and thought of your mind? That would be uncomfortable, wouldn't it? Well, you're living in that type of reality right now—and it isn't a television show. God is the audience—He is also the producer of the show. How would you describe your mind/thoughts: sin-controlled or Spirit-controlled? Let's keep it real here. You aren't going to fool God with actions that make you feel good about yourself while your thoughts are still as sinful as ever. You have two choices: You can have the mind of a sinful man who fools those around you and makes you feel good for awhile; or you can have the controlled mind of the Spirit and live a life that has real peace regardless of your circumstances—no pretending required. So what's it going to be: fake life, fake peace; or real life, real peace? You have probably seen the bumper sticker that reads "No Jesus, no peace. Know Jesus, know peace." It's up to you—for real.

209

Jump!

"But seek first the kingdom of God and His righteousness, and all these things will be provided for you." (Matthew 6:33)

Do you remember when you were little and used to run and jump into a parent or adult friend's arms with reckless abandon? Or maybe you've been at a pool and seen a small child jump from the side into someone's waiting arms in the water. Whenever I see that, I think about Jesus telling the disciples that we are to welcome the Kingdom of God like a little child—with reckless abandon. I have a friend who used to say worry was like saying, "Father, I don't believe you can handle this on Your own without me, so I'm going along too." Read Matthew 6:25–32. What does Jesus say about how you should think about what you will eat or drink, about your body, or what you will wear? What is the opposite of what He says? Now read Matthew 6:33–34. What does verse 33 have to do with the verses that precede it? How is verse 33 a link to verse 34? It's significant that Jesus started with "don't worry" and ended with "don't worry." That should be a clue for you—don't worry about it but trust in God as you go through the things in life. Tell God you trust Him in prayer.

210

Ground Floor Faith

Do what you have learned and received and heard and seen in me, and the God of peace will be with you. (Philippians 4:9)

At youth camp, we did this exciting contest: using only our own group members, we had to create a structure that the last person could climb to the top of and place a mark on the wall. The group with the highest mark on the wall won. I noticed something every year that we tackled this challenge: the teams with the best foundation always got the highest. Most times there was a solid handful of people that anchored themselves together well, and the group would strategically place others in stages above them. What is the point of a solid foundation? A solid and stable foundation was crucial as the group built higher. As you read through the stories in the Bible, one of the things you will discover are some foundations that are crucial to living confidently where God wants you. Peace is one of those things. Peace comes as you believe the things Jesus taught. These teachings form the solid foundation upon which to build life to the fullest. The firm foundation helps guard you against wavering when you reach just a little higher or when the tough winds come that try and sway you. Read Philippians 4:6–9. What are you supposed to do? What will God do for you? Consider how you can begin building a foundation today from which to grow stronger. Trust in the peace of God as you stay focused on Him.

211

Full Frame Focus

"Stop your fighting—and know that I am God, exalted among the nations, exalted on the earth." (Psalm 46:10)

Have you ever shot a photo or video that ended up out of focus? What happened? Sometimes it's hard to tell in the heat of the moment if the image is in or out of focus. Even if your camera has an auto focus feature, it can occasionally have difficulty knowing where to focus in the frame. Next thing you know, you end up with a tree in the background in perfect focus and the person in the foreground fuzzy beyond recognition. But there's a trick. When you are essentially positioned where you will be shooting, zoom in as far as the camera will zoom, focus manually, then zoom back out to frame your shot. Getting up close ensures you have a clear focus for whatever level of zoom you choose to use in the actual image you capture. How can you focus on God? You see where this is headed, right? It can be difficult to really tune in to God from a distance. So there are times when you need to dial it down to a tight zoom in your spiritual walk where God is filling your full frame. Then, once you are focused in correctly, all the other stuff in the frame that would normally distract the auto-focus won't be a distraction. What are some things that are distracting your focus from God right now? Pause right now and get alone with God. Zoom in with some time for prayer and reading the Bible.

212

Go in Peace

*He said to the woman, "Your faith
has saved you. Go in peace." (Luke 7:50)*

Read Luke 7:50, Mark 5:34, and Luke 8:48. Why do you think Jesus said, "Go in peace"? When have you experienced a time when you were not at peace? Whenever Jesus encountered someone, He wanted that person to come away from the encounter with a peaceful heart. Regardless of how much the person was hurting, if they did as Jesus asked them to do, peace was the result. Try to remember a time when you had an encounter with someone that left you feeling angry, frustrated, or deeply hurt. Now think of a time when someone had an encounter with you. How did that person walk away from your encounter? Did you show them love and compassion? Or did you come down hard on them, making them feel dirty and guilty? If you want peace in your own life you have to show others the same love and compassion that Christ has shown you. Will the people you encounter today be able to "go in peace" after the encounter? Think about it. Then, go in peace.

213

Anything But That!

If possible, on your part, live at peace
with everyone. (Romans 12:18)

Read today's verse. What are you supposed to do? Have you ever said to God, "Do I really have to do that?" And, of course, "that" is something you really need to do in order to keep the peace. Living at peace with everyone (everyone!) can be tough, but God gives you some guidance. Read 2 Corinthians 13:11. How do rejoicing, being restored, and being encouraged help you experience God's peace? Trying to live in peace—peace with each other—is probably one of the fiercest battles that occurs between your sinful nature and the peaceful nature of Christ. Why do you think that is? Living at peace with everyone requires you to have a servant's heart and let your wishes go so that peace may be possible. Remember, you are told to do whatever you can do to live at peace. It is not someone else's responsibility to live at peace with you; it is your responsibility to live at peace with them. When was the last time you gave up what you wanted in order to make someone else feel better—in order to keep the peace? What happened? Being a peacemaker is a choice. Make the right choice—live at peace. After all, that's exactly what Jesus did for you.

214

In or Out?

*"The peacemakers are blessed, for they
will be called sons of God." (Matthew 5:9)*

Keeping the peace can make others around you feel better. The decision to live at peace is up to you. But what does being a peacemaker mean for you personally? What did Jesus say about peacemakers? How does being a peacemaker impact your life? Being a peacemaker means you have an identity; you belong to God's family. He calls you His child. There is no other identity in life that out weighs your identity as a child of God. To have God single you out and call you His own is beyond any good thing you can imagine. Being a peacemaker begins inside of you—it is a spiritual quality that only comes from a relationship with the God of Peace. Blessed, in this verse, means a deep, abiding, undisturbable happiness that comes from knowing and trusting in the promises of God. Recall the last time you walked into the school cafeteria and looked around the room, hoping to find someone to sit with. How did you feel when you couldn't spot a friendly face? How did you feel when you did find a friend to sit with? The next time you have to do something you would rather not do in order to keep the peace, remember what being a peacemaker ultimately means for you. If you're truly a child of God, you'll know it's worth it.

215

Uniquely Written

*All Scripture is inspired by God and is
profitable for teaching, for rebuking, for correcting,
for training in righteousness. (2 Timothy 3:16)*

Did you know that the Bible was written over the course of 1,500 years by more than 40 authors and in 3 different languages? It is the only book in history written by so many people, over such a long time span, and under such variety of circumstances to tell one continuous, non-contradictory story! Read 2 Peter 1:20–21. Where did Scripture come from? All Scripture is inspired by God. Peter explained that even though men held the pen, God gave them the words. How did God give them the words to write? The Bible is God's primary way of documenting His eternal story. It reveals His nature, will, and promises of the past, present, and future. He could have accomplished that in any way, but He chose to speak through the Holy Spirit into the hearts of men who penned the words in Scripture. Why was it important for so many different people to be involved in the process of writing Scripture? What does that show us about how God can work through you? God's Word gives us a guide—everything we need to know about life and godliness. He gave us His Word so we could be convinced it came from Him.

216

Uniquely Perfect

For I have kept the ways of the Lord and have not turned from my God to wickedness. (2 Samuel 22:22)

There are more actual surviving manuscripts of the Bible than any ten other pieces of classical literature combined—almost 5,800 for the New Testament alone! And despite being individually hand-copied for thousands of years, differences and discrepancies between these manuscripts are virtually non-existent. How is the Word of God described? What does that mean about the Bible—God's Word? Why is it important to understand that what you're reading is accurate to the original writings? God is perfect, and because Scripture is inspired by Him, you can expect it to be flawless as well. This means everything about it must be perfect, from the original writings selected to the truths of the messages contained, to the historical details. Only a perfect God can accomplish such a task. Only a perfect God can, and did, guarantee it.

217

Uniquely Powerful

*For I am not ashamed of the gospel, because it is
God's power for salvation to everyone who believes,
first to the Jew, and also to the Greek. (Romans 1:16)*

In the book-turned-movie *Inkheart*, Mo Folchart and his daughter, Meggie, possess the ability to bring stories to life as they read aloud. Throughout the story, their voices change the course of plot lines and characters, moving them from pages to the world and then back. Can you imagine words so powerful they literally come to life? Scripture tells us this is exactly what happens with God's Word, the Bible. Read 1 Peter 1:23 and Romans 1:16. How is God's Word (and the Gospel) described? The Word of God is alive and powerful! It has the ability to literally re-birth our spirits out of a fallen human nature into an eternal, perfect one, saving us from never-ending death. When you believe the Bible and make it part of every situation, it has the power to affect the outcome. God's promises and commands always bear fruit when followed. Spiritual battles are waged in your favor when you use Scripture to confront the enemy. How does thinking about Scripture's power make you feel? When have you experienced the power of God's Word? It was God's spoken word that brought creation into existence. That kind of destiny changing power is available to you—on the pages of the Bible.

218

Truth or Error

Jesus answered them, "You are deceived, because you don't know the Scriptures or the power of God. (Matthew 22:29)

Have you ever had an argument with someone and were fully convinced you were right—only later to realize the facts and data were against your argument, and you were wrong? What did you do? Read Matthew 22:23–33. What do you see happening here? What was Jesus' admonition in verse 29? Would He say this to you? The Sadducees were experts in religion. They thought they had it all figured out. When these know-it-alls decided to show Jesus just how little He knew, they posed a hypothetical scenario to which there was no answer to—it was a trick and a trap. Have you ever faced a question you thought had no answer? What was it? Jesus busted up their game. He told them they didn't know the Scriptures, and consequently God's nature, as well as they thought. Essentially, He said to them, "Look, you've misunderstood the Scripture because you let your opinions shape what you read in the Bible instead of letting the Bible shape your opinions. As a result, you've missed the truth." Is it easier to seek out answers or convince yourself you already know them? Why? The Bible is the ultimate authority and source of truth. If you aren't in line with it, you're in error.

219

Timeless Truth

But the word of the Lord endures forever. And this is the word that was preached as the gospel to you. (1 Peter 1:25)

Although the dates and details change from story to story, history class probably has shown you there's a consistent pattern over time. Like the seasons, as time progresses things change. There are new technologies, new ideas, new trends, and new world leaders. Things only stay at the height of popularity and power for a short time before they fade away. Read 1 Peter 1:24–25. How are you described? Why? How is God's Word described? Why? Empires rise and fall. People are born and die. Everything changes. But God's Word is timeless. It transcends generations and cultures. Throughout history, the Gospel and God's principles for life have proven to be true for every people, place, and time. God's Word is true for you too. What's more, God's Word has shown itself resilient to the best attempts of humanity to destroy it. Wherever you find yourself, whatever your circumstances, God's Word is relevant to you!

220

Revealing Truth

No creature is hidden from Him, but all things
are naked and exposed to the eyes of Him to
whom we must give an account. (Hebrews 4:13)

Since the first demonstration of the laser in 1960, some of the most important uses for laser technology have been in medicine. Lasers are powerful and precise. They are able to work on tiny, delicate portions of the eye, separate brain tumors from brain tissue, repair the tiniest blood vessel, and even operate on a single cell! Read Hebrews 4:12–13. How is God's Word like a laser? How does God's Word penetrate into our lives— even into our thoughts? God's Word acts like a surgical laser in our lives, separating those things that are not of God and do not glorify Him from those things that help us grow in our relationship with God. How do you feel about nothing in your life being hidden from God? How should that impact the way you live? God knows if something is just fleeting through your mind or if you are dwelling on it. He can tell the difference between a momentary response and an underlying motive. He knows you better than you know yourself. Insight through Scripture is one of the ways He reveals the truth of your own heart to you . . . and it's one of the ways He can change it.

221

On The Offensive

Take the helmet of salvation, and the sword of the Spirit,
which is God's word. (Ephesians 6:17)

What sword is described here? Throughout the ages, swords have been an indispensable tool and weapon. The Bible tells us that God's Word is the sword of the Spirit. In other words, the Holy Spirit wields this truth through us as we do battle with the sinful things that try to consume our lives. Read Ephesians 6:13–18. What is the larger context? Paul was talking about our spiritual armor. What do you notice that is different about the purpose of the Bible from every other piece of armor? Everything else—belt, breastplate, boots, shield, helmet—are all for defensive protection. Scripture is the only offensive item listed here. Remember, God's Word is alive and powerful. When you memorize and meditate on God's Word, the Spirit uses its truth to bolster you against temptation and at times to ward off the enemy before battle ever comes. It's like sharpening your sword and practicing with it in full view of the opponent. Sharpen your spiritual sword by spending time today (and each day) reading God's Word.

222

The Source of Life

"Pay attention and come to Me; listen, so that you will live.
I will make an everlasting covenant with you,
the promises assured to David." (Isaiah 55:3)

What is your all-time favorite food, the tastiest thing you've ever eaten? Did you ever think about God's Word as a feast for your soul? The words of Scripture are like a feast for your soul. When you truly listen to what God is saying to you through the Bible, you are spiritually nourished. Like the satisfaction of a full belly after a good meal, you can take delight in how God's Word fills your heart's emptiness. Read Isaiah 55:2–3. Consider the different words used to describe God's Word and our soul's reaction to it when we take it in. Just like you have to chew and swallow your food, it's necessary to take in and chew on God's Word. You have to read it and really listen to what it says. That means learning to savor it through meditation. You need to dig out passages that enrich and enhance the flavor of your understanding, and you need to commit it to memory like a favorite recipe. Don't waste the feast God has prepared to sustain you. Learn how to take delight in His Word. Like food to the body, it is a source of life to your soul.

223

Walk The Line

How can a young man keep his way pure?
By keeping Your word. (Psalm 119:9)

Read Psalm 119:9–11. In your own words, define what you think it means to be pure. Purity has many definitions, but they all boil down to the same basic idea: to be free from contaminants, from blemishes, or from evil. You don't have to be a neurophysicist to figure out that plenty of things in this world can work their way into your life and distract you from your relationship with God. You're probably thinking of a few things you struggle with even as you read this. Take a moment to write those things here: In such a polluted world, discerning the difference between right and wrong can be confusing. The Psalmist, however, made it pretty clear. If you want to have a sin free life, line your life up with God's Word. What are some ways that you can do that? God's Word promises that when you seek Him and His will and strive to learn His commands, He will shield you from sin and keep you pure.

224

Rock Solid

"Therefore, everyone who hears these words
of Mine and acts on them will be like a sensible man
who built his house on the rock." (Matthew 7:24)

What would you design if you had an unlimited budget to build your dream house? Can you imagine building it right on the beach, like literally on the sand, right up on the water, with no foundation? As crazy as that seems, that's exactly what it's like for a Christian to read the Bible and not do what it says. Read Matthew 7:24–27. What did Jesus say about a proper foundation? Where did He say the house should be built? Why? How does this metaphor relate to putting Scripture into practice in your life? Without obedience to God's Word, your walk with God has no foundation. It is not enough to simply read the Bible—you have to act on it. Consistent obedience is the bedrock that makes the truths of God's Word a solid part of your life and keeps you from being swept away by the difficult seasons of life. It also teaches you how to withstand philosophies and moral dilemmas that seem valid but are ultimately flawed. Don't just read the Word—build your life on it.

225

A Field Guide

*Keep my commands and live; protect my teachings
as the pupil of your eye. (Proverbs 7:2)*

Time after time, the writer of Proverbs gives the same advice: "Accept my words" (2:1); "don't forget my teaching" (3:1); "listen . . . accept my words" (4:10); "pay attention to my wisdom" (5:1); and "obey my words and treasure my commands" (7:1). Each time, the reason—though explained differently—is the same: it will protect you and bring you fullness of life. Feel free to spend some time digging around in Proverbs to explore more of these verses; but for a quick snapshot, let's look at Proverbs 7:2–3 in particular. What do these verses tell you to do with God's Word? Why? The Bible is a book full of divine wisdom. God knows how He created things to operate, and His instructions teach you the best way to function within the system He laid out. Has there ever been a time in your life when you disobeyed or ignored the commands of Scripture, and it came back to bite you? God's commands and teachings are for your protection and benefit. Like a field guide written to help you successfully navigate the treacherous terrain of life, it can save you from unnecessary heartache and suffering if you will just treasure its words and center your life around them.

226

For All To Read

*Thanks be to God, who always puts us on display
in Christ and through us spreads the aroma of the
knowledge of Him in every place. (2 Corinthians 2:14)*

Have you ever applied for something (such as a job) that required personal references? Why do you think it's important to be able to provide good personal and work references to those who ask for them? Read 2 Corinthians 2:12–14 and 3:3. According to Paul, what is it that we are representing? As a believer, you are a reference letter for the knowledge of God and the power of Christ. People should be able to look at your life and plainly see the evidence of God at work. But you cannot reference what you do not know. In order to be an effective witness for Christ, you must be well acquainted with Him. There is no better way to discover who God is than to dig into His Word. What is the most recent thing you've learned about God from His Word? As you read Scripture and live it out, those truths are etched on your heart by the Holy Spirit. God's active, powerful Word transforms you, and the result of that change is on display for all to see. It is absolutely vital that the letter of Christ people are reading in your life lines up with God's Word.

227
My Own Worst Enemy

*For I know that nothing good lives in me, that is,
in my flesh. For the desire to do what is good is with me,
but there is no ability to do it. (Romans 7:18)*

Everyone has a favorite food; what's yours? Choices range from ice cream to cheeseburgers to pizza to fries or even pumpkin pie. What's at the top of your list? Imagine being on a diet and not being able to eat your favorite food. It would be easy for a little while, but eventually you would hunger for it and think about it all the time. You might even go by the local burger place just to remember how much you miss those greasy cheeseburgers. You just feel drawn to the place and can't seem to stop yourself. Inside you might feel like there's a battle going on. You want to do the right thing (like resist the greasy cheeseburger), but it's so hard to resist the wrong things. You're not alone. Read Romans 7:18–19. How did Paul feel? What is your reaction to these verses? When was the last time you felt this way? What were you struggling with? Could you be struggling because you don't want to give up your own desires? I once heard someone say, "If you are on an ice cream diet, don't sit in front of the ice cream shop." Sounds silly, but is that what you're doing when it comes to temptation? Are you feeding the wrong desires? God wants you to always examine your motives. Sometimes we can be our own worst enemy by putting ourselves in front of stuff we should not be around.

228

Dead Man Walking

*So, you too consider yourselves dead to sin
but alive to God in Christ Jesus. (Romans 6:11)*

The devil wants us dead. But if he can't have us dead, he wants us to live as if we are dead. Spiritually dead with no visible sign of a transformed life. Review John 11. Imagine what it must have been like to be Lazarus. Raised from the dead after being in the tomb for four days. How do you suppose Lazarus felt afterward? Do you think it changed his life? In what ways? There are only a few mentions of Lazarus after he was raised from the dead. But it's clear that he was very close with Jesus, and he was quite the talk of the town. Word of his resurrection spread to people all over. If you were raised from the dead, how would you act? Read Romans 6:11–13. What did Paul say you should do? Why? The fact is you have been raised from the dead if you are a Christian. You were a sinner—spiritually dead—but you were brought to life by Jesus Christ. That is fact, but do you really believe that? Why? How are you living? As someone who has been brought to life, or are you still stuck in sin? When sin rules your life, you are living like you are dead. That's exactly where Satan wants you. But if you're truly alive in Christ, why do you keep choosing to sin? It's time to start living like you are alive.

229

Don't Feed The Lions

Be serious! Be alert! Your adversary the Devil is prowling around like a roaring lion, looking for anyone he can devour. (1 Peter 5:8)

Lions are amazing. Although they're great hunters, they're actually much slower than most of their prey. But they're built for quick bursts of speed. Their trick? They hide and wait close to something their prey needs—usually water. When the time is right, the lions charge. They bite at the prey's neck and slowly strangle it. Read 1 Peter 5:8–10. What lion do you need to recognize? What attitude should you have when dealing with the devil? The devil tricks us into thinking that we need to fulfill our desires. You might be thinking "If only I had . . . " or "If only I could . . . ". What is it that the devil is telling you that you "need" right now? He could be telling you that you "need" the latest clothes or that you "need" a boyfriend. He could be telling you that you "need" to be popular. Beware—the devil is waiting for you in the bushes, crouched and ready to strike. What lies are you listening to? Where are they leading you to? Maybe you're already in the devil's grip, and he's strangling you. The Bible tells us we need to resist the devil (James 4:7–8)—but you start by first submitting to God. Know that others are with you in your struggle. You can trust that God will perfect, confirm, strengthen, and establish you as you submit to Him.

230

All You Can Eat

"Why don't you understand what I say? Because you cannot listen to My word." (John 8:43)

Imagine a huge buffet with piles of fresh shrimp, crab legs, tender roasted prime rib, fresh and steamed veggies, and trays of beautiful desserts. There's molten chocolate cake, fresh-made ice cream, along with fresh fruits and berries. You sit down and notice a half-eaten chicken drumstick under the table. Disgusted, you call the host to show it to him. To your surprise, he picks it up and begins to say how delicious it looks. In fact, it looks so good that you shouldn't waste time going to the buffet line when you have a perfectly good half-eaten drumstick right here. Then he tries to convince you that the buffet line really isn't that good. After a little while, you start to agree and decide to eat the half-eaten chicken leg from under the table. GROSS! Is this what you would do? Are you sure? Read John 8:43–44. Why can't you understand Jesus? What keeps you from hearing His word? Jesus promises a "buffet" in your life, but when you fall into temptation, it's like wanting the half-eaten drumstick. The devil's good at convincing you that the "buffet" is not good. In what ways are you giving up the best that Jesus has for you because you're listening to the devil's lies? God has great stuff in store for you. Don't settle for the devil's lies and distractions.

231

Open Your Eyes

In their case, the god of this age has blinded the minds of the unbelievers so they cannot see the light of the gospel of the glory of Christ, who is the image of God. (2 Corinthians 4:4)

There's a dining experience that's very popular in Europe. Imagine going to a restaurant where the host comes out, tells you to put one hand on his shoulder, and follow him. He opens the door, and as you enter the room, it's pitch black. You hear the discussions of other people, but no matter how hard you look, you can't see anyone or anything. There's absolutely no light anywhere. For the first time, you experience blindness. It's a miracle you made it to your table. It was even more incredible to eat an entire dinner without being able to see. Simple tasks like buttering your bread takes two or three tries. You have to consciously remember where you last placed your fork. Finally, you realize how much you take your eyesight for granted. Who prevents us from seeing the goodness of God? What things are blocking the light of Jesus in your life? What will you do to tear them down? You need to stop blocking the light, but you also have to let the light in. How are you letting the light in? Satan can blind unbelievers from the truth, but he can't make you do anything against your will. Trust in God and ask Him to give you clear vision to see Him at work around you.

232

Running Man

Although she spoke to Joseph day after day,
he refused to go to bed with her. (Genesis 39:10)

If you have ever taken martial arts or self-defense classes, you know there are a lot of ways to defend yourself if you need to. You learn to protect yourself and also how to stop an attacker. But, as my instructor once said, the best defense is to not be there. In some conflicts, it is better to avoid the conflict and run. The same is true in our spiritual lives. Joseph knew this principle very well. Read his story in Genesis 39:7–12. What did Joseph do when faced with temptation? Potiphar's wife wanted to have sex with Joseph. But when temptation came, Joseph resisted because he had made up his mind where he stood. He could never betray his master and do this great evil and sin against God. When the temptation continued, he fled. He didn't need to wait or think about it. He ran. What is your limit? What lines have you drawn? Have you made up your mind what your standards are? What are some of your standards? Are there temptations that you are resisting when you should really be running? In what areas of your life do you need to run? Set your standard. If you get too far—Run!

233

Be Prepared for the Fight

Therefore, with your minds ready for action, be serious and set your hope completely on the grace to be brought to you at the revelation of Jesus Christ. (1 Peter 1:13)

Spain began planning the Panama Canal in 1534. Then the Scottish tried to build it, but conditions were too hard. Then the French tried for eight years, but more than 22,000 workers died, mostly due to disease. But in 1904, the US took over construction and made special efforts to focus on the basic necessities of the workers. They focused on stopping the spread of disease and improving living conditions, including reading rooms, bowling alleys, gymnastics equipment, and baseball fields. The way of life in Panama was changed, and the number of workers affected by disease or quitting the project dropped every year, allowing the canal to be completed by 1914. Do you fall to temptations because you forget to take care of the basics? We need to be prepared. What temptations have you fallen to because you didn't take care of the basics? When faced with temptations, how do you normally overcome them? Read 1 Peter 1:13–16. How does the Bible say you can overcome temptation? How can you prepare your mind? Do the basics: fix your hope on Christ, don't be conformed, and be holy. Put your trust in God rather than in other things. In what do you put your trust? Are you conforming to worldly desires? What does it mean to be holy? How should that impact the way you live? You can overcome temptations if you prepare yourself before they come.

234

Stand Firm

Therefore, brothers, stand firm and hold to
the traditions you were taught, either by our message
or by our letter. (2 Thessalonians 2:15)

The Roman Empire grew in large part due to the dominance of the Roman army. Roman soldiers were known to be excellent fighters. They trained and trained to hone their skills, and their armor was considered to be some of the most advanced of their time. It was the strength of the army that led to their dominance. In the same way, we are at war with the enemy, the devil. He attacks us constantly in hopes that we will stop following God. And in many cases, he's winning. But you can stand and fight. You have incredible resources at your disposal. Read 2 Thessalonians 2:15–17. What are you instructed to do? When you stand firm (a military reference), what armor should you be wearing (remember Ephesians 6:13–17)? How does God help you stand firm? There is a way to stand and be ready for Satan's attack. Ephesians 6:18–19 says that you should be on the alert and pray. The verses in 2 Thessalonians tell us to remember what we have learned and been taught. Take the time to pray for those areas where your armor is weak. Ask God to help you stand firm with His strength.

235

Self Isn't Important

*But He answered, "It is written: Man must not live
on bread alone but on every word that comes
from the mouth of God." (Matthew 4:4)*

World Vision sponsors events called the "30 Hour Famine"—an event where students go for thirty hours without eating food so that they can experience (at least a little bit) what real hunger is like and at the same time raise money and awareness to fight hunger. Have you ever been really hungry? Maybe you've been involved in a "30 Hour Famine" experience. It's seems really easy after not eating for thirty hours to go pick up burgers at your local drive-through to satisfy your hunger. Read Matthew 4:1–4. Why would Jesus have been hungry? Who better to learn from on how to fight temptation than Jesus Himself? Thirty hours could be hard to go without food—but how about forty days? What's interesting is that the devil knows that Jesus is God and that for Him turning stone into bread is as simple as saying the word. Jesus was one hundred percent God, but He was also one hundred percent human—and He felt the same hunger that you feel. How did Jesus respond to this temptation? How would you? Would you have made bread? What do you learn from Jesus' example about how to deal with temptation? Do you really believe that God is sufficient to deliver you? Do really have all your hope in God? Why? Jesus responded with a promise from God that He will provide for all His (and your) needs. You can trust God's provision for you.

236

It's God's Fight

But the Lord is faithful; He will strengthen and guard you from the evil one. (2 Thessalonians 3:3)

David and Goliath is a famous story of how a young boy with no fighting experience defeated one of the most feared warriors of the time. Think about it—the entire Israelite army was afraid to take him on. When David walked up, you have to wonder what the two armies saw. There was a young boy with no armor, no weapons, and no experience. He had nothing but a sling and some rocks. I don't know about you, but a fifteen-year-old shepherd does not sound too threatening to me. If David had been able to step back and look at the battle scene, he would have seen something completely different. He would have seen himself standing there facing off with Goliath, but behind him he would see the towering figure of God. Read 2 Thessalonians 3:1–5. What is God's promise to you in verse 3? It really wasn't David vs. Goliath, because David was convinced that it was God who was fighting Goliath. When you are tempted, are you convinced that God will win that battle? God promises to guard and strengthen you. Does your faith rest in God and God alone? Why or why not? One way to stand against temptation is to get God involved right away. The moment you are tempted, pray immediately and ask God to take care of your situation. If your desire is not to fall into temptation, God can and will deliver you. God is there to fight for you, strengthen you, and guard you. Trust in Him and His power today.

237

Friends for Life

Jonathan then said to David, "Go in the assurance
the two of us pledged in the name of the LORD when we said:
The LORD will be a witness between you and me and between
my offspring and your offspring forever." Then David left,
and Jonathan went into the city. (1 Samuel 20:42)

No doubt, you have heard people use the term *BFF*—best friend forever. It's a term used to describe the relationship level of two people. Do you have any friends whom you would label as your "BFF"? Who? Do you consider them your true friends? Why? Building real friendships—friendships that will last—like any other relationship, requires commitment. Read 1 Samuel 20:41–42. How do you see commitment between these two friends? Jonathan was David's "BFF" (though they probably never said it that way). Jonathan made a vow to David. He didn't just commit himself to the friendship but also his descendants. Now that's a serious commitment to another person. Friendship requires commitment from both people for it to work. However, it's not the only thing that makes it work. Who was the mediator mentioned by Jonathan in his friendship with David? For Christians, Christ must be at the center of our friendships. He is the commonallly for the friendship. The bond we have with each other as fellow believers in our Lord brings a level of commitment to our relationship that we cannot have without Him. Think about your friends and your commitment to them and consider if Christ is at the center of your friendships. If not, ask Him to be at the center and then take the steps to make that happen.

238

A Shoulder To Cry On

Rejoice with those who rejoice; weep with those who weep. (Romans 12:15)

Like most people, you have probably experienced a stressful or emotional situation. You probably turned to your friends to offer you a safe place to share your feelings. When you need a shoulder to cry on, to whom do you turn? Why? Read Job 2:11–13. What comfort did Job's friends bring him? Job's friends first took action by acknowledging that he had a need—that was a good thing. Then they decided to take more action. Once they saw how severe the situation was for Job, his friends gave him the only comfort they could offer, their presence. There will be times in your friendships when you, too, will want to comfort your friend. Sometimes you can help and comfort your friends with words of encouragement or providing for a physical need. However, there will be times when words won't seem enough, and there will be nothing physically that can be done to help. In those moments, you can choose just to be there with your friend. What does today's verse instruct you to do? Sometimes you will rejoice with your friends, and other times you will cry with them. In Job's situation, his friends cried with him. Thank God for friends who know when to rejoice or cry with you.

239

Not Easily Broken

And if someone overpowers one person, two can resist him.
A cord of three strands is not easily broken. (Ecclesiastes 4:12)

Have you ever played the game Bundle, Bundle? It's where a group of people move around the room until the leader calls out a number, and then you have to find friends to be in a "bundle" of that number. Sometimes these bundles are made with great sacrifice as friends are left out. When has a friend helped you do or finish something at great personal sacrifice to themselves? Read Ecclesiastes 4:9–12. What are some of the benefits of friends? Why are two better than one? We all need other people, whether we admit our need or not. We were made for community. Solomon expressed this by giving examples of why two are better than one. He gave the example of staying warm. We all know that a person's body produces heat. If another person was next to you, you would stay warmer than if you were by yourself because your body would continue to lose heat and have no other source to get it. There is also the example of helping up someone who has fallen. Sometimes to help someone, you have to give up or sacrifice something. When have you had to sacrifice something to help a friend? Was it worth it? Why? Thank God for your friends and ask Him to show you ways that you can be a friend even when it means sacrificing.

240

Same, but Different

There is no Jew or Greek, slave or free, male or female;
for you are all one in Christ Jesus. (Galatians 3:28)

Many people would like to consider themselves unique. Despite what society tells us, most people don't really want to be like everyone else. We all want to be special. In what ways would the people who you choose as friends find you unique? In what ways do you find your friends to be unique or special? The word *choice* has a couple of meanings. One meaning, "to make a decision." The other meaning of the word is elite, special, or rare. Read Psalm 119:63. What specifically does this tell you about who should be your friends? We have relationships with people because there are things we have in common. We are friends with people because they like the same type of music, books, food, and other things. But how often do you choose friends because of your commonality in Christ? We are all different and come from different backgrounds. What does today's verse say we are in Christ? We are the same in Christ—yet we are different people. God likes variety just like you do with your friends. However, God expects one thing from all of us: to glorify Him in all we do—even in your relationships. Are your friendships glorifying God? Be wise in your choice of friends—they can either build you up or tear you down.

241

Love Without Condition

A friend loves at all times, and a brother
is born for a difficult time. (Proverbs 17:17)

Love is something that we all want and need. We get love from our parents, siblings, extended family, and our friends. Most of us know our parents and family love us. We count on that love to be constant in our lives. Would you say the love from your friend's is conditional or unconditional? Why? What does today's verse state that a friend does? A true friend loves without conditions. They love without requiring something in return. Do you love your friends this way? We can't ask something of others that we aren't willing to do ourselves. What does it mean for you to love your friends without conditions? Read 1 John 4:7–11. What do you learn about why you are to love others? We love because God loved us. Since we are His disciples, we should show love to others.

242

The Company You Keep

Do not be deceived: "Bad company corrupts
good morals." (1 Corinthians 15:33)

The wisest man, Solomon, wrote some words in the book of Proverbs giving sound wisdom about lots of things. He even talked about the kinds of friends you should and should not have in your life. Read Proverbs 22:24–25. What did Solomon say to do? Solomon shared the wisdom in finding friends who are not angered easily. He stated that if we allow ourselves to befriend a person who is easily angered, we ourselves may become the same way. You have heard the phrase *Birds of a feather, flock together*. If you are with people who behave a certain way consistently, there is a high probability that you might begin to act in a similar fashion. What is the warning in today's verse? Do you believe this is true? Why? Do you have any friends who have encouraged you to do something you knew was wrong? Making good choices about whom you spend your time with is important. Your friends tell others a lot about who you are and who you want to be in life. Make sure you are making right choices in regard to your friends.

243

Calling 'Em Out

Don't rebuke a mocker, or he will hate you;
rebuke a wise man, and he will love you. (Proverbs 9:8)

I've been told by some friends and family members, "I love you enough to tell you the truth." I find that most of the time this statement is followed with some kind of criticism. When was the last time you heard something like that? What was shared with you? Read Proverbs 27:5–6. When has a friend called you out on something you did or didn't do? How did it feel? Most of the time, you can be thankful that your friend told you the truth (even if it hurt) and that it did not come from someone you didn't know. It can be harder, though, to take criticism from a friend than from people you don't know. Why do you think that is true? Just remember that while it might be hard for you to take correction or be told you are wrong, it's just as hard for someone to share it with you. We are called as brothers and sisters in Christ to correct each other in love if one of us strays from the truth. What makes the difference between the two statements in today's verse? If a friend is wise (filled with God's wisdom and Spirit), they will welcome the correction that comes from a friend rather than a stranger.

244

Making a Point

*Iron sharpens iron, and one man
sharpens another. (Proverbs 27:17)*

If you have ever watched a cooking show on television, you will often see a chef with two knives in his or her hands, rubbing the knives together. You know, it's not always just for a cool effect before they prepare to cook—they are preparing their tools for work. What does today's verse say that iron does to iron? Have you ever felt like someone, maybe even your friend or family member, was rubbing you the wrong way? Do you think that they could have been sharpening you? Sometimes the Lord uses other people in your life to show you weak areas where you can allow Him to change your character to reflect more of Him. He uses you in similar ways with your friends when you have to hold them accountable for their actions. How has a friend sharpened you? The sharpening of iron is not a pleasant or easy thing. In fact, when sharpening real iron, sparks fly, there is loud noise, and splinters of the rough edges lay on the ground. Sometimes this is what happens when we sharpen each other. The process can be painful. However, after all the hard things are done, you have a piece of iron that can be of use. We all want to be of use to our Father and to each other. Are you sharpening someone else? Is anyone else sharpening you? Allow God to shape you into the person He desires to use.

245

Completing The Work

For this reason I kneel before
the Father. (Ephesians 3:14)

One way that you can help your friends is to pray for them. Have you ever prayed for your friends even when things are going well? Do you pray for them to be all that Christ wants them to be? Those are great things to pray about for your friends. It seems like we spend most of our time praying for friends when things are not going so well. Read Philippians 1:3–6. Paul said that he prayed for these friends every time he remembered them. I can only imagine that he was praying a lot because I know that I think of people a lot during the day. His prayer for them was to keep growing. It's evident because he said that he was confident that God would finish the work He began in each of them. Are you that confident in the work God is doing in the life of your friends? Read Ephesians 3:14–20. Paul prayed that his Ephesian friends would know the love of Christ and be filled with the fullness of God. Now that is a big prayer. Do you ask God to reveal His love to your friends who are hurting or might be running away from Him? Take a few moments to pray with confidence, knowing God hears you, for your friends. Ask God to show them His love in a special way and that they would also be filled with the fullness of Him.

246

Mercy and Love

Above all, maintain an intense love for each other,
since love covers a multitude of sins. (1 Peter 4:8)

Some people just don't know when to be quiet—and not share your "stuff." The news is full of people who had "friends" share their "stuff" with others and even the world via YouTube. Has a friend ever hurt you by gossiping about you? Read Proverbs 17:9, 17. According to these verses, what can separate friends? What can hold friends together? Proverbs tells us that a true friend loves at all times. A friend can listen to your "stuff" and help you through it without sharing it with others. We are told that love covers a multitude of sin. It can be really tough to forgive someone who has betrayed your trust. Read Luke 6:28, 31–36. What does Jesus tell us to do for those who mistreat us? Christ said to show true love—without condition—and mercy to those who sin against us. We see this even in the prayer He prayed as an example for the disciples in Matthew 6. Do you see yourself as a sinner who has been forgiven? David spoke of this in Psalm 103:12 when he said that God has removed our sins, never to remember them. Read Colossians 3:12–14. How and why should we forgive others? Forgiveness is not easy, but it does reflect the heart of God.

247

To Whom Do You Belong?

"By this all people will know that you are My disciples,
if you have love for one another." (John 13:35)

Sometimes you will see someone who is kind and loving toward people even when others don't love them back. Seeing that, you would probably think the person was a Christian because that type of attitude reflects the attitude of Christ. But there are lots of people who don't know Christ who still act kind. Read John 13:34–35. How we treat each other is very important. Other people watch us and see how we handle tough situations in our lives. They especially watch our interactions with people who are close to us—our friends and our family. As a follower of Christ, you are called to represent Him in every area of your life. That includes how you deal with relationships that don't go the way you want them to go. Read 1 Corinthians 5:17–19. The ministry of reconciliation is not easy because you will suffer sometimes in the process. The bottom line: you have been given the task of helping other people come back into a relationship with God. Jesus suffered so that you could be forgiven by a holy and just God. Take a moment and think about friends whom you need to forgive and what relationships you need to make right.

248

Never Have To Say You're Sorry?

"First go and be reconciled with your brother, and then come and offer your gift." (Matthew 5:24)

Have you ever had to say you are sorry for something but didn't know why you were the one having to apologize? How did you feel about that? Read Matthew 5:23–24. Who has sinned against whom here? Jesus taught that we must make things right with a friend before we make a sacrifice to the Lord. It says once things have been made right, you can bring your gift before the Lord. Why should we have to do this? We are only responsible for our own actions and cannot determine someone else's. You are to act as Christ and make things right even if the offense was against you. Have you ever heard the phrase *Love means you never have to say you're sorry*? This is not a true statement. True love means choosing to say you're sorry even if you were the one offended. Take a few moments to pray, asking God if there are any friends whose fellowship with you has been broken by hurt or a lack of forgiveness. Then do something about it.

249

Decision Time

Jesus told him, "I am the way, the truth, and the life.
No one comes to the Father except through Me." (John 14:6)

You are one of two types of people—you are either a follower of Christ, or you are not. So . . . which one are you? The life of a Christian is much more than a one-time decision; it is a life change that shows you recognize Jesus as the way to find hope for the future. Have you made a decision for Christ that also involves changing your lifestyle? How has Christ changed your life? Read John 14:6–9. Who did Jesus say He is? Based on these verses, what should we know about Jesus? This verse shows who Jesus claimed to be in His own words. According to this claim, Jesus is much more than a good moral teacher. Do you look at Jesus and the Bible to find direction for your life? Why or why not? To live the life that God wants, it is necessary to read and follow God's Word. It is the primary way for you to know what to do and how to really love God and others.

250

Beginning Point

"Repent," Peter said to them, "and be baptized, each of you,
in the name of Jesus Christ for the forgiveness of your sins,
and you will receive the gift of the Holy Spirit." (Acts 2:38)

Military recruits in basic training are constantly urged to stay motivated. Drill instructors know that if the recruits are not motivated, they will not succeed. What motivates you to obey God? If you aren't motivated to obey God at all, look at the beginning point: salvation. Look back at your decision to follow Christ and remember what you asked God to do in your life. Read Acts 2:38–41. What did Peter challenge the people to do? What do you think it means to repent? Have you repented? How can the Holy Spirit empower and motivate you to live for God? Repentance means you make a decision to turn away from your old life to live for Christ. Sometimes people ask God to save them, but they make no change in their lives. You must turn away from your own way to live by God's rules. Remember that at salvation, the Holy Spirit entered you, and He is the most powerful force to help you resist sin and obey God. With that power inside you, it is the motivation you need to live the life God has planned for you.

251

Following Truth

*"You will know the truth, and the truth
will set you free." (John 8:32)*

Truth, real truth, doesn't change even if you don't believe it. It is called truth because it is true, and you can trust it as truth. Read Psalm 119:29–32. What did the psalmist ask God to help him avoid? What are some deceitful ways? Why did the psalmist say he set his heart on God's law? What can truth do? Now read John 8:31. Where can you find truth? A portion of verse 32 is often quoted, even carved into the sides of some universities: "the truth will set you free." Many people don't realize that they are the words of Jesus. More importantly, they don't know what He said just before those words. The condition to being set free is to follow Jesus and His teachings. How are you putting real truth into your life? How does being a disciple of Jesus Christ set you free? Truth does not mean knowledge. Truth means Jesus Christ. Follow Him. Follow truth.

252

What Am I Giving Up?

"However, I did give them this command: Obey Me, and then I will be your God, and you will be My people. You must follow every way I command you so that it may go well with you." (Jeremiah 7:23)

Your choices reflect your priorities. The way you spend your time, money, and the focus of your relationships reflects what you have decided is important. If you say that God is the most important, then your choices should reflect it. If someone were to evaluate your choices, what would they say are your priorities? Read Jeremiah 7:22–24. What does God desire of His people? How did the people go backward? Our obedience to God shows where our allegiance is. Obedience is not just for God's convenience. It is for your own good. Obedience to God helps us to move forward on the path God desires. Have you ever been sorry that you acted in obedience to God? Why or why not? Does obeying sometimes feel like an inconvenience? When? Why? How does disobedience get you into trouble? Obedience to God does not lead to regret or trouble, it leads us to a right relationship with God. It is never a mistake to follow what is right. There is nothing more important than following God and leading others to follow Him as well.

253

Led by Love

*Your every action must be done
with love. (1 Corinthians 16:14)*

God loves you very much. The Bible tells you this over and over again in many different verses. Read this one: 2 Corinthians 5:14–15. How do you know God loves you? These verses show God's demonstration of His incredible love for you. Jesus died for you so that you can live for Him. But living for Him is your choice. How does love compel you to obey and live for God? If God's love for you and your love for Him doesn't motivate you, then think about why it doesn't. What does today's verse mean to you? List the names of five people whom you love. What have you done this week to show them that you love them? Many times we don't even demonstrate love to those we say we love. That is the challenge. Love those you already love. Love those who are difficult to love. Above all: love. Do everything in love. Your love for others is a beginning point in obedience to God's commands.

254

What Does It Take?

*Apply yourself to discipline and listen
to words of knowledge. (Proverbs 23:12)*

Lack of discipline is common. It is much easier to sleep late, text friends, and stay on Facebook than to focus on a goal. These are just a few of the many distractions that may keep you from doing what God wants. Members of an athletic team understand that discipline helps you reach your goals. It takes off-season training to stay in shape, long practices, and the willingness to be coached. The Christian life—the life of obedience to God—means you stay in spiritual shape year-round. Disciplined athletic teams can be winning teams. Talent can only take you so far. There are also benefits to spiritual discipline and obedience. When you are obedient, you are honoring God and can better enjoy His presence in your life. Write today's verse in your own words. When it comes to obedience to God, what does this verse tell you to do? Is it easy for you to listen to instruction? Why? Teams have a coach. Believers have a Lord. Show it. A life of obedience requires us to listen and obey. Decide right now what changes you need to make so that you can be obedient.

255

More Than ABCs

*They profess to know God, but they deny Him
by their works. They are detestable, disobedient,
and disqualified for any good work. (Titus 1:16)*

Do you remember the ABC song? Learning that song didn't really mean you knew your letters. You can memorize the sounds of the song and still be unable to say or recognize your letters. That's because learning letters takes more than straight memorization of sounds. Otherwise you get words like *LMNOP* (say it fast). Memorization is only the beginning of actual learning, just as getting saved is only the beginning of obedience to God. You start with the basics, apply those, learn more, obey God's Word, and as years go by, you grow and mature in your faith. If you don't do this, you could wind up a spiritual dwarf. You can know the right "things" to do but not do them. Obedience is action, not good intentions. What are three things that you know you should do but don't? What is the effect of disobedience to God? If you say something and do another, what does that mean? Obeying God is not just something you can talk about. It requires action. Even partial obedience is disobedience. Choose one thing from your list above and decide to do it today.

256

Reward of Discipline

"A thief comes only to steal and to kill and to destroy. I have come so that they may have life and have it in abundance." (John 10:10)

To accomplish great things takes self-discipline. Although some of life's rewards may seem to come easy, most don't—they require hard work over a long period of time. So it is with your spiritual growth. There is no instant trip from belief to obedience to maturity. It is a process that requires time, diligence, and effort. What is the opposite of self-discipline? Most people who are undisciplined fall into the "whatever" trap. They allow their life to be driven by their circumstances, friends, school, and activities. They don't make decisions or decide for themselves. An obedient life is a disciplined life. What type of life does God desire for you? What does it mean to have an abundant life? What is the result of living a life without self-control and diligence? Think of one area where you lack self-control. Decide now to work on this area. Enjoy living the full life that God desires you to enjoy.

257

Practical Obedience

"You must follow the Lord your God and fear Him. You must keep His commands and listen to His voice; you must worship Him and remain faithful to Him." (Deuteronomy 13:4)

The world doesn't offer a life that is anything like the life that Christ offers. Contrary to what you might think, life with Christ is not a drudge, boring, or an existence with no fun. It is one of joy, love, and decisions that God knows won't lead you into regret or bad consequences. What changes do you need to make in your life today that show your obedience to God? Read Deuteronomy 13:1–4. What are you to keep watch for? What should your response be to God? Obedience goes with faith—obey, and your faith grows stronger, and your maturity in Christ increases. Don't obey, and your faith will shrink and become weak. What kinds of things weaken your resolve to hold fast to God and His commands? What can you do this week to follow God more faithfully? Obedience is difficult for believers; it is downright impossible for unbelievers. If you are a Christian, the Holy Spirit indwells you and empowers you to resist temptation and to make decisions in line with God's Word.

258

Living with Regret

Timothy, guard what has been entrusted to you, avoiding irreverent, empty speech and contradictions from the "knowledge" that falsely bears that name. (1 Timothy 6:20)

We are bombarded with media and other outside influences that want to weaken our resolve to follow God. Obedience to God often feels like an impossibility. What are some of your bad habits? What movies or television shows would you consider a bad influence in your life? When was the last time you used language that you later regretted? Often you have bad habits or tendencies because you have allowed them into your life—you may have even paid money to allow them into your life. That's why the Bible says to carefully guard your mind because once an image is in your mind, it is difficult, if not impossible, to remove. Read 1 Timothy 6:20–21. What was Paul's challenge to Timothy? What difference would this make in your life and witness for Christ? It takes good decisions to avoid bad influences and to guard yourself against them. When you choose obedience, it won't be easy. You may have some bad habits to break. Some of those habits may have been in your life for a while. You have no secrets from God. Ask Him to help you. Tell God about your mistakes right now. Ask God to help you choose new habits that are godly.

259

Real Repentance

*But reject foolish and ignorant disputes, knowing
that they breed quarrels. (2 Timothy 2:23)*

"I've messed up" was the beginning of a long conversation Haley had with her parents. Because of her honesty, her parents forgave her and began a conversation where she could begin to rebuild the trust in her relationship with her parents. When have you messed up and felt the need to set things right? Read 2 Timothy 2:22–26. Which of these things are you doing right now? What does the devil desire to do? Not quarrelling and being kind to others may seem like a difficult task. Turning away from sin and being honest with those you have hurt is important. If the devil has you captive to something right now, you can repent and start over today. Repentance is turning away from specific sins. Saying, "forgive me for all my sins," is insufficient—ask God to forgive you and then name those sins and expose them for what they are. Face up to what you have done and make a decision to turn from them—repent—go in the opposite direction. Repent from each sin you have committed and don't go back to it. It is not what you know but what you do that counts. You can know all the right things, behaviors, and attitudes—but if you don't practice them, what good is the knowledge?

260

A New Heart

God, create a clean heart for me and renew
a steadfast spirit within me. (Psalm 51:10)

Even when you try to live an obedient life, you will sometimes mess up. That creates guilt, hurts your testimony to others, and sometimes results in negative consequences. There will always be times when you feel the need to start over. When have you felt this way? How did you respond? Sometimes it is necessary to make a fresh start spiritually. Obedience involves keeping your relationship with Christ up to date. Don't let days or weeks pass without praying and spending time reading God's Word. Read Psalm 51:11–12. What did David want from God? Why? How would you define the joy of salvation? When you allow your relationship with Christ to lapse because you neglect to deal with sin, it is easy to lose the joy you once had. Notice that the writer of the Psalm asked for a willing spirit. Do you have a willing spirit? What does that mean? Make a decision right now to maintain a daily time alone with God. You can have a fresh start every day!

261

From Dealer To Disciple

But all who heard him were astounded and said, "Isn't this the man who, in Jerusalem, was destroying those who called on this name and then came here for the purpose of taking them as prisoners to the chief priests?" (Acts 9:21)

Emilio Castillo was the boss of a large and dangerous drug ring. Emilio and his gang taunted a local pastor who tried to preach to them. Eventually, six of Emilio's associates testified against him. As a result, Emilio was sentenced to ten years in jail. For the first few months in prison, all he could think about was killing the men who had ratted him out. But the Lord had other plans. Through a prison ministry, Emilio became a Christian. After he was released, Emilio became a prominent preacher and ministered with the very pastor he used to mock. Emilio forgave the friends who had turned him in. God can use anyone as a leader, no matter where they come from or what they have done. God could use you as a leader too. Read Acts 9:1–22. How does this story relate to the above story? There is hardly a more powerful story of conversion than that of Saul. Saul would eventually become one of the most influential and wisest Christians in the history of the world. Has there ever been a time in your life that you thought you were too evil or not good enough for God to use you? When, and why? Be open to God's leadership and direction. He has a great plan for your life—a plan that will impact others.

262

Too Young?

Let no one despise your youth; instead, you should be
an example to the believers in speech, in conduct,
in love, in faith, in purity. (1 Timothy 4:12)

Read Jeremiah 1:4–10, 17–19. When did God call Jeremiah to be a leader? Jeremiah thought he was too young for the calling he received from the Lord. But God knew otherwise. God commanded Jeremiah to stand up to entire nations and promised that no one would overcome him. Two keys points are made from this calling. First, if God wants to use you, He will use you. Second, regardless of your age or experience, God knows your potential and your power in Him. What does today's verse mean to you? Have you ever felt "too young" to do something you wanted? Why? Think of one way you can set a good example for the people in your life this week. Then do it.

263

Are You Ready for This?

*Then I heard the voice of the Lord saying: Who should I send?
Who will go for Us? I said: Here I am. Send me. (Isaiah 6:8)*

In the Revolutionary War, Americans fought to gain their freedom from Great Britain. When faced with an opponent that had greater numbers, resources, and trained soldiers, America had to get creative. They selected men from all over the colonies who would be ready to fight whenever, wherever, at a moment's notice. They were called minutemen. They were usually the youngest and most mobile. The minutemen would conduct sneak attacks against the opposing troops before the British even had time to assemble themselves. The tactic proved to be extremely valuable in the unconventional war. Read Isaiah 6:1–8. When did God want Isaiah to act? What was Isaiah's response? God called Isaiah, and he was ready go to immediately. Isaiah enthusiastically volunteered for a difficult mission. His job was to tell God's people that they were about to be sent into exile and that their land would be ruined. Isaiah's role as a prophet is extremely important in the story of the Israelites as well as predicting the details of Jesus' arrival as Messiah. Are you more or less like Isaiah? Are you ready for God to use you right now? If not, why not? As a follower of Christ, you may be called at anytime. Be ready to step up to the challenge.

264

The Power of One Life

God has resurrected this Jesus.
We are all witnesses of this. (Acts 2:32)

In 1998, one individual had an idea. Jeremy Gilley dreamed about one day of peace—one day around the world when there would be a global cease fire. He envisioned millions of people in war-torn and violent countries who could receive medical aid, food, and educational materials without anyone being attacked. Jeremy made a documentary of the whole process. After years of Jeremy's efforts, the United Nations unanimously agreed to honor International Day of Peace. Now every year on September 21, the cease fire is followed by military groups and rebel armed forces in many countries. In 2008, 1.8 million children were vaccinated in Afghanistan alone on the International Peace Day. What might happen if all violence stopped for just one day? Is there something you could do in your own life on International Peace Day? Read Acts 2:32–47. What happened on this day? A single day in the early church brought 3,000 people to devote themselves to Jesus and be baptized! The Bible says that after people heard Peter's sermon they were "pierced to the heart." This church that began in the book of Acts is still the living body of Christ today. Do you believe that you have the potential to change the world? Why? To what are you passionate enough about to devote your life? Dwell on that thought for a minute, think of the first step in making it happen.

265

Invisible Children

Even while Saul was king over us, you were the one who led us out to battle and brought us back. The Lord also said to you, "You will shepherd My people Israel and be ruler over Israel." (2 Samuel 5:2)

In 2003, three college filmmakers traveled to Africa in search of a story to film. While there, they discovered northern Uganda's night commuters and child soldiers. The filmmakers called this "a tragedy where children are both the weapons and the victims." They took their footage, made a documentary called *Invisible Children,* and did not stop there. They established a non-profit organization and created international awareness of children who previously had no voice. On April 25, 2009, 85,000 activists in 10 countries gathered to request their governments' support in changing the situation.

Read 2 Samuel 5:1–5. How had David made an impact on others? How old was David when this happened? If you do not know the story of King David, you are missing out. His life is one of the most exciting, dramatic, and impressive chronicled in the Bible. The people of Israel wanted to follow David as their new king. He was courageous, a man of God, and a mighty warrior. The people were attracted to his vision and were inspired by his leadership abilities. David's life and rule were not without fail, but he continually sought God's blessing and advice. He started out as a mere shepherd but went on to become his nation's greatest king. Who is someone who inspires you? Who is someone whom you inspire? Make your life one that motivates and encourages people.

266

Your Team: Whether You Like It or Not

As Jesus went on from there, He saw a man named Matthew sitting at the tax office, and He said to him, "Follow Me!" So he got up and followed Him. (Matthew 9:9)

A leader is placed with a weird group of people they must direct toward a common goal. You have probably heard the story and seen the theme before in dozens of movies. Just a few examples of this classic story line are *The Mighty Ducks*, *The Big Green*, *Sister Act*, *Facing the Giants*, *A League of Their Own*, *Sky High*, and *Up*. A leader is shown his or her new group of followers and is unimpressed at best. The team is inexperienced, a little irritating, and not what the leader expected at all. (And sometimes the others feel the same about the leader.) When have you been forced to work with a group of people who gave you a bad first impression? The good news in all of theses movies is that the characters eventually get over themselves, pull their resources together, play to their strengths, and succeed! When is a time in your life when you accomplished something with a team or group? Read Matthew 4:18–22 and 9:9. Who did Jesus call to follow Him? The disciples were an interesting group of men chosen to change the world. Matthew was a tax collector, and several were fishermen before they became members of Jesus' team. Not exactly the first-century dream team. There are times when the people God chooses to work with you are difficult and disappointing. Realize their capability and believe in them like Jesus did.

267

Loser

"What will it benefit a man if he gains the whole world yet loses his life? Or what will a man give in exchange for his life?" (Matthew 16:26)

"He is no fool who gives what he cannot keep to gain that which he cannot lose." This quote is from Jim Elliot, who was a missionary, martyr, and a hero. Read Matthew 16:24–26. What did Jesus say would lead to a great life? Jesus makes it perfectly clear there is a cost—a big one—when it comes to following Him: your life. To be a follower of Jesus you must deny yourself. What does it mean to deny yourself? Fortunately, like most promises in the Bible, the passage ends with hope for those who are willing to make a sacrifice. In exchange for your earthly life, God promises an eternal life with Him in Heaven. Gaining the entire world is not worth it if you lose your soul in the process. What does it look like to give your life to Jesus? Your dreams, ambitions, material possessions, relationships, and actions are all secondary to loving God and pursuing His will for your life. What is the thing in your life that you would have the hardest time losing? Would you be willing to give it up if the Lord needed you too? Jesus makes it clear that it will not be easy, but it will be worth it.

268

When You Fall

*Therefore the disciple, the one Jesus loved, said to Peter,
"It is the Lord!" When Simon Peter heard that it was
the Lord, he tied his outer garment around him (for he
was stripped) and plunged into the sea. (John 21:7)*

Read John 13:37; 18:17, 25–27. What failure is noted in these verses? Peter was involved in an epic failure. Jesus told Peter that he would deny Him three times. Peter had every chance to prepare himself to be strong in the face of the accusations against him. Yet he still failed not once or even twice but three times in a row! Peter's actions were cowardly and proved he was not a man of his word. Now read John 21:7–18. What happened? Peter was so excited to see Jesus; he could not even wait for the boat to dock. He jumped into the water and swam to shore. Jesus forgave Peter for his betrayal and reinstated him. Peter went on to become a powerful speaker and pivotal leader in the early church. When is a time when you were afraid you were going to fail and did? What was the result? How did you press on? Do not let your failures get the best of you. Just because you may have faltered in the past, it does not define what you will do in the future.

269

I Will Carry You

When Moses' hands grew heavy, they took a stone and put it under him, and he sat down on it. Then Aaron and Hur supported his hands, one on one side and one on the other so that his hands remained steady until the sun went down. (Exodus 17:12)

Imagine a sports team without an offense. They could never win. Now imagine them without a defense. The other team would dominate. Sports teams are intricately designed to work together to simultaneously score and stop the other team from scoring. On their own, any player in any position would be practically useless. Read Exodus 17:8–13. Here is an example of a leader fully relying on his supporters for help. The Israelites were winning the battle as long as Moses held his arms up, but as soon as he started to put them down, the Israelites would start to lose. The battle lasted all day, and he could not hold his arms up any longer. Moses' brother Aaron and his friend, Hur, held up his arms for him. The Israelites were then victorious! In this moment, the entire Israelite army needed Moses, and Moses could not do the job without his assistants. When was a time in your life when someone supported you? When was a time in your life when you supported someone else? We cannot do everything by ourselves. Accept the assistance of others when God places them in your life. Also, remember to be there to assist other people in your life. There is honor and strength in being the leader as well as the follower.

270

Unity yet Diversity

*For as the body is one and has many parts, and all
the parts of that body, though many, are one
body—so also is Christ. (1 Corinthians 12:12)*

Little is known about Dark Ages warfare, but one military system legendarily stands above the rest. The Greek phalanx was a column formation of soldiers carrying long spears and shields. The Greeks are legendary for their vast conquests using this tactic. The phalanx's strength lied solely in the fact that every soldier marched together, shielded the soldier next to them with one hand, and held the spear with the other. Without total group participation and consistency it never would have worked. Can you imagine your life being in the hands of the person next to you at the same time you were in charge of protecting someone else's life? Read 1 Corinthians 12:12–27. Does everyone have the same role? Verse 20 says "many parts, yet one body." We are unified together through Christ. The body would not be complete or fully functional without all of its parts. How is the idea of unity similar to the idea of the phalanx? Realize that you are fully valuable and that the body would not be the same without you. Your particular gifts, talents, and thoughts complete the body in a much-needed way. Embrace this and play to your strengths. In what ways are you naturally gifted? In what ways are you spiritually gifted? How can you use your giftedness to build up the body of Christ? Decide one way you will use those gifts to benefit the body of Christ.

271

You Never Know

*When he arrived and saw the grace of God, he was glad
and encouraged all of them to remain true to the Lord
with a firm resolve of the heart. (Acts 11:23)*

Have you ever heard of Mordecai Ham? How about Billy Graham? Billy Graham became a Christian after attending a Mordecai Ham revival. Who was influential in your decision to become a Christian? Read Acts 9:26–27 and 11:22–26. What is Barnabas known for? How is he described? Barnabas was given his name because it meant "Son of Encouragement." He was the one who gave Paul a chance and convinced the apostles to do the same. Paul may be the more famous of the duo, but where would he have been without the back-up of Barnabas? You never know whose life you will impact. Seemingly small things that you do in Jesus' name may affect generations of Christians! Picture someone you have talked with about Jesus. Now picture all the places their life can go and all the people they can reach. Be on the lookout for people who have potential. Minister to them with your encouragement.

272

Nothing Hidden

LORD, You have searched me
and known me. (Psalm 139:1)

Most social networking sites allow you to determine what personal details are made public. Privacy settings let you control who can view your profile, photos, videos, and other information. If you don't want to chat with a certain person, you can appear to be "offline." If you feel like it, you can block people from ever finding your name. Is there anything you'd like to "block" God from seeing or knowing about you right now? Read Psalm 139:1–4, 13–14. What special relationship does God have with you? The psalmist wasn't perfect; there were things he surely wanted to hide from God. He realized, though, that God is all-knowing and always present. And since God had created him in the first place, it wasn't a bad thing that He also searched him and knew him completely. Instead, it was good and even a reason for praise. What does God's intimate knowledge of every detail of your life say about your value to Him? God knows everything about you. He knows it before it even happens. And still, He wants to be your friend. You are undeniably special to Him! Let that truth impact the way you see yourself and others today.

273

Kind of a Big Deal

*The one who boasts must boast
in the Lord. (1 Corinthians 1:31)*

Everybody wants to stand out in some way. We dress to impress. We spend countless hours practicing instruments and sports. We want to be good at things because it makes us feel valuable. Read 1 Corinthians 1:26–31. What's the difference between the way the world defines significance and the way God does? No matter what it looks like when you walk the halls of school, athletic skill, musical talent, intellect, social power, good looks, and wealth are not a big deal. Not in the long run, anyway. God didn't choose you because you already stood out. He chose you in order to make you stand out. Which would you say you are pursuing: boasting in your own abilities or boasting in the Lord? What would others say about you? Some of us struggle with feelings of insignificance because we think we don't stand out at all. What reason do you have to boast? It's true; you're kind of a big deal. Not because the world thinks you're cool, but because God chose you for His eternal purposes and fills you with His power and presence. Let Jesus be your reason to stand out today.

274

No Matter What

For I am persuaded that not even death or life, angels or rulers, things present or things to come, hostile powers, height or depth, or any other created thing will have the power to separate us from the love of God that is in Christ Jesus our Lord! (Romans 8:38–39)

A temptation many of us face is to base our value and God's love on present circumstances. It's like if things are going well, I am blessed and God loves me; if things are going bad, He must not really care. What gets in the way of God's love for you? There is not one life circumstance that can change the way God feels about you. It's tough for us to understand because worldly love is broken. Everyday, people get mad, turn away, and give up on relationships. But God's love isn't like that. There's nothing that has the power to get in the way of His love. What thing, past or present, makes you feel insecure about your value to God? Experience doesn't define truth. Instead, truth defines experience. So when circumstances are difficult, we can know that His love remains. When we fail, we can know that God doesn't love us any less. How would your life change if you were fully persuaded that nothing could separate you from God's love? Don't let your circumstances define your value and God's love. No matter what happens, trust Him at His Word.

275

In The Womb

For it was You who created my inward parts; You knit me together in my mother's womb. (Psalm 139:13)

You've probably seen an ultrasound picture of a baby in the womb, maybe even from when you were a baby. But with that old technology, it's a little bit hard to tell what you're looking at! These days, 4D technology adds the element of time to 3D pictures to take rapid succession photographs in the womb. This allows doctors and parents to effectively videotape the activity of babies just weeks after conception. What they see is amazing! Read Psalm 139:13–16. What do you learn here about babies? Why is God amazed at a baby in the womb? The psalmist was astonished when he considered God's pre-birth activity. But without the benefit of modern technology, how did he know? Likely, it never even crossed his mind that God, the Author of all life, would not be intimately involved in our formation before, during, and after conception. When we believe that God is Creator, there is no other option but to know that He is pro-life. God values all human life! If you were to ask the psalmist, at what point would he say that life begins? What does God's personal activity in the beginning of every human life tell you about human value? Science shows us that life begins at conception. God's law tells us that life is precious and abortion is wrong. Take time today to praise God for giving and treasuring life.

276

In His Image

So God created man in His own image; He created him in the image of God; He created them male and female. (Genesis 1:27)

Are your earlobes free or attached? Do you have dimples? Can you roll your tongue? Is your second toe longer than your first? We all have unique characteristics based upon the genetic traits passed on to us from our parents. What trait does every single one of us have in common? God made you and me to look like Him. No, not physically; the traits He passed down to you are much more important than that. "In His image" means that you look like Him in the way that you act—like having the ability to reason, the desire for relationships, and the capacity to love. In what ways can you better reflect God's image? You can hide your earlobes with long hair and refuse to smile and show off those dimples. In a similar way, people hide God's image within them. They might abuse their own bodies, condone abortion, or disrespect the elderly, but that doesn't change the fact that we were all created to mirror His character—to love His creation, to advocate for the forgotten, and to stand up for the dismissed. You can do that today. Reflect your Father's image in the way you view, value, and treat human life.

277

Always on His Mind

I chose you before I formed you in the womb;
I set you apart before you were born.
I appointed you a prophet to the nations. (Jeremiah 1:5)

Are you the kind of person who gets chosen first, last, or somewhere in between? No one likes to be picked last. Like an afterthought, getting picked last is like the world is saying, "Don't really want to, but I guess we'll take you." Read Jeremiah 1:1–5. When did God choose Jeremiah? Jeremiah was on God's mind before he was born or even conceived. Jeremiah had done nothing to earn or deserve it; before he could make a choice about God, God made a choice about him. He loved Jeremiah and set him apart for a specific purpose. In short, He picked him. How do you think it made Jeremiah feel to know that God had chosen him without merit? Do you tend to think you have to do something to earn God's favor? Why or why not? God knew you, too, and was thinking about you long before you were born. There has never been a time when your life was not valuable to Him or when He did not want you on His side. No human being is an afterthought to God. How does this understanding impact your view of yourself? How does it impact your view of other people? God loves you, and He is always thinking about you. Are you thinking about Him?

278

Like a Battlefield

"Indeed, ask about the earlier days that preceded you, from the day God created man on the earth and from one end of the heavens to the other: Has anything like this great event ever happened, or has anything like it been heard of?" (Deuteronomy 4:32)

It probably seems like the US has been at war for practically your whole life. Even so, war has been around planet Earth a lot longer than that. Read Deuteronomy 4:32–38. What happened in Egypt several thousand years ago? Why did God do these things? One consequence of Adam and Eve's decision to disobey God was that sin entered the world—and that has affected every single second of life since then. No longer do God and man enjoy perfect fellowship with one another. No longer does humankind seek or worship God alone. In short, the perfect earth God created transformed into a battlefield—both physically and spiritually. How do you think the physical and spiritual are related in war? God doesn't allow war because He's unloving or uncaring about human life. He allows war because it's a consequence of the world we've chosen. Hopefully, war will help us recognize the sinful condition we're in, turn to Him, and receive eternal life.

279

Armed Forces

*For government is God's servant for your good. But if you
do wrong, be afraid, because it does not carry the sword
for no reason. For government is God's servant, an avenger
that brings wrath on the one who does wrong. (Romans 13:4)*

Consider these situations: What if kids were openly unruly and cheated on tests, and your teachers did nothing? What if people drove excessively fast and recklessly, and police officers never stopped them? Why is it good to have leaders and rules? When we consider the alternative, we recognize leadership and rules as good and necessary. But then those same leaders are the ones who take the heat when tough choices have to be made. The apostle Paul explained it well in Romans. What is the intended role of government? God's plan for government is that it would serve and protect the people. But with that leadership comes some unpopular decisions. As God's servant, it's the duty of government to stop, and yes, even punish wrong behavior. Government leaders cannot sit by and allow evil men and women to flourish. To do so would be to neglect the calling God has placed on their lives. Can you come to terms with the necessity of war at times? Why or why not? Spend some time with God thanking Him for government leaders and asking Him to fill their hearts with the desire to serve and follow Him.

280

Epic Battle

*Then I saw heaven opened, and there was a white horse.
Its rider is called Faithful and True, and He judges and
makes war in righteousness. (Revelation 19:11)*

Quick, who won the French and Indian War? The Battle of 1812? The Battle of Gettysburg? Who will win the War on Terrorism? The Mexican Drug War? Sometimes the details of war are unmemorable, the outcome unclear, and the future uncertain. But there is a war going on right now whose conclusion is predetermined and will one day be evident to all. Read Revelation 19:11 and 20:10. What are the two sides in this war? Who wins? We are in the middle of an epic war between good and evil. For now, government is God's servant in administering justice. Evil sometimes prevails, mistakes are often made, and sometimes it is difficult to know who is winning. But one day there will be a final battle. Jesus, who is Faithful and True, will end Satan's reign with a certain and decisive victory. Sin and evil will be the final casualty of war. Jesus wins! How does the future, final outcome of this battle encourage you for today? So in the meantime, what should we do? Should we simply shrug our shoulders about war because that's just the way it is? No way! Until Jesus comes back, it's our job to pursue peace and live it out so that others will trust Him and be able to stand with us on victory's side.

281

Run, Forrest, Run!

*Listen, my son, and be wise; keep your mind
on the right course. (Proverbs 23:19)*

In the movie *Forrest Gump*, boys are chasing young Forrest. They plan to harm him. He runs to escape. As his friend, Jenny, yells, "Run, Forrest, run!" the leg braces he wears fall off, and he finds himself suddenly running free, able to outdistance the evil that had been right on his heels. Read Proverbs 23:19–21 and 1 Corinthians 5:11. How does the scene in *Forrest Gump* relate to these passages? You can choose who you hang out with. There will most definitely be people in your life who choose to disobey God by illegally drinking alcohol and who devalue the beautiful life He gives by abusing it. The Bible directs you to keep your distance from such people. Why do you think that God wants you to avoid those kinds of people and situations? Can you do that and still reach out to those who need Christ? How? Teenagers who drink alcohol are on a destructive path. Close association with such people is like wearing cumbersome leg braces, unable to move quickly enough to avoid their trap. Be bold and throw off the hindrance of unhealthy friendships so that you can run freely, for your good and His glory.

282

Alternate Plan

But put on the Lord Jesus Christ, and make no plans to satisfy the fleshly desires. (Romans 13:14)

One reason teenagers drink is out of boredom. Another is because it seems like everyone else is doing it. What Christian teenagers need, then, is an alternate plan. Read Romans 13:13–14. What did Paul instruct believers to do instead of engaging in destructive behaviors? The advice might seem a little strange. Paul didn't say, "Instead of drinking, you should go see a movie," or, "Let's get the youth group together every Friday night so you can avoid the temptation to drink." Nope, he wrote that we should "put on the Lord Jesus Christ." What do you think Paul meant by that? How do you put on Jesus? Until you decide that your relationship with Jesus is better than your relationship with the world, you're going to continue to struggle with temptations like alcohol. Busy-ness isn't the answer to the teenage drinking problem; godliness is. Would you say that you're just trying to be good, or are you trying to be godly? There is only one way to avoid the destructive path of alcohol. Love Jesus and follow Him.

283

Demonstrations of Praise

Let them praise the name of Yahweh, for His name alone is exalted.
His majesty covers heaven and earth. (Psalm 148:13)

What do the following have in common: a clear night sky with shining stars; the gorgeous array of colors as the sun sets; the sweet whistling of the wind through the trees; the sound of powerful waves crashing upon rocks; the mighty roar of a lion; and the chirping of a cricket? Give up? All these magnificent acts of God's creation are demonstrations of praising God. Check it out.

Read Psalm 148:3–13. Who and what are described as praising God? Are you included in this description? What is each thing and person in these verses instructed to do? In the hierarchy of creation, you were made just a little lower than the angels. Not only that, the Bible reveals that you are God's "possession" (Deuteronomy 7:6). Since you are valued, a natural response to your Creator is to praise Him. In fact, Jesus told the Pharisees that if the disciples chose not to praise Him that even the stones would cry out in praise (Luke 19:40). Isn't it interesting that every part of God's creation has a unique "voice"? What is your "voice" to praise God? When and where do you most enjoy praising God? Glance back over Psalm 148 and recognize the different sounds represented. You, too, have a unique voice to praise God. Not just in the sound of your voice but with your words, with your talents, and with your song. Praise Him!

284

Praise Focuses on God, Not Me

*I gaze on You in the sanctuary to see
Your strength and Your glory. (Psalm 63:2)*

A fun and ongoing social activity is updating your status on social media sites. Social media tools focus on you and your day-to-day activities—whether it is uploading a picture of you with your friends or telling where you are eating lunch. What would you list as your status right now? What is the first word of your statement? Most likely you began your statement with "I." Want to know the difference between social media and praise? Social media focuses on "I" statements (and things all about you) whereas praise focuses on "You" statements (and things all about God). King David wrote numerous Psalms. Many of his psalms could be considered an early equivalent of a status update. He penned the events of his day-to-day moments as well as his feelings. He also chose to write words of praise to the One who could deliver him from his circumstances. Read Psalm 63:1–8. How many times did David write "You" in these verses? To whom is the "You" referring? During your prayer times this week, practice "You" statements. Try to say as many things about who God is to you and what He has done for you.

285

Light in the Darkness

*About midnight Paul and Silas were praying and singing hymns
to God, and the prisoners were listening to them. (Acts 16:25)*

Take a few moments and consider these questions: Have you experienced an unjust situation? Were you falsely accused? Did you get sidelined or benched unfairly? If so, what were some of your reactions to the injustice? Did your reactions to the situation prove to be helpful? Why or why not? Paul and Silas were wrongly accused and thrown into prison. They had been fulfilling their God-given calling by "going to the place of prayer" when the trouble began. Can you relate? Were you minding your own business when someone accused you? Were you just doing your job when you were wronged? If so, how?

Read Acts 16:25–28. What was the reaction of Paul and Silas to their unjust treatment? With bleeding and chained bodies, Paul and Silas brought light and hope to their despairing situation as well as to the other prisoners. How did Paul and Silas give hope? What happened to everyone's chains? Praising God in prayer as well as in song is as powerful as an earthquake. Praise can shatter the hardest of hearts and loose the toughest chains of bondage. When you don't feel like praying or singing to God, that may be the moment you and others need it the most.

286

Relief from Regret

How joyful is the one whose transgression is forgiven,
whose sin is covered! (Psalm 32:1)

Don't you hate the feeling you get in the pit of your stomach when you know you've done something wrong and you're scared you will get caught? What a terrible feeling! When was the last time you remember feeling that way? At the time, you may have convinced yourself that your actions wouldn't hurt anyone or that no one would know, but the misery following the action wasn't as easily predictable. King David could relate. Read his complaint in Psalm 32:3–4. Why did David keep quiet about his sin (v. 3)? What did David do to find relief from the constant inner turmoil in his soul (v. 5)? What did God do for him? David made a conscious decision to own up to what he had done instead of blaming someone else or pretending he didn't do anything wrong. As soon as David confessed, God forgave. His groaning turned into a grateful attitude celebrating God's forgiveness. According to verses 1–2, how did David describe those whose sin God forgives? Would you describe yourself this way? Why or why note? David sinned. David became miserable. David stopped trying to cover up his wrongdoing. David confessed his sin. God forgave. God covered David's sin with His Son's bloodshed on the cross. God will do the same for you.

287

Confession = Freedom

Therefore, confess your sins to one another and pray for one another, so that you may be healed. The urgent request of a righteous person is very powerful in its effect. (James 5:16)

Have you found yourself asking God to forgive you for the same thing over and over again? Does it seem like every night when you put your head on your pillow you realize your wrong doing even though you had promised yourself you wouldn't do it again? You really do desire to walk in God's ways and to be a light in this dark world but are not sure what to do about your perpetual sin? God is on your side and will lead you to victory. Rick Warren in his book *The Purpose Driven Life* says, "He's not mad at you. He's mad about you." Going to God with your struggles is the first step toward freedom. What is the next step? What is the outcome? What type of person does God want you to confess your sins to? It is to your advantage that you confess your sin to someone, but it is even more important to whom you tell. God has placed godly men and women in your life to guide you and give you wisdom. These people can keep you accountable for living for God. Your Bible study teacher, student minister, mentor, or parents have your best interest at heart and want you to succeed.

288

Made Clean

Now that this has touched your lips, your wickedness
is removed and your sin is atoned for. (Isaiah 6:7)

Youth camps or retreats with a spiritual emphasis have a unique way of prodding students toward a more intimate relationship with the Lord at an accelerated pace. They provide a truly worshipful experience through the services, small groups, recreation, devotions, and other activities. Life-changing decisions are among the great things that happen at a camp or retreat. Have you experienced a time at a camp or retreat where you made an important decision? If so, what was the decision? One of the Old Testament prophets had a worshipful experience that he probably never forgot. We get the benefit of reading his intimate encounter with the Lord in Scripture. Please read slowly and soak up Isaiah 6:1–7. What was Isaiah's immediate response after being in the presence of the Lord? What did an angel proclaim to him? Sometimes during a worship experience you can be compelled to confess your sin that you may not otherwise acknowledge. Compared to the glory of the Lord, your ugliness is exposed. Through the grace of the Lord, He forgives you, and you are made clean.

289

God's Motivation

He predestined us to be adopted through Jesus Christ
for Himself, according to His favor and will. (Ephesians 1:5)

Chick-fil-A is a unique fast-food restaurant for different reasons. First, they have the original chicken sandwich (at least that is what they say). Second, they have persons dressed up in cow costumes prompting you to eat more chicken. Third, when you tell an employee thank you, their immediate reply is, "It's my pleasure." What does it mean for you to tell someone, "It's my pleasure"? Of all the amazing people in history—in the present and in the future—no one has or will ever do more for you than what God did when He sent His Son, Jesus Christ, to die for your sin. God's demonstration of His love for the world exceeds anything anyone else is capable of achieving. According to Colossians 1:19–20, how could God do such a merciful, selfless service for mankind? With what two conditions did God choose to adopt believers? Get a hold of this: the next time you thank God for what He has done for you, His response will be, "It's my pleasure." For what can you thank God today? Spend some time right now doing just that.

290

Thanks in Everything

*Give thanks in everything, for this is God's will
for you in Christ Jesus. (1 Thessalonians 5:18)*

One family's true story of devotion and heroism during the Holocaust is recorded through the eyes of the survivor Corrie Ten Boom in *The Hiding Place*. Ten Boom's unforgettable journey inspires readers to live out their faith even in the darkest of times. Ten Boom survived the harshest elements at the hands of the Nazi's in concentration camps in Germany. We may not ever have to endure such hardships as the Ten Boom family, but we will have our own problems.

Read John 16:33. What does Jesus say we will all have? What does that mean to you? The path from troubles to peace is possible through thanksgiving. That's what Ten Boom did at each and every moment of her horrific ordeal. When her sister, Betsy, chose to be thankful for the overcrowded rooms infested with fleas, Ten Boom didn't know if she could. Later she learned it was the fleas that kept the guards away from their room, providing opportunities to read aloud from their Bible and allowing the other women to hear. In what kind of circumstances does God call us to give thanks? It's tough to give thanks when things aren't going as you plan. Know that circumstances change, but you can have peace when you thank God for everything.

291

Thanks in Faith

*Give thanks to the LORD, for His faithful
love endures forever. (2 Chronicles 20:21)*

Have you ever prayed about something you were sure was God's will,
yet you hadn't received any answer after continuous prayer? You have
the faith to believe God is capable to give you what you are asking for but
wonder how much longer you can keep believing. What do you do to keep
hope alive in uncertain circumstances? King Jehoshaphat faced a life
and death predicament for himself and his people. He received bad news
that armies were on their way to make war against Judah. Jehoshaphat
inquired of the Lord and proclaimed a fast. The people of Judah gathered
together and sought divine answers. They acted not on their dismay but
instead set their eyes on what God could do for them. With the leadership
of King Jehoshaphat, singers were instructed to go ahead of the army
and sing a song of thanksgiving. Read 2 Chronicles 20:21. What song
did the people sing? How are those words comforting to you in times
when you could lose hope? One thing we can do when it seems God isn't
answering our requests is to give thanks to God for His answer ahead of
time. Lead your emotions with powerful words of hope giving thanks to
God who is able.

292

Answered Prayers

"If you then, who are evil, know how to give good gifts to your children, how much more will your Father in heaven give good things to those who ask Him!" (Matthew 7:11)

When you go to your parents to ask for something you really want but don't need, you are most likely on your best behavior and will use your manners. Even then you aren't sure they will give you what you ask for. What was the last thing you asked your parents for hoping they would say yes? We often approach God the same way—when we really want something we try praying with all kinds of "spiritual manners" thinking that might get God to answer our prayer. What about in your prayer life? When was the last time you asked God for something hoping He would say yes? How do you approach God when you are asking Him for something you really desire? God really does want to give you your desires, and He longs for you to ask Him. Remember, He is a loving God who wants to respond to His children. Read Matthew 7:9–11. To whom will your Heavenly Father give good gifts? Why does God want to give good gifts? The good gifts Jesus referred to do not necessarily mean material possessions. He does provide for our physical needs but will bless your character and emotional needs too. Prayers God will always answer affirmatively are prayers prayed according to His will. Turn the greatest commandment found in Matthew 22:37 into a personalized prayer. Because God desires you to love Him with all your heart, soul, and mind, He will gladly help you to accomplish this.

293

Even as We Sleep

I will both lie down and sleep in peace,
for You alone, LORD, make me live in safety. (Psalm 4:8)

Routine prayers are a part of many people's daily lives. Before eating and before traveling are great times to pray. Some students have made it a practice to pray before taking a test at school. But these can become routine prayers if we are not careful. What are some other examples of prayers that could be considered routine? Taking your needs and cares to the Lord in prayer is essential to your growth in your relationship with God. You will never get to a point where you don't need God anymore. As you grow up in your parents' home, your goal is to eventually become independent of them—to be able to live on your own. But that is not the case with your Heavenly Father—you will never outgrow your dependence on Him. Did you know that God isn't just concerned about your awake hours but also when you sleep? Read Psalm 4:8 and Proverbs 3:24. How do these verses describe the sleep God provides? How do these verses indicate your dependence on God even when you sleep? Sometimes the hardest part of going to sleep is when you first lie down. Thoughts from the day swarm your mind or fear of the dark grips you. God promises to give your mind peace and to keep you safe so that you will be ready for a new day.

294

Don't Give Up

"Will not God grant justice to His elect who cry out to Him day and night? Will He delay to help them?" (Luke 18:7)

Real life stories of a person's perseverance to succeed amidst numerous obstacles and set backs give hope to those also seeking to find success in a particular area. To strongly desire something and then not have it as soon as we would like can cause some serious frustration and a tendency to give up. Have you ever wanted to give up on something you a truly desired? Did you eventually give up or not? Why or why not? God wants you to pursue a godly desire through persistent prayer—over and over again. He rewards your perseverance. Read the inspiring parable Jesus told of the persistent widow in Luke 18:1–8. According to verse 1, why did Jesus tell His disciples this parable? What was the widow's request (v. 3)? What is God's promise (v. 7)? What is God looking for in believers (v. 8)? In the moments you tend to believe your prayers aren't being heard and you can't keep going, remember the widow and renew your faith in our God of the impossible. "Now faith is the reality of what is hoped for, the proof of what is not seen" (Hebrews 11:1).

295

One of Those Days

A man's heart plans his way, but the Lord determines his steps. (Proverbs 16:9)

When was the last time you had "one of those days"? You know, the kind of day where your schedule is packed from the time you wake up until the time you go to bed. Then, a teacher adds an extra assignment, and you can't remember where you left your cell phone. You haven't had time with the Lord, and if someone in need crosses your path, well, you just don't have the time or energy to help them. Days like that can cause you to question whether all the plans you make really matter. Read Proverbs 16:9 and 19:21. What do these verses say to you about all the plans that we often make? Who has the best plan? Why? God has a plan for you—not just any plan, but a good plan. It is reassuring to know that in spite of the way life seems so out of control sometimes, you can rest knowing that God is in control and you don't have to be. How does it make you feel to know God has a plan—especially a plan for you? What can you do to help you remember that God is in control and has a plan next time you are having "one of those days"? Remember, God's plan is a good plan. Try following His plan today.

296

Ask the Expert

*"You will call to Me and come and pray to Me,
and I will listen to you." (Jeremiah 29:12)*

You probably seldom read a newspaper, but if you flip through one, you will find advice columns on a wide range of issues. Today, you have more places to seek advice than ever before. Sure, you have your friends, but there are other places too. You can read magazines, read other people's blogs, or ask experts online, just to name a few. Where do you turn when you need advice? Do you think it is a wise place to look for advice? Why? Read Jeremiah 29:11–13. Where do these verses say to seek help? Why should we seek help from God? A lot of people can quote verse 11, but too often we miss the promises in verses 12 and 13. How are you supposed to seek the Lord? When you pray and seek the Lord, what do these verses say will happen? God desires for you to go to Him when you need help making wise choices. Unlike us, God sees the past, present, and future. He knows what is best for you and has good plans for you. You probably already know that He has good plans, but do you go to Him in prayer and wholeheartedly seek out His good plans? If not, take some time right now to do that.

297

Know The Word

*Be diligent to present yourself approved to God,
a worker who doesn't need to be ashamed,
correctly teaching the word of truth. (2 Timothy 2:15)*

Every good coach has a playbook and a game plan. While the playbook has all the plays that the coach knows and has taught the team, the game plan is made in preparation to face a certain opponent. The team creates a game plan to attack specific weaknesses of an opponent and to defend against specific strengths of an opponent. Through His Word, God gives you a playbook for everyday living. Sometimes, though, you may have trouble knowing the game plan because you struggle to see how God's Word speaks to the decisions you make each day and each year. For example, should you watch the latest movie or not? The Bible doesn't come out and say, "don't watch [a specific movie]," so how can you make this decision based on God's Word? Read 2 Timothy 2:15–16. What should you pursue? What are some ways that you can better handle the truth of God's Word? In order to apply God's Word, you must know His Word. If you know God's Word, you can use the principles to make good decisions every day. (For a principle that applies to what you watch, see Ephesians 5:3–4.)

298

Pleasing God or Pleasing Others

For am I now trying to win the favor of people, or God? Or am I striving to please people? If I were still trying to please people, I would not be a slave of Christ. (Galatians 1:10)

When was the last time you struggled with making a decision because you were worried about what another person or group of people would think? Everyone struggles with worrying about what other people think at some point. In the process of making a decision, you may come to a point where you know that no matter what choice is made, someone will not be satisfied. Most Christians genuinely don't want to do anything to give another believer reason to struggle, and at the same time we want to obey God in everything. God's Word speaks to this struggle that we all face. What struggle did Paul describe in today's verse? (Have you ever felt this way?) Who should you strive to please as you make decisions? What are some ways that we try to win the approval of others? Although you probably could have answered this question without reading the verse, it is good to know that Paul—who penned a good part of the New Testament—thought about this issue. He felt the pressure to please people yet chose to please God. This verse can encourage you in your decision-making struggles. Concentrate on seeking God's approval in the things you do and say today.

299

Take The Plunge

*Trust in the Lord with all your heart, and do not
rely on your own understanding. (Proverbs 3:5)*

Do you remember the first time you jumped off a diving board into a pool? How did you feel? I have to admit that the first time I took the plunge I was terrified. In spite of my fear, I jumped because my mom had promised me some sort of reward. After hitting the water, though, I realized how fun it was to jump in. Sometimes making a big decision is like jumping off the diving board. It is really scary, but after you finally do it, you wonder why it took you so long. Do you think fear sometimes keeps you from making decisions? Why? Read Hebrews 11:6. What does this verse say that it takes to please God? Go back and read Hebrews 11:1–5. What do you discover about faith in these verses? I had a mentor during college who reminded me that when you are trying to make a decision there comes a point when you just have to step out in faith and trust that God is not going to let you fall. Even if you make the wrong decision, God is still faithful. The key is to trust in God's character, not your understanding of the situation.

300

Fear and Wisdom

"The fear of the LORD is the beginning of wisdom, and the knowledge of the Holy One is understanding." (Proverbs 9:10)

I specifically remember two things that my Sunday school teachers tried to hammer into my head: not having PMS (not that kind of PMS . . . Pre-Marital Sex!) and where to get wisdom. Although pre-marital sex is a poor choice and directly goes against what God has designed, we'll stick to the topic of gaining wisdom (especially since being wise will help you to make good decisions when it comes to purity). Read Proverbs 9:10–12. From where do wisdom and understanding begin? What do you think it means to "fear the Lord"? What about "knowing the Lord"? How can wisdom reward you? To me, fearing the Lord means realizing that He is God and I am not. He is in control of everything, and I am at His mercy. When you start to realize all God is and all you are not, you will begin to be wise. The more time you spend with God, the more you will know His character—and wisdom will be the overflow of knowing Him.

301

One Way To Win

*Now if any of you lacks wisdom, he should ask God,
who gives to all generously and without criticizing,
and it will be given to him. (James 1:5)*

My five-year-old daughter and I like to play with the Wii together. Sometimes in bowling, I try to give her advice. Most of the time, she listens, and it helps her game. It usually ends up frustrating me because I'm the one giving advice, yet she ends up winning. I, on the other hand, am not always as good at taking advice from others. My husband complains because I ask his advice on fashion and then end up wearing something different. Have you ever asked for advice only to go against the advice once you were actually in the situation?

Read James 1:5–8. What promise from God is found in these verses? Have you ever prayed and asked God for wisdom? If not, why not? What condition does James give if you are going to ask God for wisdom? Why is that important? If you ask with faith for wisdom, God promises that will He give it to you. The next time God advises you, will you choose to listen and be victorious, or will you fail to take the advice you are given? Write a prayer asking God for wisdom in a specific situation you are facing right now. Date your prayer and put it somewhere that you can see it as you wait for God to answer your prayer.

302

Good vs. Best

*"One thing is necessary. Mary has made the right choice,
and it will not be taken away from her." (Luke 10:42)*

A lot of people love to read *My Utmost for His Highest* by Oswald Chambers. One of the reasons they enjoy reading his thoughts is because he often speaks to the issue of choosing what is good versus choosing what is best. You would agree, most likely, that choosing what is best would be considered choosing wisely. Have you ever been faced with a choice that put two seemingly good things against each other? As a student today, there are uncountable "good" things competing for your time and attention. *My Utmost for His Highest* states, "The things that are right, noble, and good from the natural standpoint are the very things that keep us from being God's best." Read Luke 10:38–42. So how can you choose God's best? What were the good/best choices presented to Mary and Martha? Though this a familiar story, you can learn from Mary's example. Jesus basically said that by choosing to be with Him, she had chosen the better thing. Why did Jesus say this was the best thing? Why do you think that it can be so hard to say no to being busy and yes to choosing the better thing? Take a few quiet moments now to sit and just be with the Lord.

303

Not Just Money

"'For to everyone who has, more will be given, and he will have more than enough. But from the one who does not have, even what he has will be taken away from him.'" (Matthew 25:29)

Last Sunday, I got paid fifty dollars to go to church! Okay, let me explain: Sunday morning our pastor told "The Parable of the Talents." In case you don't remember this story, read Matthew 25:14–30. To which of the three servants do you most relate? Why was the master so hard on the servant who hid his talent? The pastor gave us the fifty dollars to challenge us to be good managers. We have six weeks to "use" it. After six weeks, we will return the fifty dollars and whatever profits we have made. Then all the profits will be redistributed for us to use to bless someone else. The parable doesn't just apply to your money. It applies to being a good manager of all God gives you, including decision-making opportunities. What was the result of being faithful with little? Could you say that you are as faithful in the little decisions as you are in the big decisions? Why? Consider all that God has given you and commit to use it for Him and His glory.

304

Not Much Different

*The LORD considered what David had
done to be evil. (2 Samuel 11:27)*

Though reports seem to vary as to the number of women, Tiger Woods apparently had issues with being faithful to his wife. The day Tiger Woods married his wife, do you think that he intended to cheat on her? Probably not. Our society may be quick to judge and slow to forgive Tiger's transgressions, but he's not so different from you, other people, or numerous Bible characters. Of course, the first to come to mind is King David. Read 2 Samuel 11. What choices did David have to make in these verses? Did he have to go out of his way in order to sin? Explain. David made several choices in the verses. It would be pretty safe to assume that when David woke up that morning he did not think he would have an affair and then commit murder. One by one, however, his choices led him down a path of sin away from his God. Later, David sought God's forgiveness. Though the damage had been done, fellowship with God was restored, and David became referred to as "a man after My (God's) heart" (Acts 13:22). What area in your life is hindering your fellowship with God? What can you do about it right now? Take time to confess your sin to God and seek His forgiveness. God loves you and has a great plan for your life. Don't get sidetracked by poor decisions.

305

What Faith Can Do

If we confess our sins, He is faithful and righteous to forgive us our sins and to cleanse us from all unrighteousness. (1 John 1:9)

Have you been at a low point where you feel like you've made so many bad decisions you can't understand how God could love you enough to forgive you? It is just at that point that God wants to help you. What promise is found in today's verse? Now, read 1 John 1:8–10. What is the warning in these verses? What kind of faith do you think it takes for us to be able to rise and start over again once our hearts have been broken because of our own failures? Faith that can get up and start again must be a faith that clings to the promises of God's Word like the ones in today's verse. God's Word says that He will forgive your sin when you confess it to Him, so even when you don't think you are forgivable, be assured that God forgives, and He will empower you to start again. Take some time right now to pray about any unconfessed sin in your life. (If you are not sure if you have any unconfessed sin, ask God to reveal it to you.) Be specific in your confession because God already knows the specific sin.

306

Like a Dog

*As a dog returns to its vomit, so a fool
repeats his foolishness. (Proverbs 26:11)*

Do you like to find verses in the Bible that strike you as funny? You know, like when the Bible talks about things that we are surprised to find in it. For example, would you really think that the Bible talks about bodily functions? It does. One such verse is found in Proverbs 26:11. Since Proverbs is a book of wise sayings, what lesson do you think you can learn from this verse? Even people who are wise sometimes make mistakes. So, what separates the wise from the foolish? According to the verse you read in Proverbs, the foolish person repeats the same mistakes. This verse would also mean that a wise person learns from his or her mistakes. What is a situation in your own life that you keep making the same bad choice expecting a different outcome? Do you have a friend or relative who falls into this trap? Read Proverbs 26:17, 20. What do you learn from these verses? God wants you to learn from your mistakes. More importantly, He wants you to learn from His Word.

307

Parents Just Don't Understand

Children, obey your parents as you would the Lord,
because this is right. (Ephesians 6:1)

Is your mom leaving you embarrassing notes on social media? Is your dad trying too hard to look cool when your friends are around? Parents just don't understand. Sound familiar? Read Deuteronomy 6:6–7. What are parents told to do? When should parents instruct their children? Maybe your parents are not your favorite people to hang out with. Maybe you roll your eyes at their suggestions for quality family time. However, if you aren't spending time with your parents, you're not helping them to fulfill God's command to instruct you. Ask your parents to join you in an activity this weekend. Instead of texting the entire time, try engaging your parents in conversation about their teen years—you might be surprised what you learn! Read Ephesians 6:1–4. What instructions do you see here for you and for your parents? Just as parents are commanded to instruct, children are commanded to obey. Obeying your parents is one of the Ten Commandments—it is so important to God that He inspired Paul to quote it here. His promise is significant—by listening to your parents you honor them, and as a bonus, life is easier for you! How has your parents' advice helped you in the past? What can you do this week to honor them? Take some time right now to thank God for your parents and for the things they teach you, have taught you, and will continue to teach you.

308

Thy Word

Your word is a lamp for my feet and
a light on my path. (Psalm 119:105)

What has God given you as a guiding light? How can God's Word act as a light for you. It's easy to fall into the trap of temptation, especially in relationships. The only thing that can truly keep you from sin is obedience to God's Word. Memorizing it and meditating on it is something you may have heard of doing all your life but never seriously practiced. Whether you're just entering the world of dating or are seriously thinking *this is the one*, now's a good time to dust off those verses you learned in Vacation Bible School or Sunday school. Read Philippians 4:8. What kinds of things should occupy your thoughts? Why? TV shows, movies, music—they're not always praiseworthy by God's standard. What you think about is what you're likely to do. Take time to focus on things that are noble, right, pure, lovely, admirable, excellent, and praiseworthy, and you'll discover there's less room for thoughts that tempt you to sin. Are your thoughts praiseworthy? What thought patterns do you need to change? Read 2 Corinthians 10:5. What does it mean to take captive every thought? Ask God to bring His Word to your mind when you're tempted to sin.

309

Avoiding Temptation

How can a young man keep his way pure?
By keeping Your word. (Psalm 119:9)

Knowledge of God's Word and His desire for your life is a powerful antidote to sin. Read Psalm 119:9–11. What are keys to staying pure? On a scale of 1 (terrible) to 10 (great), how well are you doing in seeking God with all your heart? Read 1 Corinthians 15:3. What is the great truth in this verse? Merriam-webster.com says *corrupt* means, "to change from good to bad in morals, manners, or actions." Friends are powerful influences in your life, both good and bad. Has anyone ever told you it's easier for someone to pull you down from a chair than for you to pull them up from the floor? It's true—try it with a friend sometime. It's also true where sin is concerned. Read 2 Timothy 2:22. From what are you to flee? Why? God commands you to flee some things while pursuing others—and points out the best people to help you succeed. Christian friends are key in your quest to avoid sin. Ask God to surround you with friends who'll help you to remain pure in relationships.

310

High Standards

But it is from Him that you are in Christ Jesus, who became God-given wisdom for us—our righteousness, sanctification, and redemption. (1 Corinthians 1:30)

Campfire time again. The student minister is strumming his guitar and singing, "Holiness, holiness is what I long for . . . holiness is what I need . . . holiness, holiness is what you want from me." If you're singing along, do you mean it? Do you really long to live a holy life? It's easy to sing "Holiness" in a group; it's much harder to put into action every day. What's holiness, anyway? Dictionary.net says it is "the state or quality of being holy; perfect moral integrity or purity; freedom from sin; sanctity; innocence." So basically, God demands perfection. Read 1 Peter 1:13–15. What are you instructed to do? Why should you do this? Paul quotes Leviticus 11, where God commanded His people to holiness. Perfection—the highest standard imaginable. Unattainable? No! What is the source of our holiness? God demands something no one can ever give: perfection. He won't overlook your lack of holiness. He doesn't expect you to fake it. Instead, He gives you the power to be holy through His Son, Jesus. By placing your faith in Jesus, He becomes your holiness. Have you trusted Jesus as your Savior? If not, ask a Christian teacher or friend for help. If so, you can overcome the temptation to sin because you've been empowered to do so by Jesus.

311

Work in Progress

*But the Lord said to Samuel, "Do not look at his appearance
or his stature, because I have rejected him. Man does not
see what the Lord sees, or man sees what is visible,
but the Lord sees the heart." (1 Samuel 16:7)*

Is God concerned with your outward appearance? What matters
most to Him? Most people are in peak physical condition between the
ages of 16–24; after that, everything starts going downhill. Physically,
without plastic surgery, the body does decline. Spiritual life, on the
other hand, should only get better with time. Read Romans 6:22–23.
What is the benefit that you reap? Eternal life is one benefit of salvation through Jesus, but notice the other benefit: sanctification. God
demands holiness—perfection—but He helps you attain it through
Jesus! You don't have to do anything to create holiness within yourself;
in fact, you can't. Only through Jesus can we ever reach God's goal:
total transformation, stated in Romans 12:1–2.

312

Walking in Light

But if we walk in the light as He Himself is in the light,
we have fellowship with one another, and the blood
of Jesus His Son cleanses us from all sin. (1 John 1:7)

If you've ever been in a Christian bookstore, you've probably seen a variety of lighthouse gifts, artwork, and replicas. Thomas Kinkade, the Painter of Light, is especially famous for his lighthouse paintings. God, Jesus, and the Word are described as light many times in Scripture. Lighthouses illuminate and protect, ensuring salvation for those who heed its light, so it's not surprising that Christians have chosen them as a symbol throughout history. Read 1 John 1:5–7. What is the message we have received as Christians? Are you walking in light? Would your friends say your life reflects fellowship with God? Even grade school children know that the moon emits no light of its own, but reflects light from the sun. You cannot shine on your own either, but when you reflect the Son, He is able to use your life to shine His truth into others. By living out your faith in Jesus, you become a lighthouse for God among your peers, pointing to God, exposing sin, and proclaiming salvation through Jesus. Shine for Jesus today.

313

About Face

Love must be without hypocrisy. Detest evil;
cling to what is good. (Romans 12:9)

About face is defined as "a turn 180 degrees facing the opposite direction." It's not a retreat but an intentional turning from one way to another. Read Romans 12:9–10 and 1 Corinthians 6:18–20. What concepts do both passages have in common? We are to honor one another and God. So what is honor? According to Dictionary.com, "high respect, as for worth, merit, or rank." We should treat others and God with high respect. How do you communicate respect in relationship to others? To a girlfriend or boyfriend? To God? Both passages also refer to an "about face" or turning from sin. Detest evil; cling to good. Flee from sexual immorality; honor God with your body. From the initial repentance of sin and turning to God to the daily dying to self and taking up the cross (Matthew 16:24), the Christian life is filled with these "about face" moments. Read 1 Thessalonians 5:21–22. What three things are you to do? In order to do good and avoid evil, what must change in your relationships? Commit to pray and initiate those "about faces" today.

314

Actively Waiting

"Therefore don't worry about tomorrow, because tomorrow will worry about itself. Each day has enough trouble of its own." (Matthew 6:34)

John Waller broke into the Christian music world with his sophomore solo "While I'm Waiting." Maybe you heard it in the movie *Fireproof*. When asked about the song, Waller said, "The important thing to remember while we are waiting on God is to not just wait, but to actively wait. Serve, worship, and be faithful with what you have, where you are . . . even while you wait." So, what does that mean to you—to "actively wait"? As a teen, you're exposed to a variety of people, ideas, emotions, and experiences, but let's face it—there's also a lot of waiting. Wait till you're old enough for youth group, old enough to shave, to date, to drive, to marry. Waiting isn't easy. Read Matthew 6:31–34. What are you not supposed to do? It's easy to get caught up in the now of life. What does Jesus encourage you to do? Can you trust His promise? Why? Actively waiting implies a purpose in waiting; it's not passive. Now is the time to determine what's important for your future and to develop godly character. Will who you are help to attract or repel the kind of person you hope to marry? Are you willing to allow God to transform your life while you're waiting? Waiting may not be easy, but it is beneficial. Wait on the Lord today and allow Him to guide you and work in your life.

315

Clean Hands

*Let no one despise your youth; instead, you should be
an example to the believers in speech, in conduct,
in love, in faith, in purity. (1 Timothy 4:12)*

Read Psalm 24:3–6. What should you be doing? You are part of a new generation of Christian teens. Do you actively seek God? Are you leading your generation to Him? Pray for clean hands and a pure heart. From these, God provides blessings. What a powerful message it is to others to see Christian teenagers seeking after God. What is the challenge for you in today's verse? God expects His people to have pure hearts; youth are not exempt. What does it mean to be an example in your purity? If you haven't always been the greatest example, know that God is about second chances. He'll even help you resist temptation! Read 1 Corinthians 10:12–13. What should you guard against? Ask God to give you a pure heart and to equip you to be an example for your generation. Then hang on for the ride of your life. Perhaps one day you'll be commemorated as the generation who turned people back to God!

316

At Odds

"So they are no longer two, but one flesh. Therefore, what God has joined together, man must not separate." (Matthew 19:6)

Arranged Marriage: Volunteers Wanted! You in? Yeah, right! You know, in the old days, parents picked your mate. I'm glad that's changed, but it's true that an outside perspective can help to evaluate potential flaws or strengths. Opposites attract, but will it last? In twenty years, will he still be dark and mysterious, or just boring? Will she still seem perky and cheerful, or just annoying? At first, opposites enjoy their differences. Too often, though, those become struggles, then arguments ending in irreconcilable differences. Changing the other person almost never works. God tells Christians to avoid partnership with unbelievers for a practical reason: commonality and friendship last long after the initial attraction stage. But are there more reasons? Read Matthew 19:4–9. Can you be united as one with someone who doesn't share your most important belief: faith in Jesus? Some couples beat the odds, but if you can avoid heartache in your marriage, why not? Wait, you say, I'm not married, not even dating seriously! Perfect time to start working on your marriage, I promise. Ask Him to show you His purpose for your life and future relationships, to develop in you godly character and to help you recognize it in others. Pray for your future spouse and trust that God will send you a true partner in His time.

317

Bad Company

Do not be deceived: "Bad company corrupts good morals." (1 Corinthians 15:33)

"One 'bad apple' spoils the whole bunch" (Chaucer). "A man is known by the company he keeps" (Euripides). "It's easier for them to drag you down than for you to pull them up" (my mom). Surely you've heard at least one of those trusty proverbs. Chances are you've rolled your eyes at similar advice. But is it true? Read 1 Corinthians 15:33–34. What warning do you find in these verses? When have you seen this played out in real life? God inspired Paul to use a well-known proverb to make a point that still rings true today. If unhealthy friendships can have a negative impact on your character, how much more seriously should you take your dating relationships? For most people, serious dating will (hopefully) lead to eventual marriage, and that's as God intended. Jesus tells us in Matthew 19 that marriage unites us as one. That unity can be wonderful when it is with someone who shares your goals, your purpose, and your faith. If your significant other doesn't honor God, how will you honor God when your lives are intertwined? How will your relationship honor God? Pray that God will guard your heart as you reevaluate your priorities for dating. Commit to reserve serious dating only for someone you would want to marry—someone who loves God.

318

Holy Matrimony

Indeed, your husband is your Maker—His name is Yahweh of Hosts—and the Holy One of Israel is your Redeemer; He is called the God of all the earth. (Isaiah 54:5)

Checklists. We all make them: grocery lists, to-do lists, bucket lists, top ten lists. God's pretty fond of lists too: the Ten Commandments, the Beatitudes, the Fruits of the Spirit, and the spiritual gifts. In 2 Corinthians 6, He describes believers as the "sanctuary of the living God" and lists characteristics of that relationship. Read 2 Corinthians 6:16–18. What are you? What does God bring to the relationship between Himself and you? What do you contribute to the relationship? Read Jeremiah 3:14 and Isaiah 54:5. How does God describe the relationship He has with you as a believer? Does that imagery change the way you view your relationship with God? If you are the sanctuary, the dwelling-place of God, if you are "married to God," your first allegiance is to Him. His opinion of your earthly relationships is the only one that matters. Evaluate the relationships in your life. Do they honor God? Are they approved by mature Christians in your life? Do they distract from or strengthen your relationship to God?

319

Heaven Bound

*Our citizenship is in heaven, from which we also eagerly
wait for a Savior, the Lord Jesus Christ. (Philippians 3:20)*

Russian believers face laws that limit their freedom of worship.
Children must have written permission from their parents to enter a
church! Anyone attending worship or performing mission work in Russia
may face police intervention. How would you react if you could not worship freely? Read Philippians 3:18–20. What parameters define your
citizenship? Many people around the world do not know Christ. They live
as enemies of His good news of peace and redemption. They focus on
earthly things, with no plans for life beyond right now. Jesus said that His
children are "not of this world." God's desire is for Truth in the Person of
Christ to transform (or change) your life. When Saul met Jesus on the
road to Damascus, he was on his way to persecute the followers of Christ.
After he met Christ, he became one of those followers. Read Acts 8:3;
9:1–6, 18–21. Describe Saul's new loyalty after meeting Jesus. Evaluate
your loyalties. Seek fresh ways to represent your home in heaven.

320

His!

"I have revealed Your name to the men You gave Me from the world. They were Yours, You gave them to Me, and they have kept Your word." (John 17:6)

Did you ever notice that every sport has its own vocabulary? Football touts "the spread" as a good offense—rather than a huge meal. A good pass yields prime "field position" and possible "points on the board." Do you realize that followers of Christ have our own vocabulary and rulebook? Read John 17:6, 14, 17. What is the value of God's Word to you as a citizen of heaven? Christ's followers can count on some "sure things." God definitely loves us. He certainly sent His Son to die in our place. Christ lives in us. And His Spirit guides us by the Word of God. How does the Bible help you understand, know, and believe these things? How are you living out your faith? Christ's desire is for us to keep His Word. He prays for us to achieve that goal. We're not in this alone! To live by His Word, we must know what it says. Pray, then read the Bible. He will guide you to understand and apply it! We have a different playbook than the world uses. We don't live by guidelines such as "He who dies with the most stuff wins." Ours says, "I am not of the world."

321

Obliged by Law

*Everyone must submit to the governing authorities,
for there is no authority except from God, and those
that exist are instituted by God. (Romans 13:1)*

Have you ever been tempted to enter an off-limits area just because a sign warned, "Do not enter!" Read Romans 13:1–5. Why are governments and laws necessary? What connects earthly authorities to God's authority? God obliges us to follow our country's laws. He formed those structures to protect us. Like a baby confined to a playpen, legal parameters keep us safe from harm from the outside. Government serves God for the good of the people. We have government "by the people and for the people." To obey the laws actually benefits those who are rule-followers. Fear only affects the rule-breakers. How does obeying the speed limit benefit you? Obeying laws comes from an attitude of cooperation. Selfishness feeds a rogue mentality: "What do I want to do?" Laws harness evil, rather than fence in good. God formats us to abide within the law. Government is God's plan for safety.

322

Rules for a Bumpy Ride

Peter and the apostles replied, "We must obey God rather than men." (Acts 5:29)

Learning to drive involves a manual. Everyone must learn and follow the rules of the road—even if the roads are bad. Louisiana drivers cite road hazards as serious as potholes large enough to fit a mattress; as bumpy as a washboard that bounces soft drinks out of holders and onto floorboards. Bad roads? Rules still apply! How do you keep your obligation to follow God's laws—even when life is hard?

Read Acts 5:18–20, 28–31, 34, 38–39. How did Peter respond to authority in tough times? How will you? Believers need to follow God even in difficult situations. God loves you and will lead you on the right path. Trust Him even when you have to take a stand. Though the decisions you face may be difficult, choose to obey God. Seek God's protection while you are in the world. Follow your country's laws until they oppose the truth of God. Then seek how best to proceed in a way that honors God. Ask God to glorify Jesus—your Ruler and Savior—through you as you follow Him.

323

Praying for Authority

First of all, then, I urge that petitions, prayers, intercessions, and thanksgivings be made for everyone, for kings and all those who are in authority, so that we may lead a tranquil and quiet life in all godliness and dignity. (1 Timothy 2:1–2)

Admit it, sometimes you get pretty upset at the people in authority over you. From your parents to the President, they do things that make you so mad that the last thing you want to do is pray for them. But that's what you're supposed to do. Read 1 Timothy 2:1–6. For whom should you intercede (or pray)? Have you ever considered the role of your prayers in being a good citizen? God has a reason for your prayers—whether requests, appeals, worship, or thanks. You lift up everyone—from authority figures on down. Why is it important for believers to pray for those in government? What makes it difficult to remember to pray for these people? God has a purpose for quiet lives. They satisfy Him! He wants everyone to know peace through salvation and truth. Christ mediates your peace. He paid the ransom to free you from your slavery to sin. His story is a "testimony at the proper time." Your role is to pray and to live your life as a testimony of dignity and holiness.

324

Radical Rejection

About midnight Paul and Silas were praying and singing hymns to God, and the prisoners were listening to them. (Acts 16:25)

Inventors encounter the defeat of rejection. After failed attempts to invent a substitute for rubber, Thomas Adams popped a piece of the South-American tree sap, chicle, into his mouth. He liked it. Adams discovered chewing gum. His rubber-substitute inventions were rejected in favor of a sweet-tasting, long-lasting treat. When have you experienced rejection? After a sports tryout or an audition? How does rejection feel to you? Read Acts 16:16–17, 25–31, 34. How did Paul respond to rejection by the world? Why did the jailer seek salvation? Sometimes rejection comes from seeking a better path. Rejection that comes from following Christ can be painful. You get to choose which you value—being accepted by Jesus or being valued by the world. Paul's life had been "arrested" by Christ. After that, he could face rejection by the world. While he was in jail for healing a slave girl, Paul led the jailer and his family to Christ. Choose to follow Christ and tell His story no matter where you are. Start with your own personal testimony of how you came to know Jesus Christ as your Savior and what He is doing in your life right now.

325

Bridge Building

If you are ridiculed for the name of Christ, you are blessed,
because the Spirit of glory and of God rests on you. (1 Peter 4:14)

How many times would you rebuild a bridge to an isolated village? What if the bridge's name, Sebara Dildi, meant "broken bridge," because of the river's frequent flooding? Or if a villager pleaded for help: "If this bridge is broken, their lives are broken"? The bridge provides the villagers access to supplies, medical assistance, and the opportunity for commerce. The bridge is a life-line for the villagers. The villagers faced obstacles and opposition in rebuilding the bridge; what type of opposition do you face while serving in the name of Jesus? Read 1 Peter 4:12–14, 16, 19. How did Peter say we should respond to opposition? How does pressure affect your faith in Christ? When you choose to follow God, you open yourself to suffering. There may be pain for you along God's path. If so, it's for His glory! You do not choose where to serve Him—or what will happen there. But you do decide—daily—whether you will face hardships or run from them. God is always there regardless of what happens to you. Believers internationally are arrested, tortured, and killed consistently for their faith in Christ. This could happen to you. Are you willing to follow regardless? Don't be surprised when times are tough.

326

Smile for Freedom

A man who endures trials is blessed, because when he passes the test he will receive the crown of life that God has promised to those who love Him. (James 1:12)

Rescuers in Haiti struggled to coax a boy from where he had been buried for eight days. He relaxed upon hearing a nursery rhyme sung in French—"Frere Jacques." Finally he exited, spreading his freed arms wide and flashing a brilliant grin: "I smiled because I was free. I smiled because I was alive." What trials await you today or this week? Read James 1:2–3, 12; 5:10. How did James say you should respond to trials? How will you respond to the trials you will face this week? Testing serves a purpose. Enduring hardships leads to mature faith. If you "pass the test"—endure the trials—then you will receive "the crown of life" reserved for God's beloved. There will be much adversity: unappreciated, unavoidable, unpredictable trials. Ultimately, God promises to restore you, to make you strong. God pours His undeserved favor on you and calls you to eternal life: Look past the obstacle; see the opportunity! Anticipate the great joys of heaven! This refining fire serves a higher purpose. Stay under that testing. You know God's plan. Trust that nothing touches you without passing first through His hands. He's not lost sight of you; don't lose sight of Him. Persevere—and live!

327

Mirror Image

*As water reflects the face, so the heart
reflects the person. (Proverbs 27:19)*

When Shalynda Toney died of injuries sustained from being hit by a motorcycle while studying abroad in Rome, her parents decided to honor her memory with a generous donation. They donated six of her organs to help others. Shalynda's life reflected her Lord. Her memory lives on to inspire others to be generous. What image does your life portray? Read 1 Peter 2:11–12, 16 and 2 Corinthians 3:17–18. What should your life look like? How do you reflect a servant's attitude from your heart? How can God change your image? Jesus chose us to produce fruit that endures (John 15:16). Through good works, a watching world sees Christ living in and through you. They see that you are different—that you are not out to cause trouble. God imprints Christ's image onto you. He transforms you by His Spirit. Your life shows those changes. By reflecting Christ's image you reveal that there is something different about you. Make certain that your reflection is a mirror image of Christ.

328

A Good Image

Because if anyone is a hearer of the word and not a doer,
he is like a man looking at his own face in a mirror. (James 1:23)

In 1962, Sweden's only TV station broadcast a quick way to convert black-and-white images into color: to pull nylon hose over the TV screen. Thousands of people bought the joke! What effect did this prank have? What effect does God's Word have on you? Read James 1:22–25. What do these verses mean to you? What imprint has the Word left on your life? Can others see the difference? How does your life persuade others to follow Christ? Reflecting Christ begins with accepting Him as Lord and Savior then extends to obeying His Word. Spiritual forgetfulness can be avoided. The Spirit makes us sensitive to things we never considered before. When you read the Bible, ask the Holy Spirit to open the eyes of your heart to understand the words you read (Ephesians 1:18; 3:3–4). As you learn, own, and live out the truth of God's Word, you leave a positive impression of Christ. People are watching you to see if your good behavior is consistent with what you proclaim as a Christian. When God reveals Truth, you adjust your behavior to align with His Word. As a citizen of heaven, reflect Christ. That's a great impression!

329

Reflect The Light

"But anyone who lives by the truth comes to the light, so that his works may be shown to be accomplished by God." (John 3:21)

Picture balloons in a rainbow of colors against a blue sky, floating above a beige landscape of sand and clothing. Such was the sight in Kabul when balloons, kites, and music returned to Afghanistan following the fall of the Taliban. How are you a spot of color against the drab backdrop of this world? Read John 3:16–21. How is God's love for you and others described? How do you reflect Christ's love to others? Christ's light penetrates the darkness of your life and the lives of all who receive Him. Christ died to save you from your sin. He desires for you to reflect His light to those still in darkness. Whom do you know who needs the light of Christ? Is that person seeing the light from you? Why or why not? How will you reflect Christ? His light is a pathfinder. Pass it along, as torchbearers relaying beacons to waiting runners. Allow others to see the difference that Jesus is making in your life.

330

What Is Loyalty?

For Yahweh is good, and His love is eternal; His faithfulness endures through all generations. (Psalm 100:5)

Fair-weather fans show support only when their team or celebrity is successful or popular. Hard-core fans remain devoted at all times—through the good and bad. Even when a team is on a long-running losing streak, hard-core fans still go to the games to cheer them on. Or when a band drops dramatically off the charts, hard-core fans still buy and listen to their music. Who are you a fan of? Do you have a favorite singer, band, team, or celebrity? Are you a fair-weather fan or a hard-core fan?

Loyalty is like those hard-core fans. It's remaining faithful no matter what. God is like that. By His nature, God is loyal and will stick with you. Read Psalm 100:5 and 117:2. What do these verses tell you about God's character? What does it mean for God to be faithful? The Bible is packed with verses about God's unending love and faithfulness. They assure us that because of His great love for us, God will always be faithful to us—to you. No matter what, God will always love you and be faithful to you. How does that make you feel? God is loyal! It's who He is. Thank God today for His amazing love and faithfulness.

331

Forever Faithful

*"I will not vent the full fury of My anger; I will not
turn back to destroy Ephraim. For I am God and not man,
the Holy One among you; I will not come in rage." (Hosea 11:9)*

Many teens find it hard to take commitment seriously when so many adults don't keep their commitments. Politicians break their promises. Athletes and celebrities break their contracts. Husbands and wives break their marriage vows. In fact, more than forty percent of all marriages in the United States end in divorce. Do you keep your commitments? (Would others agree with you?) How has someone's lack of commitment affected you personally? Read Hosea 11:1–9. How would you describe God's level of commitment to the nation of Israel? Israel was unfaithful to God, but He never stopped loving them. Although they had to face the consequences of their disobedience, God never gave up on them. Because of His great love for them, He desired to bring them back to Him—to restore the relationship. God promises the same faithfulness to you. Even when you're unfaithful, God is working to bring you back into a right relationship with Him. He promises you the ultimate commitment—a commitment that never gives up. Why is it important to know that God will never give up on you? People will break their promises all the time, but God never will. He's forever faithful. Show your gratitude by being faithful in return—to God and to others. Ask God to help you keep your commitments, even when it's hard.

332

Never Alone

"I am with you always, to the end of the age."
(Matthew 28:20)

Have you ever heard the expression "true blue friend"? It has to do with the idea that blue is the color of constancy or dependability. Some say it refers to the unchanging blue sky. Others say it describes a blue dye that will not run. Regardless of its origin, the phrase "true blue friend" means someone you can count on. Do you have a true blue friend?

Read 2 Timothy 4:16–17. When the apostle Paul was put on trial, who came to offer support or assistance? Who stood with him? When was a time when you felt abandoned or alone? It's normal to feel that way sometimes. But the truth is, you are never really alone. Even when everyone else deserts you, God always stands with you. He alone is able to meet all your needs—just as He did for Paul. Read Matthew 28:20. What did Jesus promise in this verse? Sometimes even your very best friends may disappoint you. After all, they're only human—and you are too. But you have a true blue friend who is always there for you. Ask God to give you the confidence and courage that come from knowing He is right by your side.

333

No Other Gods

"Do not have other gods besides Me."
(Exodus 20:3)

Do you expect your friends to be loyal? That's kind of a weird question, isn't it? After all, someone who is not loyal—who is unfaithful, uncommitted, or undependable—isn't much of a friend! Loyalty is an expectation of friendship. You might say that, in one way or another, loyalty is an expectation of most relationships. Why do you think loyalty is so important when it comes to relationships? Read Exodus 20:3–4. What do these verses tell us that God expects of us? What does He promise in return? When God gave Moses the Ten Commandments, the very first thing He said was that we are not to worship any other gods besides Him. In other words, we are not to allow anything or anyone to come between God and us. He made it clear that loyalty is not a suggestion; it is an expectation. Then He promised to be loyal to us in return. Why do you think God places such importance on loyalty? God knows that relationships depend on loyalty. When there is no loyalty and no faithfulness, trust is broken. And when trust is broken, so is the relationship. Is anything in your life coming between you and God? Demonstrate your loyalty by putting God first.

334

A Sure Thing

Simon Peter answered, "Lord, who will we go to? You have the words of eternal life." (John 6:68)

Most of us like to try new things, like the latest technological gadgets or fashion trends. But when we can't afford to take chances, we'll always choose a sure thing. A sure thing is something you're certain of—you can depend on it like the rising of the sun. Maybe you have a favorite deodorant or shampoo that works better than the rest, and you won't use anything else. Or you might have a certain study habit that always brings good results. When you find a sure thing, you're wise to stick with it. What's a sure thing you've chosen to stick with?

Read John 6:66–69. When the going got tough and some of Jesus' followers turned back, why did some of the disciples stick with Jesus? What do you think Peter meant when he said Jesus was the Holy One of God who had "the words of eternal life"? Read John 14:6. What did Jesus say about Himself? Jesus is the way, truth, and life. He's the only way to God and the only source of salvation and hope. He's the surest thing of all, and He wants your love and loyalty. Spend time with Jesus today and tell Him that you want to stick with Him.

335

Trust God

If the Lord is pleased with us, He will bring us into this land, a land flowing with milk and honey, and give it to us. (Numbers 14:8)

Have you ever participated in a trust fall? You stand on a chair or table and fall backward into the arms of people you can't see. In order to fall correctly, you have to trust the people catching you. Being loyal to God is like that. Sometimes it's scary because you can't see what's going to happen. But if you want to be loyal to God, you have to trust Him. When was a time you were afraid to trust God? When the Israelites reached the Promised Land, they sent out spies and discovered that the people living there were big and powerful. They complained that it would be better to go back to Egypt than to die by the sword. Because they didn't trust God, they were quick to turn against Him. But there were two men who courageously trusted God. Read Numbers 14:6–9. What did Joshua and Caleb believe God would do? These young men had faith. They believed God had already given them the land and they simply had to take it. They remained loyal to God because they trusted Him. Will you trust God today? Ask Him for the courage to follow Him faithfully.

336

What Does Disloyalty Look Like?

"I give you a new command: Love one another. Just as I have loved you, you must also love one another." (John 13:34)

Has a friend ever been disloyal to you? Has someone done something behind your back, told lies about you, or turned others against you? With friends like that, who needs enemies? Disloyalty happens when people are self-seeking, more concerned about themselves than others, and willing to deceive others to get what they want. The Bible includes many examples of disloyalty. Jacob stole his brother's birthright through trickery and deceit. Joseph's brothers, who were jealous of him, sold him into slavery and lied to their father about it. Absalom, King David's son, schemed to gain the people's support and plotted a revolt against his father. One of Jesus' disciples betrayed Him with a kiss for thirty pieces of silver. How was the disloyalty in each situation self-seeking and deceitful? Read 1 Corinthians 10:24. What are we to seek and not seek? The Bible teaches that putting ourselves above others can lead to sin, including deceit and betrayal. But seeking the good of others is living as Jesus taught us to live. How are we to love others? Jesus loved you by dying for you. He was more concerned about your good than His good. He was selfless, not self-seeking. He was loyal, not disloyal. Ask Him to help you follow His example.

337

Let It Go

*Friends, do not avenge yourselves; instead, leave room
for His wrath. For it is written: Vengeance belongs
to Me; I will repay, says the Lord. (Romans 12:19)*

Revenge of the (fill in the blank). Do a quick Internet search, and you'll find several movie titles that fit this formula. Revenge is a popular theme not only in movies but also in life. When we're wronged, such as when someone is disloyal, our human nature is to get even. We want payback. When was a time you wanted to get even? The Bible shows us a better way. When King Saul turned against David and threatened to kill him, David fled, and Saul pursued him. On two different occasions, David had the opportunity to kill Saul. Both times, David refused. Read 1 Samuel 26:10–11. Why didn't David kill Saul when he had the chance? David knew that God would deal with Saul. David knew that God, by His very nature, is loyal and would fulfill His promise in David's life. Whose place is it to bring vengeance? It's God's responsibility to deal with those who wrong us. So when someone is disloyal, give it to God. Letting it go doesn't let the other person off the hook because God promises to handle it. Try letting go today. Write the name of anyone who has been disloyal to you on a piece of paper and then shred the paper. Give it to God, and let Him handle it.

338

Forgive and Move On

Just as the Lord has forgiven you, so you must also forgive. (Colossians 3:13)

You've heard the saying "forgive and forget." It's almost impossible to forget when someone has been disloyal to you, isn't it? But with God's help, it's possible to forgive! Forgiveness is good for you. It lowers your blood pressure, relieves stress, and frees you from harmful emotions like bitterness and resentment. But there's a more important reason to forgive. Why should you forgive? Jesus died on the cross so that your sins in the past, present, and future might be forgiven. Thinking about God's amazing forgiveness will help you be more willing to forgive others. When someone is disloyal, God wants you to forgive as He has forgiven you. Sometimes this includes working to restore the relationship. Other times, when reconciliation is impossible or unwise, it's best to forgive and move on. That was the case when David chose not to take Saul's life. Read 1 Samuel 26:12–13. What did David put between himself and Saul? Why is this a good choice sometimes? David knew there could be no reconciliation with Saul, so he wisely kept his distance. Has someone been disloyal to you? Ask God to help you forgive. Then pray for the wisdom to know whether you should try to reconcile or keep your distance. Either way, you will be moving on.

339

Unconditional Loyalty

Peter responded to Him, "Look, we have left everything and followed You. So what will there be for us?" (Matthew 19:27)

"What's in it for me?" This question could be the motto of our self-centered, materialistic culture. Yet it happens to be an age-old question. Centuries ago, the disciple Peter asked a similar question. Why do you think Peter asked Jesus this question? Peter wanted to know what the disciples would receive for being loyal to Jesus. They had given up much, and Peter wanted to know what they—what he—would get for it. What's wrong with Peter's question? Sticking with others because they can do something for you isn't true loyalty. Loyalty is offering your presence, support, and help without expecting anything in return. Being loyal means considering others' needs above your own because you care about them, not because you want something. Read Acts 27:1–3. Why did the centurion allow Paul to go to his friends? Paul was a prisoner. He was unable to give or do anything for his friends in return for their help. Still, they cared for him willingly, without expectations. They were loyal friends. This week, help meet the needs of a friend by giving of yourself with no strings attached. When you give unconditional loyalty, you are showing the character of God.

340

Through Thick and Thin

*A friend loves at all times, and a brother
is born for a difficult time. (Proverbs 17:17)*

This phrase is one of the oldest idioms in the English language. Centuries ago, when England was heavily forested, people traveled by going along paths and roads or by taking shortcuts "through thicket and thin wood." Eventually, the phrase was shortened to "through thick and thin" and was used to describe sticking with something or someone despite obstacles or difficulties. We show loyalty to others when we stick with them through thick and thin—through good and bad. In the Bible, the book of Ruth is a story of loyalty through thick and thin. Naomi's husband and two sons died in a foreign land. As she was leaving for her homeland, she encouraged her daughters-in-law to return to their mothers' homes. One returned, and one refused. Read Ruth 1:16–18. How do Ruth's words show that she planned to stick with Naomi through thick and thin? Ruth didn't know what she would experience by remaining with Naomi, yet she pledged her loyalty anyway. How has someone you know demonstrated this kind of loyalty? When does a friend love? When have you experienced this kind of love? A loyal friend loves at all times—even when it's hard. Ask God to help you be loyal to your friends through thick and thin.

341

The Loyalty Test

*My son, if sinners entice you, don't
be persuaded. (Proverbs 1:10)*

How many tests have you taken this month? How many this year? If you're like most students, you take a lot of tests! Sometimes it seems the world is obsessed with tests, which may be why there are so many books and websites that provide tips for test taking. But there's one test those resources won't help you pass: the loyalty test. The loyalty test comes whenever your friends want you to say or do something you know you shouldn't. They might even put your friendship on the line, saying you're not a real friend unless you do what they want. How can you do the right thing and remain loyal? Read Proverbs 1:10–19. What do these verses warn you not to do? Why? To what kind of peer pressure are you most susceptible? Peer pressure can lead you off God's path, and that's a dangerous place to be. Being loyal doesn't mean going along with everything your friends do. Neither does it mean abandoning them when they make wrong choices. Loyalty is looking out for their best interests and doing the most loving thing—what Jesus would have you do. Think of how a friend has tested your loyalty. If it were to happen again, how could you remain loyal while still honoring God? Ask God to show you what you should do.

342

Just Another Day

"For in those days before the flood they were eating and drinking, marrying and giving in marriage, until the day Noah boarded the ark." (Matthew 24:38)

What is a typical school day like for you? What kinds of things during your day make you happy or sad? Sometimes we live every day like nothing new is ever going to happen. We look at the events of a day with non-spiritual eyes, but God is speaking to us daily. What would you say a typical day in the world is like? Read Genesis 6:11–14, 22. What do you think makes God happy or sad? The people in Noah's day lived every day like it was just another day. They did not care that their actions were contrary to how God wanted them to live. Only Noah faithfully obeyed Him. Read Genesis 7:10–12. The consequences were harsh, but God did what He promised. Now God promises Jesus will return. We cannot live like the people from Noah's time. We cannot ignore God and expect Him not to respond to our actions. We should live as if Jesus will return today. You should take your cue from Noah by listening to God and obeying Him. Make sure your typical day includes God.

343

Thief in The Night

"This is why you also must be ready, because the Son of Man is coming at an hour you do not expect." (Matthew 24:44)

What types of events require you to prepare for all types of outcomes? Read Matthew 24:40–44. What event did Jesus describe here? You may think it is unlikely or even impossible Christ will return today. Jesus knew many of us would feel that way. Jesus' return will be like a thief in the night for many people. Many homeowners don't expect to be robbed today, but they still install alarm systems. Jesus wants us to be ready. He may not come today, but regardless, you must live your life in preparation for His return. How are you preparing for His return? As you ready your heart for Jesus' return, be sure to examine your motives. Getting ready isn't just about "covering your bases." Are you genuine in your faith? Is your trust in Him authentic? Do you desire to experience Him every day? Examine yourself and be sure.

344

Guessing Game

While He was sitting on the Mount of Olives, the disciples
approached Him privately and said, "Tell us, when will
these things happen? And what is the sign of Your coming
and of the end of the age?" (Matthew 24:3)

On February 12, 2010, Vancouver, Canada was abuzz about the opening of the XXI Winter Olympics. A point of great interest was the identity of the final torchbearer—the one person who would light the Olympic cauldron to symbolize the beginning of the games. Speculation was rampant as many names were suggested and people debated the merits of each one.

Have you read about or experienced a public event surrounded by mystery? Read Matthew 24:3–8. What did the disciples ask? Why? People have studied Jesus' words and tried to pinpoint when the "end of the age" would come. Jesus did indeed list specific things that will happen. Have you ever associated a major world event with Jesus' return? Although studying current events in light of biblical prophecy is interesting, Jesus does not want us to be distracted or obsessed with it. He wants us to focus on the greatest commandments (Matthew 22:36–40). Obeying these is more important than guessing when the end of the age will come. As you study the end times, keep your heart and mind on the most important things.

345

Christmas Part 2

"Then the sign of the Son of Man will appear in the sky, and then all the peoples of the earth will mourn; and they will see the Son of Man coming on the clouds of heaven with power and great glory." (Matthew 24:30)

How many times have you heard the Christmas story? Perhaps you've heard it many different ways and many different times. A point that is often made is that Jesus' birth was humble and lowly. He was born in a manger. He did not receive the same attention given to the birth of a king's son. Only His parents, some shepherds, and later on a few magi (the wise men) would celebrate His coming. Why do you think Jesus' birth was so humble? What will be different when He returns? When Jesus comes a second time, it will be the opposite of His birth. People all over the world will take notice, and they will see Him in power and glory. Jesus is still humble, but His overwhelming presence and glory will capture the world's attention. Read 1 Thessalonians 4:16. A group of angels sang when Jesus was born (Luke 2:13) and perhaps a few animals made some noise. The sounds of celebration were minimal at best. His second coming will be marked with shouts, the trumpet of God, and the dead rising. There will be no ignoring Him. There will be no hiding from Him. There will be no denying His existence. How can you respond now to the glory and power of Christ's second coming?

346

Disaster Scenario

*He opposes and exalts himself above every so-called god
or object of worship, so that he sits in God's sanctuary,
publicizing that he himself is God. (2 Thessalonians 2:4)*

Imagine this disaster scenario (perhaps you have lived it): You are assigned a group project at school, and your group is full of slackers. Since you are the only one who cares about a good grade, you end up doing all the work. When the project is handed in, someone else takes credit and the teacher believes it. You want to yell and scream about the faker. You want to use words like *deceitful*, *scheming*, *egotistical*, and *cheater*. Satan is like that. He is self-promoting, and he claims he knows what is best for everyone. This has happened since the dawn of time. Read Genesis 3:1–5. In what ways was the serpent egotistical? Satan wants all the glory. He wants to be God. That's why he was kicked out of heaven. Now in the last days, his pawn, the "man of lawlessness," will seek to set himself up as God. Why do you think the man of lawlessness publicizes himself to be God? Why do you think people will believe him? Before Jesus returns, the opposition to Him will come in many forms. Perhaps the most dangerous is the quiet, seductive voice of the evil one. Make your choice now to resist this evil voice. Stand strong in the courage that only Christ provides.

347

The Movies Have It Wrong

The Lord Jesus will destroy him with the breath
of His mouth and will bring him to nothing with
the brightness of His coming. (2 Thessalonians 2:8)

Hollywood movies often get their portrayal of Satan wrong. They show God and Satan as opponents on the same level. This is far from the truth. If all of your information on God and Satan came from Hollywood, how would you view each of them? Read 2 Thessalonians 2:7–8. How much greater is Jesus than Satan? Satan gives the illusion of control, but God will reveal Him easily. For almost all of us, breathing is one of the easiest things to do. That's how much effort Jesus requires to destroy Satan. Jesus uses the "breath of his mouth" (v. 8), and that is all it takes to defeat Satan. That's not all. Satan isn't just hurt or badly wounded; he becomes nothing when Jesus returns. Nothing! There's no comeback possible for Satan. Why do you think the media rarely portrays Jesus as infinitely more powerful than Satan? The next time you see a portrayal of Satan, reflect on what is said in the Bible. Perhaps the breath of your mouth can help promote what is accurate and true. Jesus is Lord!

348

Crystal Clear

*"Therefore be alert, because you don't know
either the day or the hour." (Matthew 25:13)*

If you were standing at the entrance to a corn maze and the exit was just twenty yards straight ahead of you with just one empty path, you would probably say, "Well, that's easy." The path would be pretty obvious. You might read the Bible sometimes and say to yourself, doing the right thing is so crystal clear, how can anyone miss it? Read Matthew 25:1–13. What was the obvious need for an oil lamp? Why do you think some people aren't ready for the really important things in life when it seems so obvious that you need to be ready? The five foolish virgins represent people who are not spiritually ready for Jesus' return. They had the opportunity, but made unwise choices. For believers, trusting Jesus seems like the most natural thing to do in the world. Like thinking about having extra oil for your oil lamp. Do you know anyone who isn't spiritually ready for Christ's return? Why are they like that? Why do so many people reject the message of Jesus? Take some time to reflect on the spiritual condition of yourself, your family, your friends, and your circle of influence. Pray that you can help them get ready for Christ's return.

349
Too Safe

So then, we must not sleep, like the rest, but we must stay awake and be serious. (1 Thessalonians 5:6)

Do you think comfort and easy living is eating quietly away at your soul? Read 1 Thessalonians 5:5–7. What is the warning for believers in these verses? God warns that we must stay awake and be sober. This means we must be alert and ready for His coming. Some might interpret this to mean we must protest and stand against the tide of immoral behaviors and attitudes. And we should. But we also must be aware of apathetic attitudes and becoming too comfortable. Perhaps we have become too concerned about our own wealth and possessions that we no longer love or care for those Jesus loves and cares for. When was the last time you moved outside your comfort zone to help someone? To minister to the homeless? To visit the sick or imprisoned? Do you only hang around people with the same wealth or standard of living as you? Explain. Make sure you are living in, and reflecting, the light of Christ.

350

Battle Ready

*But since we belong to the day, we must be serious and
put the armor of faith and love on our chests, and put on
a helmet of the hope of salvation. (1 Thessalonians 5:8)*

Do you have friends or relatives in the military? Have you ever felt proud of someone you see in uniform? We respect and honor those who are battle ready. The Bible calls us to get dressed for battle too. Read 1 Thessalonians 5:8–11. How are we to prepare ourselves? As people "of the day," believers are to focus on love, faith, and salvation. The politics and theology surrounding the issues for a nation to go to war against another nation can be deep, divisive, and complex. These kinds of wars need to be studied, prayed about, and debated. What cannot be debated is the need to encourage and care for one another. Believers must actively shower love on our fellow brothers and sisters in Christ regardless of where they live. Even countries at war with our country have believers needing our support and help. How can you help Christians of all nationalities "build each other up" (v. 11)? As you anticipate Jesus' return, you should not shrink from engaging in society. You cannot be satisfied in staying within the protected confines of your church boundaries. Instead, you should be awake and alert to see the injustice in your community and the world. Then, with your spiritual armor, you must dive into battle. Are you ready?

351

Make a Move

They said, "Men of Galilee, why do you stand looking up into heaven? This Jesus, who has been taken from you into heaven, will come in the same way that you have seen Him going into heaven." (Acts 1:11)

Basketball, hockey, and soccer coaches hate when their players stand around waiting for someone else to make a play. They want their players constantly moving, trying to find open space, and looking to receive a pass. Jesus had risen from the dead and was returning to heaven when He spoke some important words. Read Acts 1:9–11. What was the disciples' first reaction after Jesus ascended to heaven? Watching Jesus rise into the sky must have been inspiring. But if all we do is admire Him, we miss what Jesus commanded. Worship and singing praise songs are great, but part of Jesus' last instructions was to be witnesses for Him in your community, in your country, and in your world. He does not want you to stand still looking at Him. He wants you to move, to get involved, and to be open to His calling. Would you be willing to move to another place on earth to be a witness for Jesus? Where do you see Jesus at work around you or in the world? What places is He calling for workers? Be alert to opportunities that God presents before you each day. Remember, He has given you the power to be His witness to others.

352

What Witnessing Isn't

Every day they devoted themselves to meeting
together in the temple complex, and broke bread
from house to house. (Acts 2:46)

At the street corner, a man was loudly preaching to anyone who would stop to listen. "Repent now!" he shouted, "Or you'll go to hell! The world is going to end soon, and you are wicked." Many people walked by indifferently while others were angry at what the man said. Although the theology behind his words might have been right, his method was not working.

What type of witness turns people away from Christianity? Read Acts 2:41–47. What do you think made Christianity so attractive to the people? Witnessing isn't a game of who can win the most converts. Witnessing isn't about trying to get the seats filled in a church. Witnessing isn't about trying to get as many people as possible to repeat the words to a prayer. If there is no genuine faith and belief, there is no witness. If no meaningful relationships have been created, there is no discipleship.

The disciples shared and devoted themselves to each other. The Lord blessed their witness, and more people were saved. How can witnessing be natural or authentic rather than forced and faked? Evaluate your life this week. Are you a natural witness for Christ? Do others recognize something different in your life? Why or why not?

353

Boxed Seats

*"Everyone who believes in Him will
have eternal life." (John 3:15)*

At concerts, sporting events, or big shows, there are luxury box seats. Those fortunate enough to be in one can get special parking, have food delivered, and watch in privacy. You either need to pay lots of money or be someone important in order to get in one. There are no luxury box seats in heaven. Read John 3:1–16. Why do you think Nicodemus was so curious about the kingdom of heaven? Nicodemus was a ruler (v. 1) and a learned teacher (v. 10). He was highly respected and was probably able to get special treatment in social situations. Jesus explained that what society considers important (wealth, education, social standing) will not get you into the kingdom of heaven. The only requirement is to be born again (v. 7). What does it mean to be born again? Have you been born again? The reason John 3:16 is one of the most famous verses in the Bible is its simplicity. It is a beautiful and short summary of the message of the Bible. It is easy to forget Jesus spoke this verse to a person with a lot of power and prestige. This is someone who probably would be sitting in a luxury box seat if he lived in our time. Sometimes we act like we need our own power in order to gain entrance into the kingdom of heaven. We don't. We must simply put our faith in God's only Son.

354

Spiritual Preparation

Therefore, with your minds ready for action, be serious and set your hope completely on the grace to be brought to you at the revelation of Jesus Christ. (1 Peter 1:13)

You need to leave for school at 7:00. So, what time do you need to wake up? Well, that depends. If you need to take a shower, haven't finished your homework, have no idea what you're wearing, and like to enjoy a relaxing breakfast, you'll need to get up pretty early. But if you've already done everything to get prepared (some people even sleep in their clothes!), you can sleep until the last minute. What does your spiritual preparation look like? Do you still have a lot to do to be ready to share your faith, or have you started taking steps to help you be prepared? Spiritual preparation takes some planning. Read 1 Peter 1:13–16. Make a list of the actions required in these verses. Give yourself a grade (A through F) on how well you are performing each. Just as you probably wouldn't go to school without brushing your teeth and putting on shoes, you should not expect to successfully defend your faith without the basics: self-control, obedience, and a good understanding of God's holiness so that your life reflects Him. Are you taking the daily steps required to be ready? Do you spend time worshiping God, learning His Word, and communicating with Him in such a way that you hear Him? Make a note of the areas you need to work on to improve. Be conscious about spending time on spiritual preparation.

355

Bring It On

*The large crowd came to Him because they heard
about everything He was doing. (Mark 3:8)*

Be careful. If you really know how to defend your faith and are ready to do it in Christ's power, you may have a mob on your hands. Christ wasn't the only great teacher of His day. But He had the authority and knowledge of God, which made all kinds of people want to hear Him. Read Mark 3:7–10. How did Christ get ready for what was to come? How did He respond to the crowds? Picture the scene—there were so many people wanting to hear Jesus that He had to get in a boat so He wouldn't get pushed into the water! Crazy, right? You may also be thrown into a spotlight where you can share your choice to follow Christ and obey Him instead of living like everybody else. There are all kinds of teens who say they believe something but don't back it up with their words or actions. Even fewer are able to explain it. God intended for those who know and love Him to be so different from the rest of society that others cannot help but wonder, "What makes that person so different?" Accept the attention. Don't shy away from it. Let your light shine for others (Matthew 5:16).

356

Live It

*For there was not a needy person among them, because
all those who owned lands or houses sold them, brought
the proceeds of the things that were sold. (Acts 4:34)*

What is a testimony? As Christians, we are encouraged to share our testimony with others. But what does that mean, really? The word *witness* is a good synonym. When you give a witness, you tell what you have learned or seen or known about God. *Evidence* also has a close meaning. When you share your testimony, you're telling someone the evidence of why you believe and follow God. In your opinion, what is the most effective type of testimony? Look at the example in Acts 4:29–35. How did these believers testify to their faith? What made their testimony so powerful? You see, if you explain your testimony with words alone and do not back it up with actions and attitudes that reflect God, your testimony is weak—or even worse, hypocritical. Only when you put hands and feet to your faith will others really believe your testimony. Christ healed the sick, helped the poor, and loved all who came to Him. He is the perfect example of a testimonial life. As you continue to learn how to defend your faith, let the Holy Spirit show you how to demonstrate it as a living, breathing testimony.

357

Use Your Influence

"Go, therefore, and make disciples of all nations, baptizing them in the name of the Father and of the Son and of the Holy Spirit." (Matthew 28:19)

Whose responsibility is it to make sure people around you know the truth of Jesus? Read Matthew 28:19–20. To whom was Jesus speaking? What instructions did Jesus give them? Would you say that this verse applies to you? Why or why not? This passage is commonly referred to as the "Great Commission"—where Jesus formally gave His appointed task (His commissioning) to the disciples who were with Him. Were they all preachers and speakers? No way. They were businessmen, fishermen, and other "normal" people. They, like us, were given the task of discipling (leading), baptizing, and teaching others. It all begins with the command to make disciples—what do you think it means to make disciples? All believers in Christ have been given the same commission, or task—to spread the message of Jesus. Yes, those polished speakers and pastors may seem to be more comfortable at a pulpit or behind a microphone, but they don't hang out with your friends or have the influence you do over others. This is why it's up to each one of us to proclaim Christ in our world.

358

Led Astray

*But I fear that, as the serpent deceived Eve by his cunning,
your minds may be seduced from a complete and
pure devotion to Christ. (2 Corinthians 11:3)*

Consider Eve: God was so close to her that she talked with Him. If there was anyone who would not have been led astray by a false teaching, it would have been her, right? Well, unfortunately, even Eve was influenced to believe a lie. Read 2 Corinthians 11:3–4. How was Eve led astray? How were the recipients of Paul's letter led astray? Though Satan himself influenced Eve to believe a lie, the Corinthians simply weren't paying attention to the fact that lies were invading their beliefs. They tolerated what seemed to be the truth, and before they knew it, their beliefs weren't in line with what the Bible and Christ taught. What are some things that might lead you astray if you are not diligent in your faith? Christians—real Christians who love and want to follow Christ—can easily fall for deception when not being cautious about what is and is not truth in the face of today's society: "Sex before marriage isn't a big deal." "It's okay to cheat on this test; everyone else is." "Don't worry—your parents will never find out." Know God's Word for yourself, and be aware of falsehood. Guard your faith with truth. Read and pray James 1:5.

359

Too Good To Keep Secret

We do speak a wisdom among the mature,
but not a wisdom of this age, or of the rulers of this age,
who are coming to nothing. (1 Corinthians 2:6)

Are you any good at keeping secrets? I'm not talking about the "Oh, my mom would kill me if she knew I accidentally ran over her prize roses with the lawn mower" type of secret. I'm talking about the, "My friend is going to love it when we jump out and yell, 'surprise!'" type of secret. Some secrets are so good you just can't help telling others, right? Our relationship with Christ is supposed to be that kind of secret. It's not something we're supposed to keep to ourselves. We're supposed to be so hyped about it that we just feel like we might bust if we don't share it. Look how Paul explained it in 1 Corinthians 2:6–10. How did Paul describe the wisdom we can get from God alone? How did he describe the other type of wisdom? Wisdom that comes from God enables you to share the message of Christ with others. When you accept Christ as your Savior, it's as though your brain is uploaded with some amazing software that allows you to access all kinds of knowledge about God through the Holy Spirit. People who don't know God simply don't have access to it. The wisdom of our age sounds good and seems to make sense, but it's not truth! Possessing God's truth should inspire you to make sure that everyone you know has the secret wisdom that comes from God.

360

Courage in All Things

For me, living is Christ and dying is gain.
(Philippians 1:21)

When I was young, my family would go to a waterfall every summer. We'd splash in the pool at the bottom for a while, and then my dad would climb to the top of a small rock and slide down it. The first time he did it, he invited me to go—I told him no way. But after watching him a few more times, I went. It was SO much fun! I didn't have the courage it took to slide down the waterfall rock at first, but I gained courage from knowing my dad was there and able to help me. So where do we find the courage to stand for our faith? It's not within ourselves. We gain courage from following God, experiencing His power and plan, and knowing that we get to use His power for His purposes. Read Philippians 1:19–26. For what reason did Paul need courage? How would God be glorified if Paul was courageous in life? In death? Paul realized that he would need courage regardless of how his situation ended: Either he would live and tell others about Christ, or he would die and go to heaven forever. Both avenues took courage. Living for Christ takes courage, whether the experience seems good or bad. Depend on His strength to give you courage in all things. Consider what it would take for you to be able to say the same kinds of things Paul said in these verses.

361

Courage in Crisis

When they observed the boldness of Peter and John and realized that they were uneducated and untrained men, they were amazed and recognized that they had been with Jesus. (Acts 4:13)

Sometimes we need courage at the beginning of a challenge, such as being brave enough to strap on that roller coaster seat belt and hang on. In other times, we need courage after a challenge is over, such as not letting your legs collapse underneath you after the ride is over. What things require you to have courage? Sometimes it takes more courage to explain our God-honoring actions than it takes to be obedient. If you've ever had to explain to a friend that you didn't come to a party because there was alcohol or that you wouldn't let someone copy your homework because it was dishonest, you know what I'm talking about. Peter faced the same type of situation on a much more dramatic scale. He healed a beggar, which seemed pretty simple, but the backlash was unbelievable. Peter went through a lot. Read Acts 4:3–4, 8–13. What consequences did Peter and John face because of their willingness to heal the man? How did Peter demonstrate courage? How did his courage affect others? Courage in Christ is provided to you as a believer, whether you need it to take the step of faith or defend the step after you thought the challenge was over. Be ready to stand strong regardless of when the courage is needed.

362

Weapons of Courage

This is why you must take up the full armor of God, so that you may be able to resist in the evil day, and having prepared everything, to take your stand. (Ephesians 6:13)

You wouldn't go into a battle without gear. In the world of spiritual struggles, Christians are not weaponless. We take courage from knowing how we are armed. Read Ephesians 6:13–17. What different types/pieces of armor are mentioned? What is the purpose of this spiritual armor? The reason we can go to battle against evil is because we have been fitted with the armor necessary for our fight. The belt of truth holds our convictions firm because we know real Truth—Jesus. The breastplate of righteousness protects us from doubting that we are right before God. Peace on our feet allows us to fight without offending. The shield of faith keeps the lies of the enemy from piercing us, even when we can't explain God. The helmet of salvation lets us live in ultimate confidence that we are eternally saved. And, of course, the sword of the Spirit—God's Word—provides us with all we need to repel the enemy. We can't do it on our own; the armor of God is something we must use for defending our faith and facing evil. What piece (or pieces) of your spiritual armor needs some attention right now? As you get dressed in the morning, imagine that you are also putting on these very specific, very valuable pieces of armor. When you are challenged or tested, remember that your courage comes from the Spirit's protection.

363

The Good Fight

*Timothy, my son, I am giving you this instruction in keeping
with the prophecies previously made about you, so that by
them you may strongly engage in battle. (1 Timothy 1:18)*

As Christians, we're called to fight: We must contend for God's kingdom, fight against Satan and the world, and go into battle with other
Christians. Still, does it sound like fighting and honoring God would
be a little tricky? I mean, can you picture Christ punching Pilate in the
face? (He wouldn't.) Read 1 Timothy 1:18–20. What kind of fight does
Paul instruct his reader to fight? What two other instructions does he
include in verse 19? As believers, we don't live like the world lives, and
we don't fight like they do. We're called to fight a good fight. Do you
know what that looks like? What do you think this "good fight" looks
like? A good fight means we stay obedient to God; we don't break His
commands. A good fight means we are loving to others; we don't tear
them down or hurt them. A good fight means we are focused on others
knowing God, not on getting them to admit that we are right. A good
fight means those who are watching us see God, not our battle. What
might be two other statements you would add to the descriptions of a
good fight? As you contend for the faith this week, remember to fight
the good fight and honor Christ in your battles.

364

Spiritual Food

*Like newborn infants, desire the pure spiritual milk,
so that you may grow by it for your salvation. (1 Peter 2:2)*

Have you ever watched a little baby try to eat food for the first time? They don't really understand how to do it. They push it out of their mouths with their tongues, usually accompanied by a funny face of disgust. Babies take time to learn how to eat food, because for the first months of their lives all they get is milk. However, learning to eat food is necessary and a vital part of growing up. Read 1 Peter 2:1–3. What is spiritual milk? What does it help us do? What should make us want more hearty spiritual food? New Christians, whether age 5 or 85, start with some basic milk from the Bible: God loves you. Jesus saves you. Heaven is where you'll spend eternity. But as you grow up spiritually, what you digest from Scripture should change. You begin to understand who the Holy Spirit is and what He does. You learn how to share your faith. You learn to pray with power and hear God's voice. But the question is this: Are you choosing to grow in your spiritual food? How well are you growing? Who is helping you to grow? You don't just drink milk anymore—you like to eat a lot of other things. Learn to grow up spiritually too. Feast on God's meat in His Word this week.

365

Not Enough Time

Devote yourselves to prayer; stay alert in it with thanksgiving. (Colossians 4:2)

I never seem to have enough time. I love reading, but my stack of books grows. I have a few movies I want to watch, but the DVDs seem to just sit on the TV stand. I'd really like to spend more time in God's Word, but sometimes I only manage a short morning devo. Do you have enough time to do all you want to do for God? The Bible tells us that we've got to intentionally make the most of our time. Read Colossians 4:2–6 aloud. What does verse 5 instruct you to do? How do verses 2 and 6 give insight into how to obey God's instruction in verse 5? You make the most of your time—especially in terms of sharing Christ—when your entire lifestyle is focused on glorifying Him. Just as you see in verses 2 and 6, an attitude of prayer and thanksgiving, coupled with words that are gracious and beautiful, turn every minute of our day into a time of testimony! Whether you're riding to work, sitting on the bus, enjoying free time in class, waiting in line at a store, watching your little brother and sister, or anything else, remind yourself: I can use this moment to reflect Christ.